T0265741

On Bette Midler

On Bette Midler

An Opinionated Guide

KEVIN WINKLER

OXFORD
UNIVERSITY PRESS

OXFORD
UNIVERSITY PRESS

Oxford University Press is a department of the University of Oxford. It furthers the University's objective of excellence in research, scholarship, and education by publishing worldwide. Oxford is a registered trade mark of Oxford University Press in the UK and certain other countries.

Published in the United States of America by Oxford University Press
198 Madison Avenue, New York, NY 10016, United States of America.

Library of Congress Cataloging-in-Publication Data
Names: Winkler, Kevin, author.
Title: On Bette Midler : an opinionated guide / Kevin Winkler.
Description: [1.] | New York : Oxford University Press, 2024. |
Includes bibliographical references and index.
Identifiers: LCCN 2023038562 (print) | LCCN 2023038563 (ebook) |
ISBN 9780197668320 (hardback) | ISBN 9780197668344 (epub) |
ISBN 9780197668337 (ebook other) | ISBN 9780197668351 (ebook other)
Subjects: LCSH: Midler, Bette. | Singers—United States—Biography. |
Motion picture actors and actresses—United States—Biography.
Classification: LCC ML420.M43 W55 2024 (print) | LCC ML420.M43 (ebook) |
DDC 782.42164092 [B]—dc23/eng/20230816
LC record available at https://lccn.loc.gov/2023038562
LC ebook record available at https://lccn.loc.gov/2023038563

DOI: 10.1093/oso/9780197668320.001.0001

Printed by Sheridan Books, Inc., United States of America

Everybody deserves a divine woman in their life. If you're lucky, you get more than one. For sharing their divinity with me over the last fifty years, this book is dedicated to these women:
Susan Ball
Clovis Emblen-Scarpaci
Sandra Fleck
Kimberly Gadette
Mary Jeffries
Liz Van Doren

Contents

Preface and Acknowledgments

Sometimes you just connect with an artist from the very first encounter and instantly become her champion. I remember precisely the first time I saw Bette Midler. It was on *The Tonight Show*, and she sang Joni Mitchell's "For Free" with such soul-rattling intensity that she seemed to explode out of my little portable black-and-white television set. She reminded me of the girls I was friends with in college: not beautiful but striking and womanly, with earth mother sensuality that informed everything they did. They were funny and independent, messy and theatrical, fiercely loyal and always ready to stand up for themselves and their friends. They patiently waited for me to confide that maybe, just possibly, I might be gay. And they never tipped their hand that they knew it all the time. It didn't surprise me when I later learned that Midler's closest friends and confidants in her early New York City days were gay men.

Age and geography kept me from seeing Midler at the Continental Baths, but a few years later, rootless and lonely, living in Los Angeles at the dawn of the disco age, I experienced something like the fun and camaraderie she created at that legendary spot. On Sunday nights in the upstairs bar of a popular North Hollywood disco called Oil Can Harry's, they screened Midler's recent HBO show from a gigantic first-generation Betamax machine. Since I couldn't afford HBO or concert tickets, finally seeing her in a full-length performance was a revelation. From that Sunday on, I was a regular at the bar, nursing a Coke and laughing and singing along with a small crowd of other lonely gay boys—all of us connected by our love for this brash, funny, dramatic girl whose presence, even televised, gave off a warming, welcoming glow.

Over the years, Midler has been a touchstone in my life. I was thrilled by her successes and took her failures much too seriously. (I kept going back to see *Stella*, thinking it would get better with repeat viewings.) New York's grand Ziegfeld Theatre (now lamentably gone) will always be the spot where I saw *The Rose* for the first time. Radio City Music Hall may be home to the Rockettes, but for me it's the place where I saw Midler kill in *De Tour* in 1983 and then again, ten years later, in *Experience the Divine*.

When I got my graduate degree in theater, my thesis topic was, naturally, Midler and the Continental Baths. I adapted the thesis for articles and conference presentations. Years went by, and I was working at the New York Public Library for the Performing Arts at Lincoln Center. Midler would be an occasional presence, studiously going about her research like the librarian she always said she was inside. I thought about approaching her once or twice, but I respected her privacy (she never called any attention to herself), and besides, I figured the last thing she needed was to hear yet another middle-aged gay man tell her how much he loved her.

Now I have young nieces and nephews who know Midler only from the *Hocus Pocus* movies. They've never heard of "Boogie Woogie Bugle Boy" or "The Rose" or even "Wind beneath My Wings." Celebrity becomes more fleeting as years pass, leaving us to wonder if later generations will remember or even be aware of beloved figures of today.

On Bette Midler: An Opinionated Guide is an effort to capture what has made Midler a singular talent across media for more than fifty years. It includes no interviews with its subject or those who worked with her. Few reviews are referenced. It's not just opinionated, it's *highly* opinionated, filled with personal contemplations and deliberations on an artist and a career I've followed with religious fervor since that first black-and-white television sighting.

I thank Intellect Books and *Theatre History Studies* for their permission to quote passages from previously published works. The kind assistance of the staff at my old professional home, the

New York Public Library for the Performing Arts, always makes conducting research there a pleasure. Jeremy Megraw, the wonder man of its massive photo collections, offered his invaluable guidance. As always, Jane Klain at the Paley Center for Media was helpful and encouraging. Marathon phone conversations with Brantley Bardin, besides being a welcome break from writing, helped me work through fuzzy ideas and make them sharper. Discussing the book with Mark Frawley, John Ganun, and a new mad-about-Midler friend Tim Ziaukas gave me a boost, while Philip Shultz, not the biggest Midler fan, offered some much-appreciated perspective. Charles Kloth, who knows more about Barbra Streisand than anyone I know, helped me grapple with "the Streisand thing" as it relates to Midler. As he has done on nearly all my writing projects, Jim Wilson patiently read passages and commented with the kind of compassionate, probing insights that I treasure. My husband, Richard Schneider, kept everything running smoothly so that I could work undisturbed.

At Oxford University Press, Rachel Ruisard helped me navigate photograph clearances and deadlines with quiet assurance. Finally, all writers should have an editor as patient and encouraging as Norman Hirschy. Once again, his levelheadedness and calm authority were reassuring at every step of the writing and production process.

"Any Day Now . . . "

A Bette Midler Chronology

1945

December 1   Bette Midler is born in Honolulu, Hawaii, to Fred "Chesty" Midler and his wife, Ruth, both transplanted New Jerseyites. The third of four children, she is named for Bette Davis by her movie-loving mother, who thinks "Bette" is pronounced "Bet." The future star's name is set.

1950   First-grader Bette Midler wins a prize for her vocal rendition of "Silent Night" but feels guilty because her family is Jewish and she's not supposed to sing Christmas songs.

1956   Midler wins the two-dollar first prize in a school talent show when she sings "Lullaby of Broadway," her first performance of a song that would become an early standard for her.

1963–1965   After graduating as president of her senior class, Midler attends the University of Hawaii. She is a busy student actor, appearing in character roles in *The Way of the World* (as a maid), *The Cherry Orchard* (as a governess), and Murray Schisgal's two-hander *The Typists* (as an office drone). Her most glamourous appearance is as scheming beauty pageant winner Diana Devereux in *Of Thee I Sing*, singing "I Was the Most Beautiful Blossom." Midler yearned to be a serious actor like Ethel

Barrymore, but if musicals were casting, she was there. For the Honolulu Community Theatre, she was an ensemble member in *Show Boat* and *How to Succeed in Business without Really Trying*.

1965

August 4   Midler flies from Honolulu to Los Angeles to continue working as a background actor on the film *Hawaii*, which she had worked on when it was filmed in her native state. From there, she makes her way to New York City. Her small room at the squalid Broadway Central Hotel is fifteen dollars a week, and she pays her bills through a series of survival jobs: typist, glove salesgirl, hatcheck girl, and go-go dancer.

December 1   On her twentieth birthday, Midler makes her New York debut in Tom Eyen's *Miss Nefertiti Regrets* at La MaMa, later taking over the title role. The following year, she will appear in Eyen's *Cinderella Revisited/Sinderella Revisited*.

1966

Summer   Midler spends the summer in the Catskills entertaining vacationing New Yorkers escaping the city heat. In *An Evening of Tradition*, she performs in sketches by Sholom Aleichem and Paddy Chayefsky and makes the rounds of the area hotels, singing in showcase nights.

1968

April 21   Having been in the hit Broadway musical *Fiddler on the Roof* since 1966, first as an ensemble member and later in the role of Tevye's oldest daughter, Tzeitel, Midler makes her national television debut on the Tony Awards broadcast, singing "Matchmaker, Matchmaker."

1968–1969   Like many New York–based actors, Midler picks up random days of work on New York–based films, appearing as an extra or background actor in *The Detective*, Frank Sinatra's 1968 crime thriller, and the film version of Philip Roth's *Goodbye, Columbus*. *Stella*, a 1990 movie set in 1969, includes a *Goodbye, Columbus* Easter egg: a pregnant Midler experiences her water breaking in a crowded theater while she's watching the movie.

1969   While performing in *Fiddler*, Midler moonlights in Tom Eyen's *Alice through the Glass Lightly* as the Red Queen.

1970
July   Midler makes her first appearance at the Continental Baths.

1971
January   Midler meets Barry Manilow, who helps her focus and refine her musical performances, first at the Continental and then for the next three years. They don't much like each other at first—"Two ambitious Jews in one room" is how Midler would later describe them[1]—but they form a symbiotic musical partnership that helps blast her into stage and recording successes.

September 20   Midler makes her New York nightclub debut at the posh Downstairs at the Upstairs. The first several nights are poorly attended, and Midler takes out an ad in *Screw* magazine announcing "Bette from the Baths—At the Downstairs." Soon the engagement is packed. Though Clive Davis of Columbia Records is not impressed, Ahmet Ertegun, president of Atlantic Records, signs her to the label, where she stays for nearly twenty-five years.

1972

April

Midler goes easy on the insider gay jokes and instead leans into the Frederick's of Hollywood references during what *Variety* calls her "gabbity-gab" when she debuts in Las Vegas, opening for Johnny Carson. Neither audiences nor *Variety* know exactly what to make of her, but they love the '60s girl-group songs, and she impresses them with her "whale of a voice."[2]

June 23

Midler rents Carnegie Hall for a one-night concert that emphasizes her song repertoire over comedy. For someone without a recording to promote and a still-developing national profile, it's risky to book the prestigious hall. But the concert sells out instantly. For New York's hip, gay, show-business cognoscenti, Carnegie Hall is the only place to be that evening.

August 16

Midler performs to overwhelming audience response as part of the Schaefer Music Festival in Central Park. "When I heard the roar I thought I was in *Korea*! Entertaining the troops," she said, referencing Marilyn Monroe's frenzied welcome by soldiers during the Korean War. "That concert was the happiest night of my life. I could feel it inside, I could feel the joy . . . really physically, it was like a big *lump* in my *chest*, and it was coming OUT in huge WAVES."[3] It is the largest live audience she's ever played to, making it clear that Midler is connecting with an increasingly broad audience.

Fall

Midler is dissatisfied with her management, fearing that it is steering her in a conventional lounge-singer direction. Enter Aaron Russo, a Chicago-based nightclub owner and impresario. He becomes her take-charge manager, guiding her career at a critical moment when she is seeking to expand her audience and establish a recording career. Their combative, knock-down, drag-out relationship (including a brief, early affair) continues until the end of the decade, a period when Russo successfully steers her career into television and movies.

November 26–27   Midler makes her final appearances at the Continental Baths, just as her first album, *The Divine Miss M*, is released.

December 31   "Divine Miss M. Is Set for a Tacky Gala," the *New York Times* crows in the lead-up to two sold-out shows at New York's Philharmonic Hall at Lincoln Center.[4] She welcomes in the new year wearing a diaper emblazoned with "1973" as she rises from below the stage.

1973

June 24   When tensions between lesbians and drag queens threaten to derail the celebration in Washington Square Park after the fourth annual Gay Pride March, the event's organizer, Vito Russo, pulls a surprise by bringing out his friend Midler. Her spirited sing-along performance of "Friends" takes on special meaning for this large group of LGBTQ+ New Yorkers seeking equality. Midler is already a much-loved figure in the gay community, and her presence is a soothing balm for the frazzled and combative factions in the crowd.

1974

January   Midler achieves a certain kind of pop-culture status by topping the list of the viperish Mr. Blackwell's ten worst-dressed women for the previous year. In a group that includes Raquel Welch,

Princess Anne, and Jacqueline Kennedy Onassis—with room for the cisgender male David Bowie—Midler is singled out by Blackwell for looking "like she took pot luck in a laundromat." It isn't the last time Blackwell will unleashed his wrath on Midler, though she would turn up on his ten *best*-dressed list in the 1990s.

April 21   Midler receives a special Tony Award "for adding lustre to the Broadway season," following her record-breaking Palace Theatre run. Midler's dishy acceptance speech gets lots of laughs but turns unexpectedly serious when she says, "I'd like to address my remarks to the people who never go to the theater and to the people who've never been to the theater and to the people who don't know what theater is about. If you're watching this show and you live somewhere where there is a theater, whether it's a legitimate theater or a dinner theater or a university theater or any kind of theater, you must go and you must try and experience that because the theater is like nothing else on this whole planet . . . and the reason for that is that it is alive. And I thank you."

May 24   It turns out that *The Rose* isn't Midler's first film. In 1971, while appearing at a club in Windsor, Ontario, she is paid $252 in cash to play the Virgin Mary in a film spoof about the birth of Jesus. Her brief turn includes warbling a bit of "It's Beginning to Look a Lot Like Christmas" as Mary prepares to give birth and playing her scenes in what looks to be her stage wardrobe. The inept, unfunny comedy eventually opens in New York as *The Divine Mr. J.* with Midler billed above the title in an obvious attempt to piggyback on her current fame. Aaron

Russo springs into action, filing a lawsuit against the filmmakers and handing out flyers in front of the theater with a tell-it-like-it-is statement from Midler: "In my opinion, the movie is dreadful. However, I did it and there's nothing I can do about it except advise you of the true facts. If you still wish to see the film, c'est la vie."[5] *The Divine Mr. J.* fades quickly, though it will later be available on YouTube, billed as *The Thorn*, in clear reference to *The Rose.*

1976

January   In an interview syndicated to newspapers around the country, Laurence Olivier comments on seeing Midler in concert in Los Angeles. "Genius is a terrible word in our profession. I've spent most of my life believing that acting is not an art but an interpretive craft. But Bette Midler must be as near to being a genius as makes no matter. I know only that I sat there wearing an idiotic grin and happier than I can remember. . . . There's divinity about her. It restores your faith a lot."[6]

February 17   Harvard's Hasty Pudding Theatricals presents its twenty-sixth annual Woman of the Year award to Midler for her "great artistic skill and feminine qualities." After forcing one of the group's members to model the gold lamé bra she was given as a gift, she exits in a twirl that lifts her skirt to expose her bare ass. Years later, Midler makes the most of the notorious photo that catches the moment by using it as a punchline in her mock outrage over a new generation of trashy female singers.

1977

January   Midler is to make her debut with New York City Ballet in the Kurt Weill–Bertolt

Brecht dance-theater piece *The Seven Deadly Sins*, staged by the choreographer of its original 1933 production, George Balanchine. Midler, the "ingénue version of Lotte Lenya,"[7] as Tom Eyen first described her, would now play a singing role originated by Lenya. Rehearsals begin, but the production is eventually canceled due to a strike by the ballet company's musicians union.

September 18   In response to a wave of antigay legislation around the country, including Anita Bryant's "Save Our Children" campaign in Florida, Aaron Russo produces "A Star-Spangled Night for Rights," a fundraiser at the Hollywood Bowl with Midler, Richard Pryor, and Lily Tomlin as headliners. During the second act, Pryor's comedy monologue devolves into an obscenity-laden rant against the mostly white audience, ending with a demand to "kiss my happy, rich, black ass" as he walks off the stage. Midler, in her dressing room, hasn't heard Pryor and has planned an entrance in which the Harlettes, dressed in Ku Klux Klan robes, drag Midler, as the Statue of Liberty, onto the stage. She proceeds with the entrance, adding, "Who'd like to kiss this rich, white ass?" She gets a laugh, but the audience is in a foul mood, and Midler cuts her routine short, bringing the other performers (sans Pryor) back onstage for a quick rendition of "Friends."[8]

1978

September   After completing her first film, *The Rose*, Midler embarks on her first world tour. When she returns, she ends her tempestuous managerial relationship with Aaron Russo.

1979

May 26 Midler makes her first and only appearance on *Saturday Night Live*, singing her new single, "Married Men," and Tom Waits's "Martha." Her performance of "Martha," a song of recollection and regret, is particularly emotional, coming just a few months after the death of her mother, Ruth.

1980

Spring Insisting that a lady author should always appear in a hat, Midler attends signings for her new book, *A View from a Broad*, in a series of fanciful chapeaus, including a replica of the book, a typewriter, and a globe circled by an airplane—each perched jauntily atop her head. *A View from a Broad* eventually hits the *New York Times* nonfiction bestsellers list.

1983

Fall Midler's second book, the vividly illustrated *The Saga of Baby Divine*, is published, resulting in another round of whimsical lady-author hats at signings and another *New York Times* bestseller, this one on the fiction list.

1984

December 16 Midler marries Martin von Haselberg, a commodities broker and performance artist who appears under the name Harry Kipper. (The German von Haselberg inspires one of Midler's most oft-repeated jokes: "Every night I dress up like Poland and he invades me.") The couple is married in Las Vegas by an Elvis Presley impersonator. *People* magazine insists that of all recent celebrity marriages, the Midler–von Haselberg union will be the first to break up. The couple is still married today.

1985

January 28   Midler participates in the all-star recording of "We Are the World," which she later jokes about as "We are the rich / We are the famous," along with quips about "the soloists" (she was not one) and standing next to La Toya Jackson ("She wore a headband. I felt naked").

1986   Following the one-two box-office punch of *Down and Out in Beverly Hills* and *Ruthless People*, Midler is named one of the top ten box-office stars of 1986. She will reappear on the list in 1988.

November 14   Midler gives birth to her only child, a daughter. She describes the girl's name as "Sophie ('not for Sophie Tucker') Frederica ('for my father Fred') Alohilani ('Hawaiian for "bright sky" which is what I always wish for her') von Haselberg."[9]

1987

May 19   Midler scores big at the first annual American Comedy Awards: Funniest Record and/or Video (for her comedy album *Mud Will Be Flung Tonight!*); Funniest Female in a Motion Picture (for *Ruthless People*); Funniest Female Performer of the Year; and a Lifetime Achievement Award shared with Lily Tomlin. Of the last, she deadpans, "I certainly never expected to win a Lifetime Achievement Award. I'm only twenty-nine."

December   In the wake of the AIDS crisis, Midler expresses ambivalence regarding her breakthrough performances at the Continental Baths. In a *Vanity Fair* interview, she muses regretfully, "I mean, people go out to have fun. And there are a lot of excesses involved in having fun. Sometimes I'm really sorry that I had a part in it, that I was there. . . . I was helping to make it seem fun."[10] Her old friend and early champion, writer and activist Vito Russo, who has recently been diagnosed with HIV, holds a very different opinion and reaches out to Midler, reminding her that "it *was* fun and she should feel good about the past, present and future."[11]

1991

September 15   Midler, who cared for and financially supported her early friends Ben Gillespie and Bill Hennessy when both were diagnosed with AIDS, is always available for a donation or a performance at an AIDS fundraiser. She is honored with the Commitment to Life Award for her contribution to AIDS awareness and support by AIDS Project Los Angeles. In her remarks, she pauses to reflect, "My whole adult life I have had gay friends, I've had gay collaborators, I've had gay mentors. And if I live to be a thousand, I could never repay the debt I owe to them. They gave me my vision and they gave me my career."[12] When she sings the inevitable "Friends," the lines "I had some friends but they're gone / Something came and took them away" carry heartbreaking reverberations.

1995   "I have always picked up trash. I was born in Hawaii, when it was a pristine territory, and it was considered a sin to defile the land with so much as a gum wrapper," Midler once declared.[13] She's already been part of California's Adopt-a-Highway effort to clean up the state's public roads, but when she moves back to New York and sees how dirty the city has become, she goes even bigger. She establishes the New York Restoration Project, a nonprofit organization devoted to cleaning and reclaiming green spaces across the city. It's estimated that the NYRP has picked up more than 5 million pounds of garbage and, working with the New York City Department of Parks and Recreation, planted more than 1 million trees.

2001

September 23   Midler, who has done so much to make New York City more livable, sings a tearful and open-hearted "Wind beneath My Wings" at "A Prayer for America," an event at Yankee Stadium honoring those who lost their lives in the September 11 attack on the World Trade Center.

2003

November 26   On Larry King's show, Midler steps right in it when asked about gay marriage: "Gay men, they like to— you know, they like to move around. . . . That's part of the fun of being a gay man. So if they're married, does that mean they're not going to cheat? They're only going to be with one? . . . I'm really wondering how—what that commitment is going to be about."[14] *This* was the Divine Miss M, the belle of the baths? The one whose career had been animated by the influence and adoration of gay men? Asked later to clarify her statement, she hems and haws about needing to do more research and reading on the subject. She will eventually right her perspective and celebrate the Supreme Court ruling legalizing same-sex marriage in 2015 with an audience sing-along to "Chapel of Love" during her show at Madison Square Garden.

2008   Midler receives numerous awards and citations for her NYRP work, this year winning the Rachel Carson Award presented by the National Audubon Society's Women in Conservation Program.

2014

March 2 Midler takes the stage as a performer at the Academy Awards for the first time, singing "Wind beneath My Wings" during the "In Memoriam" segment. She returns in 2019 to sing "The Place Where Lost Things Go," from *Mary Poppins Returns*, written by Marc Shaiman, her longtime musical collaborator, and Scott Wittman.

2015 Midler takes to Twitter with a vengeance. The social-media platform's 280-character limit per post is perfect for her pithy, political, profane, and sometimes poorly judged off-the-cuff reflections. A sampling of her tweets during the fall of 2015 recalls her vintage celebrity put-downs: "Kanye West says he'll run for president in 2020. Who'd be in his cabinet? Kim Kardashian for Secretary of the Posterior?"; "Helen Mirren says she's retiring from doing nude scenes. Noooooo!! I was looking forward to *The Queen II: Regina's Vagina*"; and "People, #CaitlynJenner says she is STILL voting GOP in 2016. Regardless of gender identity, I guess she identifies most as 'uninformed.'"

2016

October Midler is a warmly encouraging, motherly guest mentor on season eleven of the popular television singing competition *The Voice*.

2019

Early June Donald Trump has trolled Midler for years, calling her "extremely unattractive" and saying her 2014 Academy Awards performance "sucked." As a major critic of his presidency, Midler never wastes an opportunity to lay into him. When she retweets a fake quote attributed to him (she later apologizes and removes the tweet), he returns fire, calling her a "washed up psycho."

June 29   Midler is the star attraction at "Stonewall 50—WorldPride NYC," the fiftieth-anniversary celebration of the Stonewall Riots. After expressing gratitude for the invitation, since she's a "washed up psycho" according to POTUS, she sings—what else?—"Friends," which plays like a beloved golden oldie nearly fifty years after she introduced it at the Continental Baths.

2021
January   Midler gets the last word in as Donald Trump leaves office, singing "Goodbye, Donnie!" with parody lyrics to the tune of "Hello, Dolly!" accompanied by images from the Trump presidency. It can be found on YouTube.

December 5   As she prepares to receive her Kennedy Center Honor, Midler is interviewed by the *New York Times* about her reading interests. Midler, who has often referred to herself as a librarian at heart, is a prodigious and informed reader. Amid a wide-ranging list of books in a variety of genres, she identifies Charles Dickens, Mark Twain, P. G. Wodehouse, and Maya Angelou as her favorite authors.

2022
October 30   As the Halloween-themed *Hocus Pocus 2* is breaking streaming records on Disney+, Midler hosts the twenty-sixth annual "Hulaween," an annual costume event benefiting the New York Restoration Project. The event, a nod to both Midler's Hawaiian heritage and her love of costume and dress-up and attended by New Yorkers sporting wildly theatrical and imaginative attire,

has raised millions for the nonprofit and is now a perennial event on New York City's calendar of fundraising functions.

2023

February 27   The Costume Designers Guild awards Midler its Distinguished Collaborator Award. In addition to remarking that she herself has had a bit of tailoring done on her face, Midler thanks the costume designers she's worked with over the years. She singles out Robert DeMora, who created, among many other Midler designs, the long-running wheelchair-driving mermaid Delores DeLago and her fish tail.

September   *The First Wives Club* may never get a follow-up, but as Midler nears her seventy-eighth birthday she begins filming another woman-centered comedy, *The Fabulous Four*, about a reunion of old friends co-starring Susan Sarandon, Megan Mullally, and Sheryl Lee Ralph.

Introduction

The Birth of the Divine

Labor Day weekend 1971. New York City. The Continental Baths in the basement of the Ansonia Hotel on West 74th Street. On this return appearance at the gay-men-only bathhouse, twenty-five-year-old Bette Midler is received like a returning champion, with her outrageous alter ego, "The Divine Miss M," in rare form. A mass of frizzy hair framing her face and her ample breasts swinging pendulously under a flimsy top, she good-naturedly dishes with the audience ("Look alive, your mother is up here working!"), jokes about Fire Island ("health spa for hairdressers") and old movie stars ("Martha Raye was mugged by the Viet Cong in the Christopher Street tearoom"), and revels in the kind of insider gay humor the towel-clad men love. Her opening number, "Friends," is already her theme song, an open-hearted embrace of the bathhouse audience, particularly on the line "Here is where I gotta stay," when she squats down and slaps the floor. Her musical selections dive deep into the detritus of American popular music, with Bessie Smith raunch and Andrews Sisters swing sitting surprisingly comfortably alongside Bob Dylan and Joni Mitchell. The cheers are loud and lusty, and in a cheeky act of solidarity, Miss M takes a final bow in a towel and flashes her derrière. Midler's show at the Continental is ground zero for a new kind of song-and-comedy cabaret entertainment— bawdy, emotionally vulnerable, and with a decidedly gay sensibility.

December 2021. Washington, D.C. The 44th Annual Kennedy Center Honors at the John F. Kennedy Center for the Performing Arts. The Kennedy Center Honors, celebrating artists for their contributions to American culture through the performing arts, is the Mount Everest of lifetime achievement awards. Among the five honorees is seventy-six-year-old Bette Midler, looking regal in white (and matching Covid mask) and with her short blond-gray hair tastefully coiffed, whom President Joe Biden salutes as "a true American treasure." At the nationally televised celebration, Midler is serenaded with a sequence of songs she is most identified with, at least a few of which she originated at the baths. Billy Porter, as brazen as Midler ever was, sings two of her signature songs, "Boogie Woogie Bugle Boy" and "From a Distance." Signifiers from the last fifty years abound: Porter emerges from a giant clam (Midler's entrance in 1975's *Clams on the Half Shell Revue*), insisting, "I'll never forget it, you know!" (Midler's deathless, dirty-mouthed "Soph" character), and calling, "Where are my girls?" (Midler's stalwart backup trio, the Staggering Harlettes). Costars from her recent hit Broadway revival of *Hello, Dolly!* sing "Friends." They don't squat down and slap the floor, but they don't have to. The performing style and ethos she embodied at the Continental have long since been absorbed into the mainstream of popular entertainment and culture, and this honor only underscores the distance Midler had traveled from there to here.

During her fifty-year journey from the Continental's subterranean showroom to the august Kennedy Center, Midler took that performing style and parlayed it into a multidecade career in concerts, films, television, and recordings. Today Midler is the very definition of a mainstream celebrity: your mother's—or grandmother's—favorite singer, known for what she calls her "inspirational ballads" such as "Wind beneath My Wings"; the brassy star of vintage "chick flicks" such as *Beaches* and *The First Wives Club*; the doyenne of shrubbery whose long-running New York Restoration Project restores parks and green spaces to the people of New York City; a Twitter warrior who takes on venal politicians and narcissistic celebrities one tweet at a time; and the beloved star

who broke box-office records in her lavishly praised Broadway return in *Hello, Dolly!*

Long before she was divine, Midler was just one of hundreds of
young women trying to get a toehold in show business. Her unconventional looks didn't help, and her apprenticeship in New York
theater was bumpy. She finally found her footing as a performer by
singing to a crowd of gay men who sought refuge at the baths from
an often cruel and dangerous world. As she later wrote, "I was able
to take chances on that stage that I could not have taken anywhere
else. Ironically, I was freed from fear by people who, at the time,
were ruled by fear. And for that I will always be grateful."[1]

The self-described "plain little fat Jewish kid"[2] who grew up as
part of a religious and racial minority on the outskirts of Honolulu
formed a kinship with the gay men who sat at her feet at the
Continental. Many had fled their small-town homes and families
for the anonymity of a big city, just as Midler had left Hawaii for
New York and the theater at the earliest opportunity. Encouraged
by them, she created a new form of cabaret performance, giving gay
male sensibility a broader expression. Her loyalty to them, even as
she expanded her audience, marked Midler as different from other
female entertainers and made her a much-loved figure.

Midler's problems growing up share a striking similarity with
those of so many gay men of her generation. She was very much an
outsider among the Samoans, Filipinos, and Chinese in her school
and community, "where there were almost no white people and no
Jews and I was both and I was made to feel at the time that I was
different, that I was not as good as the rest of them."[3] Like many
gay boys who hide their sexuality, she tried passing—in her case,
by letting some think she was Portuguese: "Because Portuguese
people were accepted. Jews were not."[4] That her breasts developed
early and prodigiously offered another opportunity for scorn. "All
these tough girls would chase me home from school and try to
beat me up just because I had bigger boobs than them," she later
recalled.[5]

For someone later deemed outrageous, Midler was a wary, bookish teenager who kept to herself, as much for self-protection as personal preference. Library visits, reading, movies, and listening to music were her solitary pursuits.

Like many a gay boy, Midler found that humor was the key to acceptance. She became a clown, a cutup, while still managing to be an honor roll student. She found her teenage métier in speech classes, talent shows, and student performances, culminating in the starring role in her senior class play, *Our Hearts Were Young and Gay*. With newfound determination to be an actor, Midler spent a year and a half as a theater major at the University of Hawaii, working summers on a pineapple factory assembly line. ("It was really sickening, but I needed the money.")[6]

Midler was too keyed up and anxious for a career to stay in school or in Hawaii, and her escape plan was launched when the production company behind the film adaptation of James Michener's *Hawaii* arrived in Honolulu for location shooting. Midler was selected as a nonspeaking bit player for the film (as a missionary's seasick wife) and was one of a smaller number chosen to travel to Los Angeles for additional filming. The money she earned financed her move to New York City in 1965. Midler was just nineteen years old, with only a small nest egg, no connections, and no real training or experience. But just like countless gay boys who made their way to the city, "I just blossomed out when I came here," she later said. "I never felt I was home till I came here. I became all the things I wanted to be. It was like I was finally free."[7]

Midler's arrival in New York coincided with a burgeoning off-off-Broadway scene, much of which was marked by gay camp humor, satire, and parody. The free-for-all atmosphere of these shows was more welcoming of her unorthodox looks and wild sense of humor than the traditional Broadway plays and musicals she auditioned for. Years before his big Broadway hit with the book and lyrics for *Dreamgirls*, Tom Eyen was a fixture of downtown experimental theater. His cheerfully anarchic plays, many of which he directed, were laced with sex and movie references and included *The White Whore and the Bit Player* and *Why Hanna's Skirt Won't Stay Down*. In the fall of 1965, he was preparing his newest, a Cleopatra musical spoof, when Midler arrived at his door to audition, looking like "an ingenue version of Lotte Lenya."[8] The Lenya connection was apt, since the teenager proceeded to sing a twelve-page arrangement of *The Threepenny Opera*'s "Pirate Jenny."

She was cast immediately, and on her twentieth birthday, Midler made her New York stage debut as "Naomi and Assorted Virgins" in *Miss Nefertiti Regrets* at La MaMa Experimental Theatre Club. The musical was revived twice in the early months of 1966, with Midler elevated to the title role.

The following summer, she joined the cast of Eyen's *Cinderella Revisited*, billed as a "Musical fantasy for demented children." An adult version, *Sinderella Revisited*, was performed in the evenings. According to Eyen, "there was no difference in the nighttime version except for one scene wherein . . . Sinderella gets gang-fucked by the evil stepsisters and a few Republican neighbors." During a matinee, "the actors forgot and put in the orgy scene . . . the kids loved it."[9]

Midler immersed herself in the work of other downtown artists who would influence her later performance aesthetic. "There were a lot of people who were doing exciting things then—[John] Vaccaro and Charles Ludlam," she later said. "As a matter of fact I got a great deal of my early inspiration from Charles Ludlam . . . the first thing I saw him do was *Turds in Hell* which blew me away. It was incredible, it was the most incredible piece of theater I had ever seen. And there was this chick in the show named Black-Eyed Susan . . . she was terrific and she really inspired me."[10]

Writer, director, and actor Ludlam was at the vanguard of this new theater movement that produced works of epic scale combining high culture (Shakespeare, Pirandello, James Joyce) with low (quotes and characterizations lifted from old Hollywood films) and featuring uninhibited nudity and simulated sex. In *Turds in*

Hell, typical of early Ludlam, a hunchbacked, penis-shaped hero searches for his lost mother in an underworld filled with depraved types rubbing elbows with sainted religious figures. For Midler, the key sequence was a 1930s number with Black-Eyed Susan as the Statue of Liberty wrapped in toilet paper and dollar bills singing Kay Starr's 1950s hit "Wheel of Fortune." This hellzapoppin' hybrid of theater of the absurd and jokey, mid-century gay humor was summed up by playwright Ronald Tavel: "We have passed beyond the absurd. Our position is absolutely preposterous."[11] Ludlam and Eyen gave Midler a glimpse of an expanded theatrical world unbounded by the strictures of commercial theater, which relied on "types" and proscribed ethnic and gender norms.*

Ever since she arrived in New York, she had been auditioning for *Fiddler on the Roof*, the Broadway musical smash based on Sholom Aleichem's stories of Tevye the Jewish milkman and his five daughters. If Midler's looks and skill set ever played in her favor, this was it, and on November 9, 1966, *Variety* carried a brief squib explaining, "Bette Midler has succeeded Irene Paris as one of the villagers in the Broadway 'Fiddler.'"[12] Midler often spoke of her difficulty in breaking into the theater, but by her first anniversary in New York, she had become a semi-regular player for an off-off-Broadway *macher*, spent the summer as a performer in *An Evening of Tradition* on the "Borscht Belt" circuit in the Catskills, and made it to Broadway in the street's biggest hit. If not exactly a "Star Is Born" storyline, it was a solid accomplishment that paid off from hard work and perseverance.

The *Fiddler* gig was as a temporary replacement for an ensemble member, but Midler got to understudy the role of Tzeitel, Tevye's

---

* John Vaccaro's Play-House of the Ridiculous, which staged works by Tavel and others, numbered Charles Ludlam, a recent graduate of Hofstra University's drama department, as a company actor. After a falling out with Vaccaro, the twenty-four-year-old Ludlam established his own company, the Ridiculous Theatrical Company, and took with him several key members from Vaccaro's company. *Turds in Hell* was among the new company's first productions.

oldest daughter, a big supporting role with musical and dramatic opportunities. Later, after auditioning for the show's director-choreographer, Jerome Robbins, she was hired to play the role permanently. "I thought, well, this is my chance. . . . I'm on my way now," she later said. "And I wasn't. I was in *Fiddler*."[13]

Midler stayed with the show for three full years. The ambitious young actor had hoped to use her Broadway perch as a platform for other jobs, but "I couldn't get into agent's [sic] offices. And when they would send me out for auditions the people wouldn't like the way I looked, or the way I sounded."[14] Midler had run up against age-old show-business biases. She was a "character" type (i.e., she looked Jewish). She wasn't "pretty." She had a big nose. She wasn't a typical ingénue (at least, not outside *Fiddler*). Midler's photograph in *Fiddler*'s souvenir program was a carefully lighted portrait downplaying her nose and presenting her in a conservative, high-necked dress and sensible short bob. She admitted, "I used to look at those pictures of myself and no matter what angle they shot, I still couldn't get my foot in the door. I just decided I had to let that little dream go because it was destroying me."[15]

Marta Heflin, another *Fiddler* cast member, often sang at showcase cabaret rooms where performers could get up and try out songs. Midler began going with her and eventually began singing herself. One night, at a room in Greenwich Village called Hilly's, Midler experienced a turning point. "The first two songs I sang, nothing happened. But in the third song ["God Bless the Child"], something happened to me in the middle. I suddenly knew what the song was about. I had an experience, some kind of breakthrough. And when I came out at the end, I knew I had to do that. For as long as the trip will be, I had to live it out."[16]

Midler now had a passion, something to keep her going through her eight-show weeks in *Fiddler*. Afternoons were spent searching for obscure songs at the New York Public Library for the Performing Arts at Lincoln Center or rifling through thrift shops and Salvation Army stores for the long velvet dresses and vintage gowns that now made up her wardrobe. After the show, she'd head to a club to sing in her retro finery. This torch singer style was adopted by way of her boyfriend Ben Gillespie, a dancer in *Fiddler* who introduced her to recordings by Helen Morgan, Libby Holman, and Aretha Franklin with her tribute album to Dinah Washington. These were singers she'd never heard before, and she found herself drawn to their dramatic performances of vintage torch songs. Her repertoire shifted exclusively to songs like "Am I Blue?" and "Ten Cents a Dance," which she later characterized as "I lost this person/I lost that person."[17]

Like Eyen, Gillespie, who later came out as gay, was an important early gay male mentor to Midler. He encouraged her to find her own interpretation of these songs by stripping them to their emotional core. Gillespie coached her on the physical and dramatic presentation of her material. "He taught me a grandeur I had never known before," she said. "He inspired me not to be afraid and to understand what the past had to offer me."[18]

Midler frequently sang at the Improv on West 44th Street, a tough, show-business insiders club better known as a showcase for comedians than for singers. Its owner, Budd Friedman, was excited by Midler's potential and signed her to a management contract. By now, she had left *Fiddler* and, after a brief stint as a replacement in *Salvation*, an off-Broadway rock musical, she began to concentrate exclusively on her singing. Friedman negotiated her first paying jobs, including a few out-of-town club dates and television spots on *The David Frost Show* and *The Merv Griffin Show*.

Midler was a hard worker who was always taking classes, researching new music, or checking out Hollywood films from the 1930s and '40s at revival houses with Gillespie and another gay friend, Bill Hennessy, a hairdresser on *Fiddler*. "Afterward, Bette would do take-offs of people like Charlotte Greenwood, Martha Raye, and Joan Davis," Hennessy recalled.[19] Midler was inadvertently prepping for the next act of her career.

Doin' the Continental

Bathhouses were as much a part of gay social life as bars in New York City—and their owners just as contemptuous of their clientele. The "tubs," as they were called, were straight-owned and -operated, often with mob money, and subject to police raids, just like the bars. There was little incentive to upgrade their dank, run-down facilities, even at the most popular bathhouses like the Everard on West 28th Street (sometimes referred to as the Ever*hard*).

The situation was duly noted by Steve Ostrow, a married, openly bisexual entrepreneur and bathhouse regular, who was convinced that a new place offering clean, well-maintained facilities and respectful treatment could dominate this lucrative niche market. Ostrow found a suitable location in the basement of the Ansonia Hotel, a landmark residential building and home to many performing artists, located on Broadway between 73rd and 74th Streets. The previous tenant had been a health club featuring a forty-five-foot swimming pool, with a gym, steam room, and showers nearby. Ostrow leased two other floors in which he installed more than a hundred private rooms with beds and one hundred fifty lockers, all available for twelve-hour stays.[20]

When the Continental Bath and Health Club opened in September 1968, it was New York's largest gay bathhouse, boasting unheard-of amenities. The pool area included a restaurant, library, tanning booth, and TV room. Nearby was a jukebox and a dance floor where weekend dance contests were followed by free buffet meals. The orgy room was (dimly) illuminated by chandelier. Twenty-nine floors above, the Continental's "Sun and Sky Club" offered a sun roof for sunbathing.[21]

The Continental was an immediate success, but it also attracted the attention of the police, who staged frequent raids and entrapment arrests. "They'd wear handcuffs underneath their towels, waiting for someone to touch them," Ostrow said.[22] The raids eventually stopped, but not because of payoffs. Instead, the landscape of gay New York had changed. That change began on a sultry night in June 1969, when the patrons of the Stonewall, a gay bar in the Village, refused to file into paddy wagons after a by-then-routine police raid and instead fought back, serving notice that gays and lesbians and trans persons would no longer submit to police harassment. The Stonewall Riots, as they were later termed, were the cornerstone of the contemporary gay rights movement.

The Continental, with its image as an inviting social haven "for sophisticated males only,"[23] was well positioned to take advantage of the new sense of freedom and self-respect in the city's gay community. Articles in the local gay press lavishly praised Ostrow's Upper West Side pleasure palace, noting not only its cleanliness and amenities but also the feeling of community it offered gay men on the cusp of a new era of liberation.

Ostrow took all this praise very seriously, and his vision for the Continental soon acquired a grandiosity far beyond its original conception. He was eager to add "show business impresario" to his CV and decided that the Continental would add live entertainment to its list of attractions.

Ostrow's choice of entertainment reveals a desire to position the bathhouse as a legitimate performance venue offering the best professional talent he could afford. The Continental's first performers were a husband-and-wife folk-singing duo named Rosalie and Lowell Mark, who sang on weekends in early 1970. The Marks came to the Continental via singing and acting classes taught by Robert Elston, whose classes at the Herbert Berghof Studio in the Village served as a talent pool for the Continental in its early days.

Scouting for an act to follow the Marks, Ostrow again turned to Elston, who recommended another of his students. Ostrow heard her sing at the Improv, made an offer, and settled on a date for her first appearance. Starting in July, Midler would perform at the Continental for eight Fridays and Saturdays at one a.m. for fifty dollars a weekend.

Divine

On a visit to the Continental, Bill Hennessy saw an announcement of Midler's upcoming appearance. Assuming it couldn't possibly be her, he immediately phoned to tell her that a drag queen
was appearing at the Continental using her name.[24] Midler roared
with laughter and used the line during her first performance. It
was probably the only laugh she got that weekend. Her torch songs
were politely received by the twenty or so men sitting on the floor
near the swimming pool. The second night's reception was noticeably cooler, and she realized that many of the men were weekend
regulars who expected a different show each night.

Midler also recognized that the Continental wasn't Hilly's or the
Improv. It was noisy and unfocused, with men coming and going
from the nearby steam room or splashing in the pool while she sang.
And entertainment was secondary to the baths' primary purpose.
"The audience there wouldn't settle for half-ass," she reasoned. "If
I'd kept my distance, they'd have lost interest because there were too
many other things going on in the building that were more fun."[25]

This unorthodox setting required an entirely different energy
and approach, and it also offered Midler opportunities she'd never
had, as one of her biographers, James Spada, observed. "Bette
realized early on that here was a chance to be raunchy and sexy and
wild without having to appear in a show; at the baths, she could be
like Black-Eyed Susan and yet not have to keep to a script."[26] Soon
her act was nearly unrecognizable from her first appearance.

The biggest change was her appropriation of gay camp elements
into every facet of her performance. What is camp? People seem to
know it when they see it but find it hard to explain. And it's different
for different people. Susan Sontag laid down a marker with her
influential 1964 essay "Notes on Camp," but she only grudgingly
acknowledged its strong link to homosexuals.[27] Journalist Jack
Babuscio later claimed camp was central to gay male sensibility,
calling it "a heightened awareness of certain human complications

of feeling that spring from the fact of social oppression."[28] Camp, he wrote, is "those elements of a person, situation, or activity that express, or are created by, a gay sensibility."[29] The gay camp elements incorporated by Midler into her act included humor, visuals, and a whole new musical repertoire.

She had never talked much between songs, but Hennessy began working with her to create jokes, gags, and characters, and she quickly found her own speed and rhythm as a comedian. Midler began referring to a character based on Hennessy himself named Mr. Gerard, or "The Divine Mr. G," her hairdresser who worked in a salon in the 34th Street subway station (and sometimes in between the tracks).

Her comedy also encompassed bits of Jewish, feminist, and show-business humor and found its perfect embodiment in a newly created alter ego, "The Divine Miss M." Originally a female counterpart to Hennessy's Divine Mr. G, "Miss M" was the means by which she could directly connect with the men. "At the Continental Baths I was playing to people who are always on the outside looking in," she later said. "To create the *semblance* of someone like that can be wonderful. And so I created the character of The Divine Miss M. She's just a fantasy, but she's useful at showing people what that outsider's perspective is."[30]

The unattractive Jewish girl from Hawaii who left home seeking success in the theater but couldn't find a place in mainstream show business had much in common with the men who regularly came to the baths seeking sex and a sense of community. As the Divine Miss M, she joked about sex the same way gay men did, dishing their mating habits at the baths ("Even Josephine the Plumber couldn't get the stains out of these sinks"). Miss M spoke in an exaggerated, drag queen manner, cajoling or dishing everyone, including herself (in response to subway graffiti that read, "Miss Midler is a drag queen from Chicago," she insisted, "I am not from Chicago").[31] She took up the knowing, insider manner that gay men often used about show-business figures ("I ripped this dress off Joan Crawford's back"). She adopted familiar gay camp expressions, calling the Continental "the pits," and joked about her attire as "tacky." She referred to herself and to anything deserving the highest praise as "divine," another camp term (think Tallulah Bankhead), and the expression soon shot into the gay slang pantheon.

In fact, the Divine Miss M, with her mincing, sashaying stage manner, had much in common with female impersonator Ty Bennett, a headliner throughout the 1960s at Club 82, a popular mob-run drag nightclub on the Lower East Side. Whether or not Hennessy was familiar with Bennett's act, elements of Bennett's dry, double-entendre-laden asides to audience members could be heard in Midler's dishing with the Continental audience. The portly Bennett, who looked much like Sophie Tucker in drag, also performed in Tucker's style, and his risqué stories share similarities with Midler's later Soph jokes. Bennett exemplified a popular female-impersonator hostess type, one who mixed droll one-liners with songs. The comedy material Hennessy created with Midler shared obvious similarities with the style and manner of drag performers like Bennett.

Yet Midler also exuded a strong female sexuality, reveling in her body and as much concerned with sexual liberation as the gay men in her audience. She was unquestionably a straight woman with strong appetites, but she made it clear that her sexual desires were no different from theirs. Her appraisals of the physical attributes of men were directed to an audience of equals. Her humor, an increasingly important part of her performances, could be sarcastic, but Midler tempered it with a genuinely warm personality and self-deprecating wit.

In footage of an appearance at the Continental, what's most striking is her apparent nervousness amid the brashness and vulgarity of her act. When she introduces a new song, she confides her apprehension at singing it for the first time. Later, in misjudging a music cue, she ends a song ahead of the band and readily admits, "I fucked it up!" She implores the crowd to come and see her in an upcoming engagement at another club because "I don't know too many people in that neighborhood." The vulnerability beneath the bravado helped Midler communicate with the men in a manner that ultra-serious female singers of the time such as Peggy Lee or Sarah Vaughan did not. She had a sensuality that funny women such as Joan Rivers and Phyllis Diller lacked. And her presence was more humanistic than that of the drag performers whose style she borrowed.

Trash with Flash

The camp element of Midler's act took visual form when she ditched the long velvet dresses. She still got her clothes at thrift shops, but now they were a lively hodgepodge of different eras. Merry Widow corsets, halter tops with no bra, wraparound skirts slit to the thigh, and skintight lamé pants all contributed to her new "trash with flash" look. Her mincing walk was facilitated by Spring-o-Lator shoes (a type of platform shoe that sat dangerously atop an extra-long, narrow heel). She also stopped straightening her curly hair and instead let it provide a frizzy frame to her face, adding to the animation of her features.

Her new look was a form of drag that differed significantly from drag performers, most of whom sought to create the illusion of female-ness while camouflaging their biological gender. Midler's drag boldly emphasized her own physical attributes—a full, lush bosom, which she would shake or sensuously caress, and slim legs and hips—and made her appear a more vibrant and sexualized woman. By boldly wearing "trashy" clothes and using vulgar gestures, Midler subverted the notion of passing for straight (e.g., conforming to conventional feminine standards of decorum) and further underlined the outsider status she shared with her audience.

When she began at the Continental, Midler had less than a half hour's worth of songs and was desperate to add new material.

She called on Gillespie and Billy Cunningham, the Continental's house pianist, to help her find comedy and novelty songs to enliven what she called a "fairly negative, bluesy down trip."[32] Her earlier repertoire was confined to the 1920s and '30s, but with their help, she began to explore other eras. As with her humor and costuming, Midler's songs further accommodated a gay camp sensibility. Babuscio wrote that "while camp advocates the dissolution of hard and inflexible moral rules, it pleads, too, for a morality of sympathy."[33] Midler's "morality of sympathy" led her to explore the value in forgotten rock and roll, girl-group jingles, and 1940s swing.

Midler had always loved girl groups of the 1960s such as the Shangri-Las, the Shirelles, and the Ronettes, and she began singing songs that they and others of the period had made popular, including "Leader of the Pack," "Sh-Boom," and "Chapel of Love." From 1940s movies, she added the Glenn Miller swing hit "Chattanooga Choo Choo" and the Andrews Sisters' "Boogie Woogie Bugle Boy." Camp novelties like "Marahuana" and Mae West's "Come Up and See Me Sometime" became staples of her act. But she also gave authentic readings of rock numbers such as the Beatles' "Lady Madonna" and the Rolling Stones' "Honky Tonk Woman," blues such as Bessie Smith's "Empty Bed Blues," and contemporary songs by Joni Mitchell and Leon Russell.

Midler's act became a panorama of American popular music, but rather than a mishmash of different styles and eras, the songs were unified by her sense of purpose as a singing actor. She didn't condescend to "Leader of the Pack" or "Chattanooga Choo Choo" but sang them with intensity and commitment. Midler instinctively grasped how to physicalize each song. For "Chattanooga Choo Choo," she single-handedly recreated the energy of all three Andrew Sisters, featuring a full round of bosom shaking and ending with a collapse onto the floor. Midler's embrace of songs and musical genres that other singers found of dubious quality demonstrated her "morality of sympathy" for outsiders and underdogs.

These songs, along with her comedy, provided a pointed and devastating contrast to her more serious singing. Before long, a young songwriter and pianist named Barry Manilow began working with Midler as her musical director and arranger. His charts brought a discipline and focus to Midler's musical performances. Now she began to truly distinguish herself as a ballad interpreter, delivering songs such as "Superstar," "Hello in There," and "Am I Blue?" (one of the few holdovers from her old repertoire) in a naked, deeply personal manner. Since she purposely pitched her performance to acknowledge and embrace her audience's sexuality, her raw-nerve ballads hit them hard and further marked her as different from other female singers.

The Streisand Thing

From the moment Midler began to be talked and written about, she was repeatedly compared to Barbra Streisand. Most of the comparisons were reductive, if not downright biased. Both were identifiable, forthright Jewish women with prominent noses. Both sang out-of-left-field songs with emotive intensity. Both were idolized by gay men. There were other similarities beyond the obvious—as well as some major differences.

Streisand was the Brooklyn diva who gained attention by winning a talent contest at the Lion, a Greenwich Village gay bar. This led to a breakout engagement at the Bon Soir, a Village nightclub also heavily attended by a voluble gay male audience. In fact, gay men formed the nucleus of her early fan base. Then it was on to other nightclubs, television appearances, a Columbia Records contract, and Broadway renown, followed by major movie stardom. By the time Midler played her first fifty-dollar gig at the Continental, Streisand was an Oscar–Emmy–Grammy–(honorary)Tony Award–winning entertainment icon and had created the template for the kind of cross-media stardom Midler would seek.

But when she was just starting out with ambitions of succeeding as a dramatic actor, Streisand, like Midler, knew that singing was the key to opening doors and getting noticed. She was aided immeasurably by actor-singer Barry Dennen, who introduced her to recordings by great chanteuses of an earlier era, selected her song repertoire, and coached her in phrasing and interpretation. Dennen and Streisand were lovers, similar to Midler's relationship with Gillespie, and Dennen later come out as gay. Streisand also acquired an accompanist, Peter Daniels, whose sympathetic piano allowed her room for interpretive flights within his skilled backing.

Both Streisand and Midler often sang obscure songs, but Streisand's were mostly neglected items from the great American songbook by Harold Arlen, Rodgers and Hart, and Sigmund Romberg. She seldom engaged with the music of her contemporaries. Midler, on the other hand, was an enthusiastic dumpster diver, rooting through several decades of discarded pop and novelty songs to discover hidden gems. Streisand's repertoire was more elevated and upwardly mobile, and Daniels provided the perfect musical settings for her vocal dramatizations. Midler had broader, more egalitarian tastes and treated Kurt Weill, the Dixie Cups, Bob Dylan, and Glenn Miller with equal respect. Manilow's arrangements found the ideal musical profile for each song, showcasing her voice to its best advantage.

"If it hadn't been for certain gay friends of mine, I wouldn't know nothing from nothing," Midler declared in 1998. "If Ben Gillespie hadn't played Aretha Franklin for me, I'd still be singing in *Fiddler on the Roof*."[34] Midler readily credited Gillespie, Hennessy, and Manilow for introducing her to a world of songs and singers she'd never experienced, for helping channel her natural wit and humor into a comic persona, and for providing the musical discipline that helped reveal her gifts as a singer. Streisand, on the other hand, always downplayed the importance of Dennen and Daniels to the development of her early repertoire and musical profile, instead preferring the narrative that she emerged fully formed as an artist

in her earliest appearances. It would fall to other, later writers, including Dennen himself, to quantify the foundational assistance
she received but never fully acknowledged.[†]

As for their voices, there was really no comparison. Streisand's
powerful, piercing voice with its crystalline tone had no peer in
popular music. Midler sometimes had pitch problems and strained
to hit high notes. At times, she could be strident. She was the first
to admit her vocal shortcomings—and to compliment Streisand,
opining "she has it all above me technically and musically, but I try
to get as much feeling as possible into my small range."[35]

Streisand's pristine vocals were of a piece with her visual presentation. Just like Midler, she went for thrift-store finery in her
early days but quickly jettisoned this look for a sleek, tailored style.
Streisand was a fashion trendsetter (she picked up her Oscar in designer Arnold Scaasi's glittering see-through pajamas) who leaned
into looks that showed her at her most glamorous. Midler couldn't
compete with Streisand's chic. She was an Everywoman who wasn't
afraid to look spent or disheveled on stage. Her "trash with flash"
style was strictly mix-and-match.

Where Streisand was composed and slightly aloof, Midler was
in constant motion, stalking the stage and engaging with the audience. Streisand's vocalism was controlled; Midler's was often on a
hair trigger. (It's hard to imagine Streisand ever admitting "I fucked
it up!") Streisand *allowed* the audience to experience her extraordinary talent; she could just as easily sing for herself or for five thousand people. Midler warmly *welcomed* her audience into a shared
experience, and her creativity fed off their involvement.

There was one other, crucial area in which the two had little in
common. Streisand's early success happened in the pre-Stonewall

---

[†] In *My Life with Barbra: A Love Story* (Amherst, NY: Prometheus, 1997), Barry
Dennen identifies himself as part of a triumvirate of gay men who contributed to
Streisand's breakthrough performances, including designer Terry Leong, who styled
Streisand's memorable stage costumes from thrift-shop finds, and Bob Schulenberg, the
originator of Streisand's striking makeup and hairstyles.

era, and she quickly put distance between herself and her early gay fans, never acknowledging their early support even in later, more liberated times. Midler, on the other hand, was like every mouthy girl who stood up for her gay friends when they were bullied in school. "The boys from the baths were the start—they were really the beginning of my career, and I'll say that from now till the day I die . . . and they are still the foundation of my audience. They're very loyal, and I would never give them up—they're a great audience."[36] Midler became the first post-Stonewall star, closing the distance that Streisand kept from gay audiences and emphasizing her similarities to them.

"I Shall Be Released"

The plaintive yet determined melody of Bob Dylan's "I Shall Be Released" accompanies lyrics that appear to reference a man's yearning for freedom from incarceration. "They say ev'ry man needs protection / They say ev'ry man must fall," he sings with irony before insisting, "So I remember ev'ry face / Of ev'ry man who put me here." He tries to find hope somewhere above the walls that hold him. Finally, he observes, "Standing next to me in this lonely crowd / Is a man who swears he's not to blame / All day long I hear him shout so loud / Crying out that he was framed," before returning to the song's determined refrain: "Any day now, any day now / I shall be released."

The Band included "I Shall Be Released" on its 1968 debut album, and Dylan himself recorded it in 1971. Women also performed the song. Cass Elliot, Mary Travers, and Joni Mitchell blended in sisterly harmonies on Elliot's 1969 television special, while Nina Simone's stately interpretation was a demand for racial dignity. But they kept Dylan's lyrics intact. When Midler added it to her set list in 1971, it was with a complete overhaul.

Manilow's arrangement built slowly from a mournful piano line, following Midler as she sang barely above a whisper but soon built in power. "I remember ev'ry face / Of ev'ry man who put me here" as sung by a woman instantly takes the song in a new, unexpected direction. She swapped genders to add a recriminating edge, singing, "They say ev'ry woman needs protection / And then they turn around and tell you ev'ry woman's got to fall." Midler turned the final verse inside out, furiously reworking the lyric: "Now yonder stands there in that lonely crowd / A man who swears he's not to blame / And if you ask him, has he ever seen this lonely woman / He'll tell you no, no, and what's more, he does not know my name."

Now when she sang, "Any day now, any day now / I shall be released," it was with the fury of every woman who had ever been mistreated, lied to, abandoned. She doubled down on the lyric about women needing protection, repeating it mockingly before adding, "And then they turn around and say, no, I'm gonna make that woman fall!" She turned Dylan's song into a howling cri de coeur, with fists clenched and beating the air. As she exhorted the men at the Continental, repeating "Any day now" over and over, the song became a fierce declaration of emancipation for women and gay men alike. As the audience jumped to its feet and cheered, she bowed deeply from the waist with her arms at her side—an oddly formal gesture that reinforced her kinship with her audience. It was a moment that resonated with deep emotion.

Midler's original eight weeks at the Continental extended into sixteen, and her reception in the gay press took on a particularly proud and proprietary air. Author and activist Vito Russo, a friend and early supporter, gushed, "I am now convinced that Bette Midler is destined to be numbered among the great performers of our time. . . . I have heard *no one* sing as she sang . . . not Joplin, not Garland, not Piaf, not Streisand, *no one*."[37] Ostrow soon began announcing Midler—with typical, if now justified, bombast—as "the first great superstar of the Continental Baths."

By 1971, Midler's acclaim had moved beyond the gay scene, and Ostrow, who had upgraded the Continental's interior with gleaming Lucite and chrome finishes and dramatic lighting, began to open her performances to women and straight men. The only woman who had ever been seen on the premises was Ostrow's wife (though his daughter did chores there on Saturdays). Ostrow knew that opening the baths to the general public would imbue it with insider cachet and media attention. "Ladies Welcome," the sign at the door soon read—but for the show only, after which they were kindly, but firmly, asked to leave. As if on cue, the show-business and media elite soon arrived: Mick Jagger, David Bowie, Andy Warhol, Helen Gurley Brown, columnists from *Women's Wear Daily*. A gallery space with chairs was set up for clothed audiences and sometimes roped off, not unlike a VIP area. Suddenly, a late-night show at a gay male bathhouse was the hippest, most "in" event in town, commanding mainstream media attention for Bette and the baths.

By now, Midler had added a new number that would become her theme song. When she was hired to do a backers' audition for a new musical, her scene partner, singer-writer Buzzy Linhart, played her a song he had written with Moogy Klingman. "(You Got to Have) Friends" was a jaunty sing-along ode to the importance of friendship, and Midler immediately saw its potential for her act. "Friends," as it was thereafter called, carried a bittersweet undercur-rent for Midler and the Continental's audience. "Standing at the end of the road, boy / Waiting for my new friends to come" held as much meaning for this young woman still finding her way in show busi-ness as it did for the men sitting at her feet each weekend (no VIP area for them) while outside making their way through a straight world that was only marginally beginning to welcome them.

In fact, they only had to read some of the coverage Midler was getting in the mainstream press to see just how far they still had to go. The toxic antigay attitudes on display in the rock press of the 1970s is shocking in the twenty-first century, but it was standard commentary for outlets such as *Rolling Stone*, which sent Ed McCormack to profile Midler and the Continental. After denigrating her appearance (she looked "like a girl who doesn't get asked out on Saturday night"), McCormack focused his scorn on the Continental's gay patrons, referring to them as "hunkering, buggering manmeat herds," who reminded him of William S. Burroughs's novel *The Wild Boys*, "in which wild boypacks raised in a womanless society run amok and lay waste to the remnants of Western Civilization."[38] "Any day now" couldn't come fast enough.

The Gay Show-Biz Sensibility

Midler was being recognized as a new kind of chanteuse, one whose performances were a synthesis of rock and theater. She had seen Janis Joplin and Tina Turner whip audiences into a frenzy with their raw power and soulful intensity. Midler was willing to scream and shout, to collapse on the floor, to risk looking ridiculous to move an audience. She was a savvy show person whose vivid, over-the-top performing style struck a chord with both gay men and the straight audiences she was now reaching. "We were in North Carolina a couple of weeks ago and this chick came up to me and she said, 'You know, you remind me so much of myself,'" Midler recalled. "'When I go to a party I get drunk and I carry on just exactly the way you carry on.'"[39] The connection Midler forged with fans went beyond the stage.

It turned out that camp sells, not just to gays but to everyone in some form or other. When *Ms.* magazine put her on its cover and asked several women to weigh in with thoughts on the Bette Midler phenomenon, nearly all invoked some analysis of camp in her work. "She's given camp back to women," declared novelist-playwright Roslyn Dexter."[40] The performing ethos she developed at the Continental played surprisingly well with mixed audiences, whether in a Midwest nightclub, in a Las Vegas showroom, or in front of Johnny Carson's nationwide viewers. Midler took on outlandish subjects that, while not specifically gay-identified, had a kind of trash-culture veneer that marked them as "queer." She switched out bathhouse and Fire Island jokes for comic observations on the exotic lingerie of Frederick's of Hollywood and her own prodigious bosom.

Midler recognized in her performing alter ego the potential to liberate and broaden the consciousness of everyone. "I have that sense of humor. I mean, what they [gay men] think is funny, I think is funny," she told Warhol. "Actually everybody has the potential for that humor. I used to go to the Ridiculous Theater [Charles Ludlam's Ridiculous Theatrical Company] and *die* laughing. But most people are never exposed to that kind of humor. In their day-to-day living they don't see it. They're not told, 'This is funny.' I'm talking about 'camp.' But as soon as they see it, they—change. And they—learn."[41]

This was the "gay show-biz sensibility"[42] that Richard Goldstein in the *Village Voice* credited Midler with transmitting from the baths to straight audiences: mocking the deadly serious, reveling in show-business references, gleefully slipping in and out of new identities, picking through musical trash heaps for hidden treasures, pushing emotional boundaries, upending the whole notion of a diva's relationship to her fans. In a sense, Midler took the boys from the baths with her everywhere and acclimated straight audiences to *their* sensibilities.

The excitement Midler generated at the Continental also led to a rebirth in the city's nightclub scene. Intimate cabaret rooms and clubs began to borrow from what was perceived as the Continental formula: mostly female performers with a strong appeal to gay men singing oddball settings of old or obscure songs (think "Tea for Two" as a husky ballad) in relaxed, informal settings. The circuit boasted its own stars, including Ellen Greene, Alaina Reed, Judith Cohen, Baby Jane Dexter, and Gotham, a gay male Andrews Sisters–style trio. They and others adopted, to varying degrees,

Midler's camp-nostalgia repertoire, eclectic fashion sense, and emotional way with ballads. Of course, there was always the hope of discovering a new, unknown performer like Midler. Clubs such as Reno Sweeney, Grand Finale, Brothers and Sisters, Trude Heller's, and others made up an informal cabaret network referred to as the "K-Y Circuit," named for a lubricant popular with gay men—which could be purchased from a vending machine at the Continental. A man buying a tube of K-Y while Midler sings "I Shall Be Released" is an image worthy of Susan Sontag.

By the time Midler took the stage for her final farewell performance at the Continental on November 27, 1972, she had given a sold-out concert at Carnegie Hall, released her long-awaited debut album, played important dates at pop-rock venues across the country, and was practically a semi-regular guest on Carson's late-night talk show. The two concerts she was scheduled to perform on New Year's Eve at Lincoln Center's Philharmonic Hall had sold out within hours.

The bathhouse regulars who jostled for room next to the jet-setters, show-biz insiders, and curious straights were bidding farewell to a performer they had nurtured and loved, one who was now poised to bring the performance style she had created for and with them to a larger audience. Those few square feet of space Midler and her audience occupied at the Continental was the site of a head-on collision between post-Stonewall gay liberation and the whole of contemporary show business. And when the wreckage was cleared, a performer emerged who would do more than any other contemporary performer to bring the "gay show-biz sensibility" to the mainstream.

1

"And Me, I Was Your Hostess!"

Bette Midler's Theater

"The girl who gave the most exciting auditions (she did three of them) for the role of Mary Magdalene in [*Jesus Christ*] *Superstar* was Bette Midler," wrote casting director Michael Shurtleff. "[She] sang 'I Don't Know How to Love Him' like no one else: disillusioned, hurt, vulnerable" and was "regal and mysterious." But director Tom O'Horgan ultimately decided against casting her in the 1971 Broadway production when "he realized this mature, voluptuous, womanly interpretation of the role would not fit in with his cast of hippies and flower children."[1]

Even as she was building her name as a singer, Midler was still interested in appearing in stage musicals. She had already done the first fully staged production of *The Who's Tommy* at the Seattle Opera in the spring of 1971. Double cast as both Tommy's mother, Mrs. Walker, and the Acid Queen, she much preferred the latter role, in which she jumped out of a box in only a G-string and bra and shrieked her introductory song. Midler was praised for her "great Janis Joplin-y voice"[2] and "extraordinary performance."[3] But *The Who's Tommy* would be her last time in a musical not of her own creation until *Hello, Dolly!* in 2017.

It's interesting to speculate what path Midler might have taken had she continued to actively seek stage work. She would have been ideal casting as Gittel Mosca, the tough, ulcer-ridden New Yorker in love with a transplanted Midwesterner in *Seesaw* (1973). She might have been a sexy Old Lady in Harold Prince's revival of *Candide* (1974). By 1973, she was a star big enough to have a show written especially for her, but she wisely rejected *Rachael Lily Rosenbloom and Don't You Ever Forget It!*, a camp musical about a Streisand-loving Brooklynite who rises from fish-market drudge to Hollywood stardom. *Rachael's* director and co-book-writer was none other than Midler's downtown discoverer, Tom Eyen. But what could have been high-spirited silliness at La MaMa was a chaotic mess on Broadway, and *Rachael* closed in previews. By the time she turned down the role of Mabel Normand in the new Jerry Herman musical *Mack and Mabel* (1974), Midler had become her own auteur, working with a select group of collaborators to craft solo performances that showcased the full range of her talents in a way no musical ever could.

Midler at the Continental Baths on September 6, 1971 is still the holy grail among the faithful. That's because Vito Russo borrowed video equipment from the Gay Activists Alliance and taped this Labor Day weekend return engagement (her "800th farewell performance," she joked) in its entirety. The grainy black-and-white footage made the rounds of collectors over the years and now sits grandly on YouTube, where the entire performance as well as individual songs spliced out and available on their own have been viewed half a million times.

Midler opens with "Friends," by now not just her theme song but a covenant between her and the men at the Continental. She begins the song slowly, pensively, before exploding into the chorus, reaching out and shaking hands with those sitting at her feet. There's a DIY flair to the performance, with Barry Manilow on piano and Joey Mitchell on drums, and a broken microphone stand to contend with. She's loose and spontaneous, recognizing actor Marilyn Sokol in the audience ("It's the Divine Marilyn Sokol!") and dishing Steve Ostrow, "the owner of this dump," about his attempts "to fill my shoes . . . and my blouses" with another star attraction. When a joke doesn't land, she good-naturedly demands a response: "Laugh, you motherfucker, you're sitting in the front row!"

"Fat Stuff," a new song for her, gets a pounding blues treatment, and she gives "Chattanooga Choo Choo" plenty of hubba-hubba. Introducing Leon Russell and Bonnie Bramlett's "Superstar," she's sardonic: "This is the song where everybody always gets up and leaves. . . . Well, the span of attention in this place is so short anyway . . . it only takes a song, right?" The rueful ballad, about a groupie who's been seduced and abandoned by a rock star, was a current chart hit, with a steady, straightforward delivery by Karen Carpenter. Midler turns it into the mature retrospection of a woman who's waiting in vain for a lover to return. Midway through, Manilow takes the tempo down even further, and Midler's delivery becomes pleading and broken, before softly fading away. It's a deft and devastating contrast to the raucous vibe she'd created moments before. No one in the audience gets up and leaves.

"Empty Bed Blues" gets the rock treatment, one that doesn't entirely give the double-entendre lyrics their due. She's genuinely Janis Joplin-y, with some rock riffs that don't always land. But she's a dervish, running around the stage and revving the audience up before announcing intermission: "I have to go off and change my clothes . . . into even greater drag!"

Midler bursts out of her dressing room (actually, Ostrow's office) in a towel and with plastic fruit on her head in a ludicrous recreation of Carmen Miranda, singing Miranda's bouncing "Cuanto Le Gusta" before segueing into "Marahuana," from the pre-Code musical *Murder at the Vanities*. Singing of her cannabis enslavement with mock seriousness, she preens and poses like Barbra Streisand at her most dramatic, pausing only to vigorously shake a pair of maracas with an "over it" attitude that's pure camp.

With the laughter and applause still ringing, Manilow and Mitchell strike up a deliberate waltz rhythm, and Midler begins Joni Mitchell's "For Free." Mitchell sang her song as a delicate reflection on the difference between herself as a highly paid professional musician and "the one man band by the quick lunch stand" whom no one noticed as he was "playing real good for free." Midler, backed by the insistent beat, captures the drama in the narrative and becomes an advocate for the lonely busker ignored by the passersby because he wasn't a familiar face from television. "For Free" became a harrowing plea for every performer, herself included, seeking recognition by singing "real good," for free or otherwise.

A sing-along girl-group medley of "Easier Said Than Done" and "Chapel of Love" is followed by "I Shall Be Released." She ends just as she started, with "Friends." She begins in the wrong key, and when Manilow eventually gets her back on track, she endearingly acknowledges his help. But mistakes don't matter. The standing ovation is tumultuous, followed by her now de rigueur brief reappearance in a towel with a flash of ass.

Many performers, even the most adored and acclaimed, stay within a safe emotional register, rarely, if ever, straying past the guardrails they erect themselves. Midler dared to push against any such safety measures. She wasn't afraid to be too big, too loud, too sensitive—to be *too much*. For fifty-four minutes, she held nothing back, not her voice, not her humor, not her insecurities, not her emotions. What she gave was the unfaltering truth.

"Make Me a Legend!"

Midler sang only ten songs that night. But she was already curating the act that she would expand and revise and reshape for the next fifty years. Things began to accelerate for Midler with successful engagements at Mister Kelly's in Chicago, first as an opening act, then as a headliner. It was during that first engagement, opening for comedian Jackie Vernon, that she met a man who would come to play a key role in enlarging her comedic persona.

Midler burst out of the kitchen wearing a shirt tied at the waist with no bra and singing "Sh-Boom." "It was a political statement not to wear a bra, but in Bette's case, it was a terrorist act," Bruce Vilanch recalled. "She was every diva I had ever loved rolled into one. Plus, it was the most eclectic musical presentation I'd ever seen one person do."[4] Vilanch, who was working for a Chicago newspaper, told her that she was funny and needed to talk more in her act. When she asked if he had any jokes, he gave her one, which she delivered at her next performance: "I love Chicago because I love Mayor Daley. He reminds me of one of my childhood toys: Mr. Potato Head."[5] City-specific jokes became a staple of Midler's act, as she referenced local places and figures for broad laughs. By the time she left Chicago, Midler and Vilanch had recognized a shared sense of humor, and he began contributing to her act, a partnership that has lasted for more than fifty years. In *Get Bruce* (1999), a documentary about Vilanch, Midler insisted, "Bruce was the first man to put something in my mouth that actually made us both money."

Following a tour of small clubs and college venues, Midler, Manilow, and her band picked up gigs in and around New York, including a week's run at a free theater in a Paramus, New Jersey shopping mall. During a dire Saturday matinee, she played to an audience of Girl Scouts. When one particularly disinterested Scout scrunched down in her front-row seat and stuck her tongue out at Midler, the star had had it. She looked down and said, "Don't slouch, honey, your tits'll sag," and dramatically exited the stage.[6] Midler was adept at withering comebacks to obnoxious audience members, even prepubescent Girl Scouts.

Soon two important additions were made to the traveling Bette Midler show. She loved the interplay between Tina Turner and her Ikettes, three hip, sexy backup singer-dancers. "I like the strength of a lot of women on stage," Midler said. "When you see a lot of women on stage the 'woman thing' is accentuated, thrust out at you, quadrupled."[7]

She put together a three-woman backing group she called the Harlettes (often the Staggering Harlettes)—clearly in homage to Turner's group. Like the Ikettes, they had attitude to spare and soon became musical and comedic foils for Midler. When they weren't singing and dancing (solid musicianship and stage presence were prerequisites for the job), they were being playfully dished to filth by their boss. They started out in demure prom gowns but soon shifted to "trash with flash" styles closer to Midler's. In all the years since, a few dozen women have cycled in and out of the Harlettes, making the job a show-business rite of passage for a certain type of brash female singer.

The other addition to the Midler team was one who had a profound influence on her career for the remainder of the decade. Aaron Russo was a New York–born rock promoter and impresario, the owner-operator of a popular Chicago rock venue and nightclub called the Kinetic Playground. The refrigerator-sized Russo had a take-charge manner and outsized devotion to Midler, which immediately endeared him to the star, whose current management was pushing her in the Vegas showroom direction. He was a tough, experienced negotiator with an instinctive grasp of how to take Midler's career in a new, more high-powered direction. When he first proposed himself as her manager, she had only one half-joking request: "Make me a legend!"[8] Midler didn't want to be just another girl singer working the club circuit. She wanted Russo to clear the decks for her so that she was free to make her mark not just as an actor or singer but as an artist.

Russo was more than game for the challenge, and Midler became his only client. Almost immediately, they began an affair that ran its course quickly (and proved a problem for his marriage). Theirs was an especially combative relationship. Screaming and yelling scenes were common, and his controlling attitude alienated many of her collaborators. But he was her tough-guy protector and quickly steered her career upward.

One of Russo's earliest gambits was to confirm Midler's credibility with the rock crowd, booking her into the Troubadour in Los Angeles, the Boarding House in San Francisco, and Philadelphia's Club Bijou—all established rock venues. All were sellouts, with the response as tumultuous as ever. They loved the boogie-woogie, they loved the ballads, they loved the jokes about Frederick's of

Hollywood and Richard Nixon ("The Divine Dick"), all delivered with full-on gay innuendo. Everyone from rockers to grandmothers was apparently ready for her brand of "gay show-biz sensibility" as the Midler bandwagon picked up momentum.

The Palace Tour

The show that Midler opened on Broadway at the Palace Theatre in December 1973 was both a consolidation and an expansion of the act she'd been doing around the country for three years. The Palace was actually the final stop on a cross-country tour that took Midler, for the first time, to major auditoriums and arenas. One of those stops was her hometown of Honolulu, with her mother, sister, and brother in the audience leading the cheers. (Another sister had been tragically killed a few years earlier.) Missing was Midler's father, who, because of the outrageousness of her performances, refused to attend and, in fact, never saw his daughter perform live. "He's very conservative, kind of an ultra-right-wing Republican," she later said. "He's the only Jewish Republican in the world. He has a plaque that says so."[9]

The highlight of her Los Angeles engagement was a celebratory performance by the two remaining Andrews Sisters with Midler on "Boogie Woogie Bugle Boy." The popularity of Midler's recording prompted a resurgence of interest in the now-middle-aged singers. Two albums of hits by the original trio had just been reissued, and Patty and Maxene (sister LaVerne died in 1967) would soon star in the nostalgic 1940s musical *Over Here!* on Broadway.

Midler was, in fact, at the apex of the nostalgia trend sweeping America. *Life* magazine devoted half its February 19, 1971, issue to the topic, including features on the current hit revival of the 1925 musical *No, No, Nanette* and the renewed popularity of tap dancing, the rediscovered grandeur of art deco movie palaces, and a new appreciation of the glamourous fashion styles of the 1930s and 1940s.

Charles Ludlam's and Tom Eyen's adoration of old movies, clichés and all, had made it to the center of the culture. The pre-Code Hollywood films that Midler and Bill Hennessy and Ben Gillespie used to see at revival houses were being rediscovered. It was now hip to get stoned and go to an old Busby Berkeley musical.

In the wake of Midler's success, new musical acts such as Manhattan Transfer and the Pointer Sisters referenced earlier musical styles and fashions, with nostalgia filtered through a contemporary lens. Harry Nilsson revisited American Songbook classics for his hit album *A Little Touch of Schmilsson in the Night*. Peter Allen crafted songs of urban ennui like a 1970s Cole Porter and performed them with hedonistic flair. *Grease* delivered the 1950s to Broadway. *Follies*, *Irene*, and *Good News* all brought old movie stars to the Great White Way.

In this atmosphere of celebrating the past in contemporary terms, Midler at the Palace seemed almost predestined. On the stage of the legendary entertainment temple, Midler took her place alongside Fanny Brice, Sophie Tucker, Al Jolson, Judy Garland, and other stand-and-deliver show-business greats.

By the standards of her later, more elaborate stage shows, the Palace act was small-scale, with judiciously placed stage effects. Opening act two, Midler appeared at the top of a giant high-heeled shoe against a New York City skyline, singing "Lullaby of Broadway" as she descended its built-in staircase.

Hennessy and Vilanch came up with a steady stream of political jokes ("I sent Tricia Nixon a man-eating plant for a wedding present. I thought she could learn something from it. After all, she did marry a man named Cox") and lacerating celebrity put-downs (Helen Reddy was arrested "for loitering in front of an orchestra"). Midler's stage wardrobe, including a gown that looked like aluminum foil ("my 'baked potato' dress,"[10] she called it, designed for her by Norma Kamali) with a high front slit worn with stone marten furs and platform shoes, along with her high-energy travels across the stage, had her looking, according to the *New York Times*, like "a cross between Sadie Thompson and Martha Raye."[11]

The Harlettes were now a well-tooled backing trio, with tightly synced movements and serious attitude. Choreography was courtesy of André De Shields, later a Tony Award–winning and much-lauded Broadway actor, but in 1973 their self-described "boogie master."[12] De Shields worked with the trio on movements that complemented songs of whatever period or style. Under his direction, they trucked, they Suzie Q'd, they jived, they funked. When De Shields was unsure about particular period styles, he called in none other than Broadway choreographer-director Michael Bennett in his pre–*A Chorus Line* days.

The first act was heavy on comedy, while the second gave Midler room to stretch out as a dramatic vocalist, with songs she'd been singing since the baths and those from her just-released second album, including the 1940s swing number "In the Mood" and Kurt Weill's "Surabaya Johnny," in which she once again became a young Lotte Lenya.

Each act built to a volcanic climax, with "I Shall Be Released" in the first act and the slow-burning "(Your Love Keeps Lifting Me) Higher and Higher" in the second. "Chapel of Love," once again an audience sing-along, brought the show to a joyous close. When Midler was voted a special Tony Award "for adding lustre to the Broadway season," it felt altogether inevitable.

She once said, "I would like to see what is happening in music today combined with a theatrical kind of experience."[13] The sold-out three-week engagement did just that, and her achievement was noted even by the rock press. *Rolling Stone*'s 1973 music awards named Midler and Elton John "Rock Stars of the Year," adding, "In 1973, Bette Midler did her damnedest to put the show business back in rock. Her New York Palace Theater engagement resulted not only in a personal triumph but an increased awareness on the part of artists and audiences alike of the still-unexplored potential for new ways of presenting pop music. In a year filled with bogus cults, hers is real and will last."[14]

Clams on the Half Shell

In what must count as one of the most mystifying disappearing acts in show-business history, Midler vanished in 1974. She was overwhelmed and exhausted by her meteor-like rise to pop stardom, and her relationship with Russo had remained volatile even as career pressures mounted. (When he poured a glass of Coke over her head just before a performance at the Palace, it was business as usual.) She showed up to accept her Tony and then again when she won a Grammy as Best New Artist, but otherwise she was missing in action the entire year. There were big-time television and film offers brewing and a successful recording career that required tending while Midler traveled and relaxed. Finally, to jolt her back into action, Russo booked the Minskoff, one of Broadway's largest theaters, and announced a new Bette Midler show would open in the spring of 1975.

Bette Midler's Clams on the Half Shell Revue was a full-fledged Broadway musical built around the singular talents of its star. Midler had a whole new creative crew, starting with musical director Don York. (Manilow had departed after the Palace shows in order to concentrate on his own flourishing recording career.) Joe Layton, an experienced Broadway hand who had devised Barbra Streisand's early, acclaimed television specials, came aboard as director-choreographer. Celebrated scenic designer Tony Walton created lavish and imaginative settings. The cast included not only the Harlettes but a gospel choir, the Michael Powell Ensemble, and legendary bandleader and vibraphonist Lionel Hampton. Demand for Midler hadn't abated in her absence. The first day the box office opened, it broke the Broadway record for one-day sales—the previous record having been set by Midler's 1973 Palace show—and the show extended for a total of ten weeks.

Midler originally wanted to do a smaller show with a group of sketch players, one in which she could act in scenes and vignettes as well as sing. *Clams on the Half Shell* grew out of this concept, with set pieces designed to show off her musical and dramatic versatility. The camp quotient was through the roof in the opening Layton staged, one that spoofed Broadway showstoppers with the knowingness of someone who had spent a career devising them.

After a rousing *Oklahoma!* overture, the curtain rose on Michael Powell's choir dressed as dockworkers on a levee setting out of *Show Boat*. The workers sing "Ol' Man River" as they gather their catches in fishnets. Finally, a large clam is caught and deposited downstage, where, to themes from *South Pacific*, it is ceremoniously opened to reveal the star. Like Lorelei emerging from the sea, Midler launches into the old Dorothy Lamour movie song "The Moon of Manakoora." During rehearsals, Layton had watched Midler demonstrating Maori poi balls, which she learned to twirl as a child in Hawaii. The weighted balls, attached to strings, can be spun in a variety of rhythmic and geometric patterns. It's likely no one in the audience had ever seen or heard of poi balls, but Layton equipped the star with a pair, which she now twirled with great dramatic precision, climaxing an opening number that turned Broadway's most revered musicals on their heads.

Clams on the Half Shell featured all the conventions of high-powered Broadway staging—the elaborately contrived star entrance, eye-popping scenic effects, set pieces calculated to present the star in a variety of moods. Yet Midler blew a hole in all this theatrical pizzazz, playing off the musical-theater contrivances in a way she couldn't in a concert setting. Her singing and comedy took on a sharper, wittier tone amid all the pageantry.

She welcomed the audience with Elton John's self-explanatory "The Bitch Is Back." A Philadelphia medley with the Harlettes presented a new set of old girl-group songs. A barroom sequence found Midler singing songs of romantic longing and disillusionment while surrounded by life-size mannequins of men in various states of inebriation or disinterest. Act two opened with Walton's giant jukebox set, complete with turntable, as the setting for a series of tight-harmony 1940s numbers with Hampton and the Harlettes. Walton pulled off a genuine coup de théâtre to close the first act. As a New York City skyline unfurled as if going up into the clouds, the top of the Empire State Building gradually appeared, with King Kong himself perched at the top. His arm swung around from behind with Midler in his grip. Stroking the simian's large thumb and gazing into his eyes with something between shock and erotic fascination, Midler shrieked: "Nicky Arnstein, Nicky Arnstein, Nicky Arnstein!" If, after all this time, she was still being compared to Streisand, she made sure to send up the star's now-familiar, breathless exhortation from *Funny Girl* in devastating fashion.

"Ernie, Get Off My Back!"

Clams on the Half Shell was retooled and simplified for a tour that began in late 1975. Dubbed *The Depression Tour*, to align with her new album, *Songs for the New Depression*, the show featured several new elements that would become regular features of Midler tours. At the Minskoff, she had included a few jokes in the style of Sophie Tucker, the late singer and comedian, known as the "Last of the Red Hot Mamas." Tucker, a Jewish woman of sizable girth and coarse features, sang famously ribald songs with titles like "No One Man Is Ever Going to Worry Me" (about the virtues of having more than one sexual partner), "I Don't Want to Get Thin" (reveling in her plush figure, which Latin and Greek men found particularly sexy), and "You've Got to See Mama Ev'ry Night" (in which she demands sex from her lover nightly). Through her songs and observations about men, Tucker established herself as a good-humored woman of frank sexual appetites.

The substance and delivery of Midler's "Soph" jokes were in Tucker's hearty style, conveying her lusty outlook and down-to-earth perspective on relations between men and women. Soph's boyfriend, Ernie, was her eternal stooge, as in one of her most repeated jokes: "I was in bed last night with my boyfriend Ernie. And he said to me, 'Soph, you got no tits and a tight box.' I said to him, 'Ernie, get off my back!'" In drawing on Tucker's early style and attitude, Midler created a line from the "Last of the Red Hot Mamas" to the "Divine Miss M," from one unruly Jewish woman with unconventional looks and personality to another.

Earlier, Midler quoted another comedian when she responded to a heckler, "Belle Barth used to say, 'Shut your hole honey, mine's making money!'" It was a classic put-down in keeping with Midler's comic moxie. As Midler's comedy evolved, it owed much to Jewish female comedians such as Barth and Pearl Williams and Rusty Warren, who earned reputations for their off-color, or "blue," comedy routines, often preserved on "adult party records" recorded live at after-hours clubs. Midler soon took to prefacing her Soph jokes with "I will never forget it, you know!" much as Barth used to say, "This next story is a little risqué," before launching into another filthy tale. Like Warren, famous for her exhortation "Knockers up!," Midler both joked about and celebrated her own prodigious breasts ("In a spasm of sisterly generosity, I donated my tits to Cher!"). And like the others, Midler peppered her comedy with Yiddishisms ("Kiss my tuchus" was a favorite comeback). But there was one area in which she parted with her spiritual heirs in comedy. Barth and Williams freely joked about "faggots," but this new-generation funny woman who came into her own in front of gay male audiences would have none of that.

While the older women's material often sought to puncture the pretensions—sexual and otherwise—of men, Midler confined these jokes to her Soph routines. She was as capable as ever of delivering sarcastic put-downs of celebrities and politicians (Neil Young, Shelley Winters, Gerald Ford, and Ronald Reagan were some of her recent targets). But her humor had become more varied, more humanistic, offering commentary on popular culture and the absurdities of contemporary life. Hennessy was gone, and Jerry Blatt, a composer-lyricist who had earlier contributed songs to *Sesame Street*, was now writing Midler's act along with Vilanch. Both men became key architects in constructing Midler's stage shows, with Blatt contributing to her early films as well.

John Prine's "Hello in There" was a poignant ballad about an old couple facing the end of an uneventful life, their children grown and moved away, or on the road, or killed in war. Midler the actor made a meal of Prine's song, evoking a world of worn-down routine, of a woman dazed by events in life that once seemed momentous but have receded in memory and importance, with nothing but monotony and isolation left. She ends with a plea for recognition of often-ignored senior citizens like herself: "So if you're walking down the street sometime / And spot some hollow ancient eyes / Please don't just pass them by and stare / As if you didn't care, say, 'Hello in there, hello.'"

Here she prefaced the song with an outlandish monologue about a giant, bald-headed woman on the streets of New York wearing a fried egg on her head. Milking the ridiculous image for maximum comic impact, she deadpanned, "Oh, God, don't let me wake up tomorrow and want to put a fried egg on my head." But the laughs slowly fade as she turns the fried egg into a metaphor for the existential anxieties of our era. "You can call it a fried egg. You can call it anything you like. But everybody gets one. Some people wear 'em on the outside. Some people, they wear 'em on the inside." After that introduction, "Hello in There" was more moving than ever.

A new character allowed Midler to spoof the kind of nightclub performers her success had played a part in making obsolete. Vicki Eydie, "definitely a lounge act," was a hard-working road warrior whose unflagging energy couldn't quite mask her minimal skills or taste levels. She sang in the insistent style of Frances Faye, the veteran nightclub singer-pianist whose emphatic way with everything from "Summertime" to "All the Things You Are," set to swingin', ring-a-ding-ding arrangements, bulldozed over the songs' sentiments. Vicki Eydie embodied a can-do show business that wasn't afraid to dip into "blue" material. Her "global revue" included "Fiesta in Rio," a Brazilian samba about coping with venereal disease ("I thought I was dying, but I just had the clap") and "South Seas Scene," a Polynesian chant about sexual deprivation ("If you're cracking up from having lack of shacking up") that served as an audience sing-along—all delivered with face-front, up-to-the-rafters enthusiasm.

Vicki Eydie was abetted by a backup trio called the Dazzling Eydettes, who bore a suspicious similarity to Midler's own Staggering Harlettes. This 1976 edition of the trio proved to be the ultimate Harlettes, for both their chemistry with Midler and the opportunities they were given to assert their own personalities. Tall, bodacious Charlotte Crossley ("the oldest living Harlette") and tiny Sharon Redd, both Black, were joined by Ula Hedwig, a gangly white singer with a resemblance to Popeye's girlfriend, Olive Oyl. Their harmonies were tight and carried the weight of group numbers when Midler's voice tired. Their sizes and shapes gave them an oddball effect that nevertheless worked, because each looked fully capable of replacing Midler at a moment's notice. Whether in tight, shiny cocktail dresses or bikinis and towering headpieces, they exuded indolent, trashy attitude, serving as perfect foils for their exacting boss.

"And me, I was your hostess!" she proclaimed after introducing the Harlettes and her band at the end of the show. As presiding hostess of this hybrid Broadway musical/rock concert/cabaret performance, Midler was without peer among other female singers out on the road in the mid-1970s. Compared with hers, Linda Ronstadt's, Helen Reddy's, Donna Summer's, and Olivia Newton-John's acts were stately and composed, without the freewheeling fun and drama of a Midler concert. The dazzling Diana Ross and Liza Minnelli embraced all the "sincere" show-business tropes that Midler joyously tweaked.

A few Black performers matched the exhilaration of Midler in concert. The soaring rock-funk vocals and flamboyant space age costumes of Patti Labelle, Nona Hendryx, and Sarah Dash, collectively known as Labelle, made for vividly theatrical stage shows. Queer disco/R&B/gospel diva Sylvester and his plus-size backup singers Martha Wash and Izora Rhodes (later variously known as Two Tons O' Fun and the Weather Girls) paired powerful voices and achieved the sisterhood in song that Midler had with the Harlettes. Millie Jackson, the ribald R&B singer, had Midler's timing and comedy chops and was adept at stitching scathing monologues about male–female relations into song medleys. She was sometimes called the "Black Bette Midler," but with all the chutzpah of Midler, Tucker, and other disruptive female comedians, she insisted instead that Midler was the "white Millie Jackson."[15]

"I Stand before You Nipples to the Wind!"

The theatrical excitement of Midler's performances made her a major concert draw even when she wasn't selling a lot of records. In 1977, she could have gone back to large concert halls but instead embarked on a tour of small clubs. This "intimate evening," as it was billed, was a return to the cozy settings of the small nightclubs she played years earlier. There were no sets, no props, and no costume changes during the ninety-minute show performed twice nightly. Redd, Hedwig, and Crossley had now gone out on their own, under the cumbersome name "Formerly of the Harlettes." Midler gave them the opportunity to open the show with a short set and then do backup vocals for her. (She gave Manilow a similar showcase when he was launching his own solo career while serving as her musical director.)

The Harlettes stood at ease for much of the performance, while this unplugged Midler bantered with the audience almost as much as she sang. She was a more freewheeling and confident raconteur than the girl who took the stage seven years earlier at the Continental. After an introductory "Friends," taken at a hundred miles an hour, Midler usually greeted her audience with "I stand before you nipples to the wind!" and never let up. She gave fresh spontaneity to scripted lines she'd spoken many times before, always with the perfect comeback or put-down to any audience crack.

Midler had long tailored her comedy material to include local references, and she outdid herself this time around. Her Los Angeles stint was filled with outrageous observations on Southern California traffic ("I haven't got a clue about merging, but I've got a real good handle on yield"), grooming styles ("I always know when I'm approaching Los Angeles because I can hear the sounds of thousands upon thousands of blow dryers"), and less-esteemed local communities (when Soph told Ernie to "kiss me where it smells," he took her to Anaheim).

Midler's voice was noticeably ragged, strained from two shows nightly, but seeing her perform at close proximity, it was impossible not to be overwhelmed by the emotional range of her singing. After "Long John Blues," a double-entendre song about a seven-foot-tall dentist whose drill could fill any cavity, and a spate of Soph jokes that left the audience screaming with laughter, she segued to the poignant "Let's Shoot the Breeze," a song she had debuted on her recent NBC television special. To a melody written years earlier by Dustin Hoffman, Midler contributed lyrics about a woman's aimless discontent ("It's not my man or the kids, you see / To tell the truth it's a mystery / Why I'm so damned dissatisfied").

Her plaintive performance was followed by a passage from Carl Sandburg's *The People, Yes*, first published in 1936. Sandburg's epic prose poem was a paean to American resilience during the height of the Depression. With understated pathos, Midler told the story of Mildred Klinghofer, an elderly woman about to die who longed to hold the baby she had borne years ago. Her cries for her baby were such that a rag doll was given to her, which she clutched contentedly as she took her last breath. As Midler spoke the last lines,

"There are dreams stronger than death / Men and women die holding these dreams," the underscoring for "I Shall Be Released" slowly began. Her performance of this familiar song cast it in an entirely new light, its refrain, "Any day now," becoming the furious plea of a woman facing an existential void and begging God for mercy. Moments earlier, Midler was the funniest woman on the face of the earth. Now she was the most moving of singing actors. Twice nightly, Midler turned entertainment into transcendent art.

The End of the '70s

After completing her first film, *The Rose*, a dramatic musical about a self-destructive rock singer not unlike Janis Joplin, Midler launched her first international tour, performing sold-out concerts in England, France, Germany, Sweden, Denmark, and Australia, where her appearances resulted in pandemonium ("Midler Hottest Aussie Import in Long Time," blared *Variety*).[16] At the London Palladium, audience members held up signs that read, "WE LOVE YOUR TITS," which naturally resulted in Midler obliging with an impromptu flash of the referenced body parts.[17]

A US tour was coordinated with the release of *The Rose* in late 1979 and included a month's stay at the Majestic Theatre on Broadway. Following the overseas tour, Midler severed her ties with Russo, and *Bette! Divine Madness* was her first project without his guidance. Staged by Midler and Jerry Blatt, it was a hard-driving two and a half hours that opened with the big-band disco of "Big Noise from Winnetka" from her new album, *Thighs and Whispers*, and kept accelerating. (It also featured the dancing-est set of Harlettes yet.)

Midler looked smashing in a tight sequined cocktail dress designed by Bob Mackie in high Frederick's of Hollywood style. The top of the dress opened to reveal a flesh-colored bra that, from a distance, made her look topless. Her hair was the same bright blond as in *The Rose*, and she was in fighting trim. If anything, she sashayed around the stage with more exultant confidence than ever. But she also made sport of her own aging (she was thirty-four on December 1). Examining the sagging flesh of her underarms, she deadpanned, "How old a woman would you say I was? Isn't it terrible how once you reach thirty, your body wants a life of its own?" Midler gloried in her own figure and wasn't shy about an occasional flash, as she did in Paris. But her appeal was never about her looks, and her remarks were a refreshing acknowledgment of the passing of time for herself and her audience.

Midler referenced Pearl Williams's raunchy party album *A Trip around the World Is Not a Cruise* when she announced, "I went around the world. Of course, I'm famous for that. But this time we did it in a plane!" She dished the Harlettes ("They thought the inflationary spiral was an intrauterine device") and told priceless stories about her foreign adventures (she tried to be gracious when visiting Germany, but instead, "My little Jewish heart was leaping up screaming, 'Get me the fuck out of here!'").

Midler traded in celebrity jokes for cracks about the royal family. "What has she got in that purse?" she demanded about "Her Maj," the queen. "You know she hasn't got car fare." "Boy, is he rich, and man, is he ugly," was her dismissal of Prince Charles. The "outdoorsy" Princess Anne gave her age by stomping her foot like a horse.

"I am now a screen goddess in the great tradition of Shirley Temple, Liv Ullmann, and Miss Piggy!" Midler joked in reference to her film debut, and the show featured several songs from *The Rose*. The film's big, dramatic ballad, "Stay with Me," was delivered as a final, desperate gasp of life just before Rose dies. Onstage, Midler did "Stay with Me" nightly with every ounce of passion and lung power, collapsing on the floor and screaming the last lines on her back. This spellbinding display of energy and showmanship would be a finale for anybody else, but here it came early, with Midler carrying on for another two hours.

Vicki Eydie had now rather awkwardly metamorphosed into Delores DeLago, the Toast of Chicago, a mermaid in a motorized wheelchair with a tinseled palm tree attached. (In Copenhagen, audiences took Delores as a tribute to their own Little Mermaid.)[18] Like Vicki, Delores practices "the lowest form of show business humanly possible," in this case a "Revue Tropicale," complete with poi balls. Midler/Delores got a good bit of comic mileage out of a pair of coconuts on the palm tree suspiciously shaped like testicles. And she distinguished herself as an expert wheelchair operator, executing hairpin swirls and stops with aplomb.

The barroom sequence from *Clams on the Half Shell* became a song-and-pantomime routine featuring the Magic Lady, a homeless woman decked out in a long, baggy overcoat, with a winter scarf fashioned from Christmas tinsel and an umbrella made of rainbow-colored strips. Seated at a park bench, she fed the birds and fashioned a rain hat for herself out of paper. Midler had often edged toward sentimentality, with her astringency always pulling her back. But the Chaplinesque sketch felt overstretched and soggy in its determination to show the indomitable spirit of this "little person."

The 1979 Bette Midler was a self-assured and creatively restless performer who was now, literally, a world-class concert star. She had long since established a unique intimacy with audiences. (This time around, the crowd even "serenaded" her with punchlines from earlier Soph jokes.) *Bette! Divine Madness* was the final, high-powered iteration of the act she had been polishing for a decade.

Pondering Mahler and Picasso

The debacle of her 1982 film *Jinxed* sent Midler into a nervous collapse. She spent long hours reading and immersing herself in art books. She also began exploring new musical sounds, spending months recording a new wave–ish rock album called *No Frills*. When she was ready to return to live performance, she wanted the show to reflect these interests. *De Tour*, which debuted at the end of 1982, was one big, expensively mounted art-school project, with Midler the A-plus student at its center.

In design, costume, stage movement, and musical profile, *De Tour* was a true conceptual presentation. Opening with Bruce Springsteen's strutting "Pink Cadillac," she was a vision in a bright red, architecturally constructed short tunic. Costumes (and a variety of wigs for the Harlettes) were in primary colors that often used bodies as canvases. The stage deck was painted in bold geometric shapes. Stylized props were everywhere, their meanings often inscrutable. Choreography was sharp-edged, stylized, and ever-so-slightly pretentious. Even Midler's hair was a short, angular crop. But leave it to her to pop the balloon of pomposity: "Some of this show is so modern, so daring, so metaphysical, so overwhelmingly artsy-fartsy, even I don't get it!"

De Tour included more new music than any Midler concert, including half of the upcoming *No Frills* album. The show's happiest surprise was Midler's strong, confident singing. In the past, her vocal reach had sometimes exceeded her grasp, but now the voice had deepened, allowing her to sing with new power and consistency.

Her overhaul of Keith Richards and Mick Jagger's "Beast of Burden" was a revelation. The Rolling Stones' recording was a teasing, mock-pleading riff aimed at a reluctant lover ("Am I hard enough? / Am I rough enough? / Am I rich enough?"). Midler took the song apart and put it back together, redefining it as a woman's demand for respect and stating her case right from the start, with a furious exhortation: "Now write this down!" The burden she carries is the one all women carry, striving always to be hard and rough and rich enough for any man. When Jagger made the invitation to go home, put on some music, and make sweet love, you knew it would be accepted. When Midler made it, it was with pronounced anxiety, as if it might not happen—and didn't her lover owe her at least this for all the burdens she's borne?

The original, nonsensical lyrics of the third verse repeat "pretty girl" over and over and end with "Come on baby, please, please, please." Midler's rewrite made explicit the objectification and brutality just below the surface of Jagger's louche delivery.

> My little sister
> Is a pretty, pretty, girl
> My little sister is a pretty, pretty, girl
> She love to ride, she loves to crawl
> They love to take her out, behind the garden wall
> And when they're done, they just throw her away
> And she don't have an awful lot to say
> It hurts her so bad to come to the end
> I remember all the times she spent sayin', "Please!"

Midler's little sister was every groupie who ever hung out at a rock concert, hoping to connect with her favorite singer, only to be enjoyed and then abandoned when the gig was finished. (It was a rock variation on "Superstar," which preceded "Beast of Burden" in the concert.) The physicality of Midler's performance matched the ferocity of this new interpretation. She angrily swung the microphone over her head before carrying it off on her back, stooped with the continuing weight of being a woman in an unfair world. As with Bob Dylan's "I Shall Be Released," Midler's renovation of "Beast of Burden" revealed nuances and meanings Jagger and Richards never imagined.

Midler's habit of pulling up a stool and talking for an extended stretch was now so familiar that audiences began applauding when the stool appeared. She didn't disappoint. Her comic observations, delivered as if to an auditorium of intimate friends, were more screamingly hilarious than ever. She took on subjects as diverse as the tendency of cocaine users to grind their teeth ("Some have ground their teeth so fine they can snort their own bicuspids"), bewildering new technologies ("I don't know a VCR from an IUD"), and her concert's high ticket prices (responding to an "I love you!" from the audience, she replied, "I hope so, at these prices").

Midler was on fire rattling off a slew of Soph jokes that climaxed not with Soph and Ernie but with a truly filthy and delirious story about Queen Elizabeth's and Princess Diana's attempts to hide the royal jewels on their persons as they elude a highway robber. Midler had always been funny, but on *De Tour*, her jokes sent audiences into comic euphoria.

The saying "Revenge is a dish best served cold" was inspiration for a wicked sendup of *Jinxed*, which had recently opened and quickly flopped. A scene from the film, dubbed into Italian, was accompanied by English subtitles that spoofed not only Midler (she's mistaken for Diana Ross) but her director, Don Siegel (here a drunken buffoon with sexual performance issues), and the whole misbegotten enterprise. If she couldn't make *Jinxed* a hit, she could at least make fun of it.

Midler's interest in high art intersected with her ongoing pre-occupation with breasts. "Art and art alone is my pursuit," she solemnly intoned. "I studied form and line, I worshipped at its shrine. Art is the tree and I am just a fruit. Oh yes, I pondered Mahler and Picasso. I owed some money on a Grecian urn. I read some Gertrude Stein, up to page sixty-nine. And now I'm here to tell you what I have learned." And with that, she and the Harlettes launched into a new song, "Pretty Legs, Great Big Knockers," a catchy, up-tempo tribute to the universal appeal of the title attributes ("That's what sells them tickets at the door"). It said the quiet part out loud and used outrageous visual and lyrical humor to make the case that art is art, whether high or low. Midler brought out bigger and bigger breast-shaped balloons (complete with areolae), comically wrestling them to the floor in a feat of acrobatics.

Everything went bigger and more colorful on *De Tour*, including Delores DeLago, this time with the Harlettes as her three sisters, all in motorized wheelchairs roaming the stage in intricate patterns. A performance of "In the Mood" had the four DeLago sisters dancing on their fins, rolling on the floor, and finally flat on their backs as they posed below a giant mirror for a Busby Berkeley overhead effect.

The show's final suite of songs was indeed staged in the artsy-fartsy manner Midler joked about, with the star in a Grecian tunic and the Harlettes unrecognizable as harlequins and chess pieces brandishing hula hoops. Somehow it all worked. The thematic selections set a mood of nostalgic loss and apocalyptic forecast. Peter Gabriel's "Here Comes the Flood" ended with the haunting words "Drink up, dreamers, you're running dry," speaking of a day when human thoughts are visible to others and those not open to this concept will drown in their opposition.

That was too esoteric for Midler, who rewrote parts of the lyric and ended with a more hopeful refrain, "Drink up to human kind!" Her full-throated singing and stylized movements, including a sequence in which her head disappeared, Martha Graham–style, into her tunic, were like some kind of inspired art rock performance. Her immediate segue from impassioned humanist to pleading lover with "Stay with Me" was breathtaking enough to bring a roar from the audience. The seamlessness of her emotional transition was also pure showmanship. Midler knew how to build to a performance peak—and then top it.

"Stay with Me" was a revelation, because at last, Midler's voice matched her interpretive skills. Her new vocal muscularity allowed her to give the emotive lyrics their full value without shouting, and here she achieved the rock power of Joplin. *De Tour* was Midler's most financially successful show to date and an artistic triumph. It made it clear that she was a creatively evolving artist and that the stage was her true métier. The audiences who made every show a sellout didn't care about her Hollywood status, and their enthusiasm seemed to bolster her.

A Divine Experience

De Tour turned out to be Midler's last live show for ten years. That decade marked a complete turnaround in her career and her personal life. In the mid-1980s, she returned to films and, to everyone's surprise, became a genuine, box-office-topping movie star in a series of comedies for—of all places—Walt Disney Studios. The soundtrack album for *Beaches*, another Disney hit, this one a weeper, revitalized her recording career. Its showcase ballad, "Wind beneath My Wings," became her biggest hit, and a year later, she had her second-biggest hit, the anthemic "From a Distance." She also married and had a child. It was a happy life of nesting with the family and making hit movies and records.

By 1993, Midler's film status had dimmed following several underperforming vehicles. Unlike with films, Midler was the creative driving force of her stage shows, and it was where she felt most in control and most in touch with an audience. "The foundation of my career has been those shows," she later said. "My audience has never left—they're very familial. And when I feel I'm getting bitter, I go back on tour. It's always and forever O.K. on the road."[19]

In a stroke of synergy, her new show, *Experience the Divine*, was named for her recently released greatest-hits album. The show itself was a greatest-hits package, with Delores DeLago and Soph returning, along with a new generation of Harlettes. New music mostly took a back seat as the star rolled out a string of hits and fan favorites. Its title acknowledged Midler's long-standing divinity among the faithful, and the show was studded with signposts underscoring the point. A quartet of showgirls heralded her arrival during an overture of signature Midler songs. When she appeared, it was from on high among the clouds, like a goddess. Midler made sport of her status as the Divine (as if the Divine Miss M was too cumbersome an honorific), by regularly striking a studied showgirl pose, allowing the audiences that packed every performance to savor her fabulosity.

The gay audience had stuck with her for more than twenty years ("I've never seen such a turnout of middle-aged gay couples," a critic noted in surveying the show's crowds),[20] and the hippest people in any town she played always supported her, but she now had a new fan demographic. Her Disney film hits and sentimental, chart-topping ballads introduced her to audiences that had no idea of her celebrated stage performances. (Even some in the media were clueless; in an interview with Midler to promote *Beaches*, Oprah Winfrey proved thoroughly unfamiliar with this part of the star's background.) Soccer moms, firefighters, church ladies, conservative married couples—now everyone wanted to experience the Divine, even if they were shocked by her salty language. (They got over it.)

Midler played the whole I-am-a-goddess-worship-me shtick with her tongue glued to her cheek, but the fact that it got uproarious laughs from the broad and diverse audience only pointed to how thoroughly her style of humor had penetrated the mainstream. Midler opened a record-breaking six-week, thirty-performance run at the massive Radio City Music Hall just days after the Wigstock festival on Manhattan's Lower East Side. The annual outdoor festival (its name a takeoff on Woodstock), celebrating drag in all its many-splendored and diverse glory, was started in 1985 by performers from the Pyramid Club. That Avenue A nightspot was incubator to a generation of punk, drag, and avant-garde theater artists like RuPaul, John Sex, and Lypsinka who, much as Midler had done at the Continental Baths and Ludlam and Eyen before her, discovered the value of pop-culture castoffs and reveled in an anarchic spirit of camp as they toyed with new representations of gender and sexuality. A whole new legion of Divine Miss Ms was launched at the Pyramid Club and Wigstock, while the copyright holder brought that aesthetic further into Middle America.

Experience the Divine was both a primer for her new fans and a reminder to the old ones that her caustic wit and camp showmanship were undimmed. She and the Harlettes introduced "I

Look Good," a rollicking new rap song stuffed with biographical details about the last ten years. Despite being "compromised, Walt Disneyized, dried out, detoxed, and Jurassified," Bette Midler 1993 looked not only good but sensational, sleek and slim. ("I'll bet you were expecting a beefier girl," she knowingly quipped.)

"Trash with flash" was a thing of the past. The star was decked out with glittering jewelry and a high-end coif. But she was as energetic as ever, the mincing sashay in place, along with jokes about her breasts ("This is the last stop on my World Cups tour") and the audience ("yuppie swine," she called the front-row American Express Gold Card holders who had to watch the show looking straight up). A new generation of tabloid celebrities was ripe for Midler's mockery: Tonya Harding, Joey Buttafuoco ("I still can't believe there were actually *two* women who were willing to have sex with him"), Anna Nicole Smith, Dr. Jack Kevorkian, and Lisa Marie Presley (on her marriage to Michael Jackson: "I don't think she understands why they call it Neverland").

Midler also took time for humorous ruminations about the environment, politics, culture, and obsessions with physical fitness and cosmetic surgery. The self-described "Queen of Composting" was both funny and pointed in laying out the global benefits of the practice: "If you have your own fruits and vegetables that you grow yourself and that you don't have pesticides on, then you'll feel a lot better and you won't hate your neighbor so much and you won't want to get a gun and shoot your neighbor. And I just envision world peace through composting!"

Midler undertook vocal coaching prior to filming a television version of the classic Broadway musical *Gypsy* just before *Experience the Divine*. Her voice sounded better than ever, and she sang a demanding two-and-a-half-hour program with no apparent strain. A sequence paying tribute to *Gypsy*'s burlesque world of strippers and low comics featured Midler as house mother, wrangling recalcitrant strippers and Harlettes. Her Soph jokes were delivered as interjections to "Pretty Legs, Great Big Knockers," much in the manner of Pearl Williams, who punctuated her jokes with her own piano playing.

Finally, and appropriately, she recreated *Gypsy*'s eleven o'clock number, "Rose's Turn," the wrenching culmination of Rose's single-minded efforts to make her daughters show-business stars, only to be shunted aside. It was every bit as ballsy as "Stay with Me," the other big workout of the evening—and she ended it in rock style, collapsing to her knees at its climax. Midler traveled the emotional and stylistic terrain between show tune and R&B raver with some kind of genius dexterity.

Delores DeLago returned in even more bombastic style. Joining the current mania for home shopping, she and her three sisters presented an "inspirational infomercial" for Delores's new self-help program, "Twelve Strokes to Satisfaction." Everyone twirled poi balls ("Balling to the Oldies"), the showgirls joined in for a mermaids-in-wheelchairs Rockettes-style kickline to "New York, New York," and the whole thing was labored and overextended. What had started in the 1970s as a witty takedown of lounge acts and the deluded stars who perform them had become in the 1990s a bloated production number that threatened to embody the very values Midler had originally spoofed. It took all of Midler's and Vilanch's comic invention to keep the lengthy routine afloat. (Blatt, her longtime comedy collaborator, died of AIDS in 1989.)

Experience the Divine ended with Midler alone, running through songs that had become standards for her—but each with a twist. "Hello in There" was now less a character study than a motherly instruction on kindness. "Stay with Me" rocked as hard as ever (even in an evening gown) but became the plea of a mature woman fearing the departure of a longtime lover or spouse. "Wind beneath My Wings," was a thank-you to audiences both new and old.

Experience the Divine was a pinnacle in Midler's career. She was now a true movie star and bestselling recording artist making a triumphant return to the medium that launched her. Her audience was broader and more adoring than ever. She had matured and mellowed but still kept her topical edge. She seemed capable of just about anything.

Mellowing, but Not Really

Midler's tours became increasingly elaborate, even as they loosely followed the *Experience the Divine* template: A splashy, specially written opening sequence, a mix of songs both old and new (usually from her latest album) and comedy (Soph and increasingly pointed politics and culture jokes) in the first act, Delores DeLago and a selection of favorites in the second. *The Divine Miss Millennium* tour of 1999–2000 spoofed Y2K fears ("I personally don't care if the computers knock off one hundred years, this act played just as well in 1900") and presented the star as a benevolent earth mother managing a troubled planet. A decade before Beyoncé insisted that girls run the world, Midler presided over a stage filled with women—not only the Harlettes but a troupe of dancers of various sizes, shapes, and ethnicities—a fierce female force of strength.

She resembled a World War II entertainment unit commander as she corralled her young company through "Boogie Woogie Bugle Boy." Her motherly spirit drove stately, majestic readings of Patty Griffin's "Mary" (the Jewish mother of a teenager, like herself, Midler pointed out) and "Sunrise, Sunset" ("for my tribe") from *Fiddler on the Roof*. She took time during "Stay with Me" to speak of her concerns over climate change and hate crimes, in an indirect reference to the recent killing of Matthew Shepard.

The show's visuals evoked a strand of the current "gay show-biz sensibility" courtesy of Mark Waldrop, the director and lyricist of the recent hit off-Broadway revue *Howard Crabtree's When Pigs Fly*. Waldrop and Howard Crabtree, a dancer-turned-costume-fabulist, created a series of camp romps built around Crabtree's mind-altering designs—Ziegfeldian concoctions trimmed in bathroom and gardening equipment, towering wigs and headdresses, a hunky shirtless centaur, dancing playing cards (all queens, natch)—and Waldrop's witty and well-crafted lyrics which expressed both the joys and the peculiarities of contemporary gay life. Waldrop and Crabtree brought musical-theater discipline and precision to the kind of hectic camp Midler had first been exposed to when she worked with Tom Eyen thirty years earlier. *When Pigs Fly* was the last of their collaborations; Crabtree died of AIDS at the age of forty-one just before the show opened in 1996.

Waldrop joined *The Divine Miss Millennium* as production supervisor and writer (along with Vilanch, Jonathan Tolins, and Midler), and his influence extended to a "Club Pits" sequence in which a nightclub table and chair emerge from a performer's costume, and Midler revisited "Marahuana" with the assistance of two large dancing marijuana blunts ("the Doobie Brothers"). She led the cast in a full-on Hawaiian dance number that ended with her towering over them in a face-devouring sun-goddess headdress singing Frank Sinatra's "My Way." ("I gave my all / I went for broke / So fuck 'em if they / Can't take a joke / The record shows / Though my taste blows / I did it my way!")

Delores, in a new guise as a presidential candidate, delivered *When Pigs Fly*'s "Laughing Matters," a warm but exasperated call to keep a sense of humor when politicians let us down. She repurposed that show's running series of cheeky torch songs to famously hypocritical conservatives such as Newt Gingrich, Strom Thurmond, and Rush Limbaugh to include an ode to Ken Starr, the grandstanding investigator of the Bill Clinton–Monica Lewinsky scandal: "You look so bland but goodness gracious / Underneath you're just salacious." A gallery of comically grotesque celebrity puppets supported Delores's political campaign, including Clinton (with sunglasses and saxophone, grabbing at the nearest girl), the pope, and Barbra Streisand and Queen Elizabeth street fighting over the microphone (Barbra won!). Waldrop added to *The Divine Miss Millennium* a touch of delirious gay camp that had gone missing from Midler's shows.

It wasn't that Midler had scrubbed all the gay content or innu-endo from her act. Rather, she had transferred the arch, knowing, sarcastic humor from her Continental Baths days to a wider audi-ence so successfully that it no longer read as specifically gay. Midler and the middle-of-the-road had somehow met left-of-center. The Divine Miss M had matured into a wise, outspokenly liberal, middle-aged wife and mother, albeit with a crack writing team pro-viding ever-choice bons mots delivered with plenty of F-bombs.

Her observations about politicians and celebrities now carried a shake-your-head-throw-up-your-hands weariness. During her 2003–2004 *Kiss My Brass* tour, she joked about Saddam Hussein: "This is of course a huge coup that George W. Bush captured him. You know, they're saying that he might even win the next election the old-fashioned way—with votes." With mock aggrievement, she bemoaned current pop stars who dress and act in a manner not unlike her earlier persona: "Do any of these girls drop a line and say thank you? I opened the door for trashy singers with bad taste and big tits!"

Kiss My Brass, as its name suggests, added a horn section to her orchestra and was the most sumptuous of her tours. A light-filled, turn-of-the-century Coney Island was the setting, complete with midway freak attractions (one of which was Delores DeLago) and a stage deck that looked like a wooden boardwalk. The stage cur-tain recalled Paul Cadmus's 1934 painting *The Fleet's In*, filled with sailors, whores, cruising gays, and other louche characters. The star, looking svelte and sparkling, made her entrance atop a grand merry-go-round pony.

Musically, Midler was as strong as ever, rocking hard with "When a Man Loves a Woman" and celebrating the decency and tolerance of Mister Rogers with his "I Like to Be Told." She did a wicked takedown of Jennifer Holliday's *Dreamgirls* showstopper, "And I Am Telling You I'm Not Going" in an otherwise endless Delores DeLago sequence.

Her peers who worked the same arena circuit with splashy catalog retrospectives may have sold out more shows or longer tours
(Streisand, Cher, Tina Turner), but only Midler consistently
showcased a unique mix of comedy (both current and comfortably old school), imaginative production concepts and designs,
characterizations, new musical material, and era-spanning song
selections. With *Experience the Divine*, *The Divine Miss Millennium*,
and *Kiss My Brass*, Midler had polished and (mostly) perfected a
large-scale contemporary vaudeville performance. How much
bigger could the Divine Miss M go?

Even Bigger

The answer was *The Showgirl Must Go On*, which opened in 2008
on the ginormous stage of the Colosseum at Caesars Palace in Las
Vegas. The $10 million show was set to play five performances a
week (with regularly scheduled layoffs) for two years in the 4,300-
seat auditorium at a top ticket price of $250. Las Vegas residencies
were lavish paydays for legacy stars like Midler ("There's money,
and then there's 'fuck you' money," according to a *New York* magazine story hinting that her take was of the latter variety,)[21] which
likely led to her interest in spending all that time in a town she had
famously dismissed as "Lost Wages."

The Showgirl Must Go On took all her recent arena shows and
supersized them into a ninety-minute career highlight reel.
To fill the massive stage, Midler and Toni Basil, who had been
choreographing her shows since the 1970s, added eighteen
showgirls they dubbed the Caesar Salad Girls ("each and every
one a tomato and always served with as little dressing as possible"),
along with the ubiquitous Harlettes.

The sixty-two-year-old Midler swaggered across the monster
stage like a modern-day Mae West, leading her all-female troupe
through a Delores DeLago bit to end all Delores DeLago bits. Las

Vegas was Delores's natural habitat, and she staged a lavish tribute to the legendary city, complete with cameos by Elvis and the *American Idol* judges and backed up by a chorus line of twenty-one wheelchair-riding mermaids.

Soph was introduced as a ninety-three-year-old showgirl, arriving in a colossal headdress (actually a piece of hanging scenery) that outdid Carmen Miranda's famous towering banana hat in Busby Berkeley's *The Gang's All Here*. Midler's Soph delivery was once a rapid-fire Borscht Belt bleat, but as Midler aged, she slowed Soph down. Her setups became more leisurely, and she savored the punchlines, still presented with bawdy gusto. Here she delivered her jokes in a series of showgirl tableaux that looked to feature every pink feather on the Vegas Strip.

Midler never met a floor she didn't want to lie down on, and all her concerts featured some variation of her reclining from mock fatigue. She had reason to be tired from rushing around the 120-foot stage and at one point resorted to a rolling sofa pushed by the Harlettes. Her comedy was as outrageous as ever, if no longer very shocking. Noting that she alternated the Colosseum stage with shows headlining Elton John and Cher, she joked, "Does it get any gayer?"

Midler worked harder than John, who seldom got up from his piano, or Cher, who mostly remained stationary and surrounded by acrobatic dancers. Maybe that's why Midler called herself the People's Diva. She wasn't afraid to let audiences see her break a sweat or pause to catch her breath. She made sport of her age ("I was taking a shower and something bumped me behind my knee. It was my ass") as well as that of her fans ("Thirty years ago my audiences were on drugs. Now they're on medication"). But for the first time, her jokes about being perpetually pooped sounded all too real, and her relief was notable when the show ended its run in early 2010 after around 170 performances.

The Showgirl Must Go On, with its long-stemmed chorus line and Midler's brand of brash comedy and sentimental song, was refreshingly old-school Vegas, in contrast to the chilly, Cirque du Soleil–style spectacles that had become the norm on the Strip. The large-scale *The Showgirl Must Go On* felt like an appropriate conclusion to Midler's brilliant stage career.

It was a surprise when she announced she was going back on the road in 2015 in yet another big show, this time called *Divine Intervention*. It had been five years since her Vegas show ended and ten since she had toured. (She took *Kiss My Brass* to Australia in 2005.) *Divine Intervention* was similar in scale to pre-Vegas shows like *Experience the Divine*, with a proscenium arch and a stage curtain that doubled as a projection screen. The show's theme was apparent in its first, cheeky image, that of Michelangelo's *The Creation of Adam* with Midler taking the place of God giving life to Adam.

That serene moment was violently interrupted by a montage of special-effects destruction: fires, hurricanes, tornadoes, and other natural and unnatural disasters. The curtain opened to reveal Midler sitting serenely amid an apocalyptic setting. As she and the Harlettes, who emerged from the wreckage, began the title song, it was clear Midler had weighty thoughts on her mind in what might be her final concert magnum opus: "I heard your S.O.S. / I'm aware of your distress / So before it's time to go collect my pension / I'll make some time / For some divine / Intervention."[22]

It was all hands on deck, with a rockin' horn section taking the stage alongside Midler and the Harlettes. That these tall young men and the youthful Harlettes were led by a woman just shy of her seventieth birthday gave *Divine Intervention* the air of a musical Boy and Girl Scout pilgrimage led by the coolest den mother in town. The den mother set the tone for the next two and a half hours: discipline and musical detail mixed with joking high spirits and a touch of civics thrown in.

As Midler got older, the Harlettes stayed the same age, and her relationship with them changed. No longer her peers, they treated her with daughterly deference and served in a more generic capacity as skilled backup singers and dancers. (Their trashy manner of the old days would have been redundant, since, as Midler liked to point out, now everyone in show business was trashy.)

She sang more new material than in some time, including selections from *It's the Girls!*, her new tribute album to several generations of girl groups. The most striking was "Waterfalls," introduced in 1995 by the hip-hop trio TLC. Midler turned this rambling scenario about mothers' inability to keep their sons safe from the horrors of street crime and AIDS into a stripped-down, mournful ballad. She sang with quiet desperation, as if she were ready to block the door to keep her son at home, transforming the contemporary hip-hop classic into a dramatic monologue.

Midler's comic observations were more barbed than ever, particularly about the insidious influence of social media: "Remember when people were *afraid* if they were being followed?" According to her, Sally Field invented Facebook by exclaiming, "You like me, you really like me!" Dick pics now flooded Midler's inbox ("Mug shots of little old bald men, and don't be fooled, the camera adds ten pounds"), along with endless updates on the Kardashians, whose prominent and highly promoted posteriors had, to Midler's chagrin, replaced breasts as erotic symbols.

Noting that the Kardashians' celebrity began with a sex tape, she lamented that she hadn't had the foresight to publicize for profit her own libidinous past. Cue the comically photoshopped images of Midler in bed with a rogues' gallery of notorious celebrities, including Richard Nixon ("He was fantastic! Why do you think they called him Tricky Dick?"), Vladimir Putin (who insisted she call him "Vlad the Impaler," though "Vlad the Imputent" was more accurate), Dick Cheney, Chris Christie, Caitlyn Jenner back when she was Bruce, and Tom Brady ("I was the first to suggest that he might want to deflate his balls").

With the audience's laughter still ringing at this marathon comic riff, Midler paused to reflect on the proliferation of time-guzzling social-media platforms, calling them "a perfect storm of useless information" because everybody knows most of it already. As she spoke, the first strains of Leonard Cohen's brooding, prophetic "Everybody Knows" crept in. Midler's chilling intensity situated the song's day-of-reckoning vision squarely in the current media-saturated landscape. Like so many times before, she moved imperceptibly from comedy to piercing drama, her interpretive skills and theatrical instincts undiminished. Midler refused to leave things so grim. She followed "Everybody Knows" with a healing "I Think It's Going to Rain Today," singing the lines "Human kindness is overflowing / And I think it's going to rain today" as a cry for humanity's better instincts.

Soph returned with jokes as lewd as ever, but Delores DeLago appeared only in an "In Memoriam" video tribute. No cause of death was given, but it was likely that Delores reached her apotheosis in Las Vegas and Midler had decided it was time to retire her wheelchair and fins.

During the thirty-five years that Midler had been singing "Stay with Me," the song's emotional temperature had shifted. What was once a knock-down, drag-out demand made to a departing lover had become a reflective consideration of the world around her. Over the years, she used its spoken interlude to ruminate on personal and family relationships or the earth itself or acts of inhumanity she felt powerless to stop. Here she paused to remember the ghosts of friends who had died, filling her with love but also rage. She sang the song more carefully now but with deeper, elegiac power.

And her sixty-nine-year-old, red-sequined-gowned self kicked "Beast of Burden" in the balls, making it a mother's ferocious lament for young women's mistreatment by men. The inevitable "Wind beneath My Wings" was followed by a tearful thank-you to the audience, as if the star knew this would be the last of her big shows.

As usual, she ended on an up note, introducing "the song that started it all," "Boogie Woogie Bugle Boy," with the Harlettes and the full band joining her onstage. When Midler first did the song in the early 1970s, she and the Harlettes performed it as a knowing gloss on 1940s harmonies and dance moves. Over the years, Midler used it as a Delores DeLago specialty, a group number, and a spirited encore, sometimes affectionately referring to it as "the national anthem." It always took pride of place in her shows. By 2015, she had been singing it for more than forty years—longer than the original distance between her first performance and that of the Andrews Sisters. It had established its own nostalgia, not for the 1940s but for a glorious moment of youth shared by Midler and her audience. Her singers and musicians, most not even born when their boss first sang it, didn't try to emulate 1940s moves, they just grooved on it, sailing on its joyous waves. When Midler and the gang took their final bow, she glowed like a proud mom who had just treated her brood to a grand adventure. Her work here was done. Her intervention was truly divine.

I'll Eat *Hello, Dolly!* Last

Those of us who were there at the beginning of Midler's career thought she could, and would, do everything in the theater: star as the ultimate Rose in a stage revival of *Gypsy*, pursue her early interest in Lotte Lenya by exploring the works of Kurt Weill and Bertolt Brecht. (She'd have made a great Jenny in *The Threepenny Opera*.) We thought she, not Meryl Streep, would play *Mother Courage* in Central Park. This, of course, while she was also making records, doing concerts, and starring in movies. Being blown away by her phenomenal talents gave us license to dream big about all she would accomplish.

Of course, she *did* accomplish a lot. But her stage career took her in a different direction as she created her own theatrical world. Singers and musicians and even showgirls were part of that world, but she essentially worked alone and appeared to prefer it.

It came as a complete surprise when it was announced that Midler would appear on Broadway in 2013, not in a concert or a musical comedy but in a play. An eighty-minute, one-woman play, at that. The title of John Logan's *I'll Eat You Last: A Chat with Sue Mengers* was a bit misleading. It wasn't so much a chat as a monologue delivered from the sofa of her Beverly Hills home by Mengers, a top Hollywood agent in the 1970s, a star in her own right with a powerhouse roster: Barbra Streisand, Faye Dunaway, Ryan O'Neal, Burt Reynolds, Candice Bergen, Michael Caine, and many more.

Midler's earlier dramatic ambitions had long since passed as she settled into a comfort zone with her concerts and divine diva persona. "By the '90s I wasn't really an actor anymore. I was someone who went on the road with these gigantic concerts," she admitted by way of explaining her fears of doing something so different after so long. "I mean, can I really create a full, three-dimensional character? I don't know anymore. I'm certainly going to try."[23]

The role of Sue Mengers was a good fit for Midler. Both were Jewish women who persevered and succeeded in show business. Just as Midler called herself a "plain little fat Jewish kid,"[24] Mengers described herself as a "fat little German Jewess."[25] Both Mengers and Midler (at least onstage) were exuberantly foul-mouthed, though the Divine Miss Mengers took first prize for her baroque vulgarities. (Elton John was an ideal dinner guest because "he'll eat anything but pussy.")

Mengers fled Nazi Germany with her parents in the late 1930s, arriving in the United States not knowing a word of English. Chutzpah and stick-to-itiveness took her from talent agency secretary in the 1960s to superstar agent in the 1970s. *I'll Eat You Last* is set at a very particular moment in 1981. Mengers has just been fired by Streisand, not only her star client but a longtime friend, and is awaiting a telephone call from the diva, presumably to explain the decision. Her client list has already been shrinking, and a new breed of corporate, college-educated talent representatives is taking over Hollywood, marginalizing freewheeling mavericks like Mengers. The ever-savvy agent sees the credits rolling, and it's not a happy ending.

Midler as Mengers was inspired casting, not only for her iden-
tification with a woman who declared, "You want to be a thing?
Make yourself that thing," but for the immense public persona she
brought to the role. Logan's work was less a play than a series of
anecdotes padded out to barely reach eighty minutes.

Guided by director Joe Mantello, Midler gave a precisely
modulated performance in which Mengers's stories played like a
series of set pieces, not unlike Midler's carefully crafted concerts.
She brought depths of emotion to Mengers's recollections of her
awkward childhood as a barely literate immigrant and of her
father's shocking suicide. Her story of losing client Ali MacGraw at
the height of her career to marriage and domesticity with "that cunt
Steve McQueen" played like an aria of comic rage that slowly turned
pensive and resigned when she realized how happy MacGraw was.
It was an emotional arc Midler had traveled many times in song,
now applied to story.

In a role that kept her sitting the entire time, Midler gave a highly
physical performance, making the most of Mengers's smoking of
cigarettes and pot, sometimes simultaneously—all impeccably
timed for maximum comic effect. No one could have been as funny
delivering lines like Mengers's description of her own marriage: "On
a good night we're Nick and Nora Charles; on a bad night we're
Nick and Nora Charles Manson." A phone call in which Mengers
tries to sell Sissy Spacek on a role was a riot, Midler's interjected
"uh-huh, uh-huh, uh-huh" even funnier than the agent's frantic
wooing of the hesitant star. The story of landing Gene Hackman
the lead in *The French Connection* was relayed with such delirious
comic energy that it earned Midler a hearty round of applause, like
a showstopping song. Even those with only a passing knowledge of
Midler's own complicated history with Hollywood could note the
blistering edge she brought to Mengers's tales of industry backstab-
bing and chicanery.

I'll Eat You Last was lucky to have Midler, whose appearance gave
it a heft and a sense of occasion that its subject didn't necessarily

earn. Mengers's "dish" about the stars was juicy but trivial, like flipping through back issues of *Vanity Fair* or *People* and spotting all the boldface names. Her heyday was strictly the 1970s, and stories about MacGraw, Spacek, Hackman, Ann-Margret, Charles Bronson, and William Friedkin carried little currency in the second decade of the twenty-first century. It was Midler who made it seem funnier and more relevant than it was, which may explain why the play, a sellout smash with Midler on Broadway, has had so few productions since, despite its modest cast and production requirements.

Midler's performance in *I'll Eat You Last* was widely lauded, but sandwiched between her Vegas residency and the *Divine Intervention* tour, it was more a palate cleanser than a decisive new career direction. Yet immediately after *Divine Intervention*, she was announced as the star of a major new revival of *Hello, Dolly!*

Hello, Dolly!, the story of multiple couples joined in marriage through the machinations of Dolly Levi, the widowed buttinsky who gets the biggest prize for herself, carried just enough traces of its source material, Thornton Wilder's play *The Matchmaker*, to give it a tiny dose of vinegar amid all the musical sweetening. When it first opened in 1964, starring Carol Channing, it quickly became the standard for a singing and dancing Broadway musical built around a big lady star.

In the intervening fifty years, several generations of celebrated women (and a couple of men) had appeared at the top of the Harmonia Gardens staircase to make their triumphal appearance in the title song, one of the most recognizable in the Broadway canon. The role was roomy enough to accommodate Channing's eccentricity, Mary Martin's warmth, Martha Raye's clowning, Pearl Bailey's sardonic earthiness, and every other quality possessed by the many stage, TV, and film stars who played it over the years.

Dolly felt like a role just waiting for Midler to step into, even if, at seventy-one, she was one of the oldest to play it. (Channing was seventy-four in 1995 when she returned in the previous Broadway revival.) As always, she was pragmatic: "It's a lot—I'm no spring chicken—but I'm curious, and I love to do all the things this character is required to do."[26]

The $16 million production that opened on Broadway in the spring of 2017 was a sumptuous reworking of director-choreographer Gower Champion's original production, with painterly vistas of turn-of-the-century New York, an endless parade of colorful costumes, a large cast, and a big orchestra. In the current landscape of scaled-down revivals of classic musicals featuring reduced casts and orchestras, this *Hello, Dolly!* was as close to golden age Broadway as most audiences would ever experience. And the star at the center gave them their money's worth.

While Barbra Streisand channeled Mae West in the film version, Midler channeled—guess who?—Sophie Tucker by way of the persona she had perfected over the years. She was earthly and ribald and landed every laugh, as expected. Some Dollys might have been more affecting during their introspective moments, and others might have been vocally fresher, but it's hard to imagine anyone being funnier. In interviews, Midler stressed that she was not much of a dancer, but her body language and gesticulation reflected the rhythm and pulse and, yes, the humor in Dolly's songs. It was a physical, dance-y performance, even when she was standing still.

Jerry Zaks's direction hit the comedy beats particularly hard, leaving little room for charm or the unforced humor built into the script. Occasionally, Midler went right along with it. In the hat shop scene where most of the romantic couples converge, everyone had a case of the cutes. Dolly's famous eating scene in the Harmonia Gardens was as funny as expected, but Midler (and Zaks) drew it out to exhausting lengths.

You can take the girl out of the concert stage, but you can't take the concert stage out of the girl. The role's presentational moments, in which Dolly speaks to the spirit of her late husband, suited Midler, who had been connecting directly with audiences for decades. She didn't shy away from breaking the fourth wall even when it wasn't in the script. When she tripped exiting a doorway, she shrugged and announced, "It's live!" During the title number, she fell back on her mock-fatigue shtick by collapsing against the proscenium, though in truth, its cakewalk steps were nothing compared with the frantic cavorting of Delores DeLago.

When Midler made her first appearance, it was to a whooping, foot-stomping, rock-star welcome, not unlike one of her concerts. Cheers and sustained applause greeted her throughout the evening. This over-the-top audience response was by now the norm at musicals, but here it felt genuine. The "Hello, Dolly!" number, with the star serenaded as she promenaded the runway around the orchestra pit, always blurred Dolly's celebration with that of the actor playing her. This time, the audience was more than happy to let the distinction slide and erupted in a roof-rattling roar.

The combination of Midler and *Hello, Dolly!* led to a stampede for tickets, and just like her 1970s Broadway engagements, the show broke box-office records for first-day sales. Premium tickets went for as much as a thousand dollars, and the show was a constant sellout. Midler stayed with the show through the beginning of 2018, playing a reduced schedule of seven shows weekly (Broadway stalwart Donna Murphy played the eighth performance), and returned in July to headline the final four weeks.

By any measure, *Hello, Dolly!* was a triumph for Midler, who won the Tony Award for her performance (leaving her just an Oscar short of an EGOT). While it was a thrill to see her at last in a Broadway-musical role that fit her so snugly, one couldn't help but wish that she had played Dolly ten or fifteen years earlier. For all her talent and verve, there was an undercurrent of caution, a husbanding of energy, and a noticeable weakening of her voice. (Maybe she really was tired during the title number.) Midler bestowed on *Hello, Dolly!* every ounce of her star personality and made it a true event. But it and *I'll Eat You Last* also left open the question of all she might have accomplished as an actor had she returned to scripted theater earlier.

And yet. Did it really matter what stage she was on? She touched audiences wherever she performed. She had been a singing actor all those years in her concerts, playing roles far beyond the scope of any one character. She had now come full circle: from Tom Eyen and *Miss Nefertiti Regrets* at La MaMa, to nightclubs and rock arenas, to *Hello, Dolly!* on Broadway—all her travels and triumphs across the globe had landed her back where she started more than fifty years earlier. Broadway was just an address. Bette Midler's theater was wherever she could commune with an audience. She was still our hostess.

2

"Some Say Love . . ."

Bette Midler's Recordings

In one of her first interviews after breaking through at the Continental Baths, Bette Midler was asked about her favorite singers. After namechecking Judy Garland, Edith Piaf, Billie Holiday, and "my all-time favorite," Aretha Franklin, she added, "I don't have any male favorites because male singers don't really show it to you like the women do."[1] Showing it to us was what Midler excelled at onstage, with emotions bubbling out of her in response to the collective energy of her audience. The perceived wisdom was that if you wanted Midler to show it to you, you had to see her live.

Midler's recording career has been a fifty-year effort to harness that onstage alchemy for listeners. Sometimes she made great records that clicked with the public. Sometimes she made great records that no one bought. Sometimes she recorded what she thought record buyers wanted, but they didn't. And sometimes her records were wildly inconsistent and wrongheaded. Being a Midler fan meant being alternately delighted and bewildered by her efforts to show it to you on disc.

After Atlantic Records president Ahmet Ertegun signed her in late 1971, he had to come up with a plan for capturing the excitement of Midler's live performances on record. Steve Ostrow wanted Midler to record her first album live at the Continental Baths, the place where it all started. But *Bette at the Baths* would have been too easy, too on-the-nose. To establish herself as a recording artist, she needed to work with a simpatico producer to translate her onstage appeal to the studio.

Ertegun looked close to home for the answer: Atlantic staff producer Joel Dorn had created just the right setting for Roberta Flack's elegant, crystalline vocals on her early albums. Flack had been singing and playing piano in Washington, DC, clubs before she began recording, so Dorn looked like the right person to present another live performer in the studio. The songs on Midler's first album would come almost exclusively from those she and Barry Manilow had developed and shaped onstage. But Dorn commissioned new arrangements, effectively cutting Manilow out entirely.

Midler was insecure, afraid the studio microphone would reveal vocal shortcomings that her live performances obscured. After several months, she and Ertegun were less than thrilled with the results of the Dorn sessions, feeling they captured little of Midler's onstage essence. In the meantime, Manilow had surreptitiously recorded Midler's triumphant concert at Carnegie Hall. After playing the tape for Ertegun, Manilow was invited to produce additional songs for the album. He set out to create an atmosphere in the recording studio that approximated the immediacy of Midler's live performances. He brought in her band, rather than studio musicians, and her current Harlettes for background vocals. Theatrical lighting was installed, and a small audience was invited and served food and drink. The trick worked, and Midler, Ertegun, and Manilow were all happy with the fresh, spontaneous results.[2]

When *The Divine Miss M*, sporting an idealized cover drawing of Midler by artist Richard Amsel, was released near the end of 1972, four producers were credited. Five of Dorn's cuts were retained from the original sessions, and Manilow, with Ertegun and Geoffrey Haslam, was responsible for six cuts.

The placement of Midler's sultry, slowed-down version of Bobby Freeman's 1958 R&B hit "Do You Want to Dance?" as *The Divine Miss M*'s first song announced that it would be an album showcasing a singer, not just a stage performer. Here Dorn's immaculate production, all soft percussion and soulful background vocals led by Cissy Houston, provides an intimate setting for Midler, whose first words are a breathy, whisper-in-the-ear plea ("Do you want to dance / And hold my hand / Tell me baby, you're my lover man / Oh baby, do you want to dance?"). "Do You Want to Dance?" which Midler called both "sexy and sad,"[3] builds slowly, finally reaching a crescendo of swirling strings as she grows more insistent, bolstered by her female chorus. Lots of artists recorded Freeman's song over the years: Sonny and Cher, the Beach Boys, the Mamas & the Papas, John Lennon. But no one brought out its sensuality like Midler, and Dorn's production made her performance a slow-dance classic.

Three Manilow tracks followed, with "Chapel of Love" capturing the sing-along zest of Midler in concert, as well as a bit of Miss M attitude. "That is the pits ending for a really terrific song," she deadpans after the final harmonies. On "Superstar," she's both fragile and tingling with erotic yearning, leaving little doubt what she means when she insists, "What can I say to have you come again?" Manilow's delicate arrangement catches Midler's voice suspended in air before trailing off in despair. "Daytime Hustler," the one song on the album she'd never sung before, is down-and-dirty R&B that transports Midler to a Times Square corner where she and a posse of equally furious women make short work of yet another man working a hustle.

Dorn's production of "Am I Blue?" sounds as if it's taking place in one of the late-night clubs Midler sang in before the Continental Baths. With the piano tinkling around her, Midler luxuriates in the story of her lover's abandonment, adding just a bit of fray to her voice. Dorn keeps the mood crisp and matter-of-fact until the end, when Midler, sounding frail and resigned, goes off script, adlibbing, "Would you believe it if I told you I'm blue?" and stretching the note out till it evaporates.

Side two opens and closes with variations on "Friends." Dorn's lively production features Midler in conversation with herself, her voice multitracked as she opines on the value of friendship with a wisdom that sounds hard-earned. ("I am speaking cuz I know / It's going too fast / We're all going too fast / I'm tryin' to tell you to slow down / Those friends are hard to come by.") These multiple Midlers are followed by "Hello in There." In concert, Midler could sometimes overplay the song's emotions, but here she's at her most disciplined. Against Dorn's poignant piano and string ensemble, she sounds dry and wintry, with the weight of the years hanging heavily upon her. Listening to Midler's heart-wrenching performance more than fifty years later, it's hard to fathom her insecurities in the studio.

Manilow's production of "Leader of the Pack" features Midler in what she liked to call her "tough shiksa voice," milking every ounce of teenage melodrama from this tale of doomed romance between a girl and a motorcycle bad boy. Her performance is the very essence of camp: treating trivial material with immaculate musicianship and fulsome emotion, while also standing at a slight remove from it all. Her sense of irony manages to make "Leader of the Pack" both a sendup and a satisfying slice of classic girl-group pop.

"Delta Dawn" is a country ballad about an aging, delusional Southern belle straight out of Tennessee Williams. It's a juicy story of a "faded rose" who waits "with her suitcase in her hand" for "a mysterious dark-haired man" to "take her to his mansion in the sky." With this much drama, all Helen Reddy and Tanya Tucker had to do to get big hits out of "Delta Dawn" was to sing it straight. They told the story from the outside; Midler inhabits it, embodying the delusional Delta Dawn and turning the song into a one-act, white-gospel melodrama with a chilling climactic primal scream.

Suddenly, it's 1941, and we're at the Decca Records studio as Patty, Maxene, and LaVerne Midler lay down "Boogie Woogie Bugle Boy." Midler's triple-tracked vocals get the trio's harmonies perfectly in Dorn's tight, period production which plays like a vintage 78-rpm record.*

---

* Manilow recut "Boogie Woogie Bugle Boy" when Midler performed it on a Burt Bacharach special, giving it a looser, more spacious feel and opening up Midler's vocals so that each of the three voices became more distinct. It was a contemporary take on a

It's a joyous eleven o'clock number, with Manilow's straightforward singer-and-chorus version of "Friends" as the curtain call. The friends Midler sings about could be all the characters she played during the previous ten cuts, a gallery of musical and dramatic performances that displayed her astonishing versatility.

The Divine Miss M was an immediate hit, going platinum and winning Midler the Grammy Award for Best New Artist. It had a cohesion and artistic integrity that belied the chaos of its production and the number of hands involved. The initial misgivings about Dorn's production seem overblown in retrospect, as his cuts fit smoothly with those of Manilow and company. Though vastly different in style and substance, *The Divine Miss M* shared similarities with the introductory albums of her Atlantic label mates Aretha Franklin (*I Never Loved a Man the Way I Love You*) and Roberta Flack (*First Take*). It was both an engaging record with a new sound and a complete artistic statement from the artist.

A year later, Midler was back with the unimaginatively titled *Bette Midler*, produced by Manilow and Atlantic Records arranger-producer Arif Mardin. Manilow also arranged and conducted all of *Bette Midler*, and it carries his musical imprimatur even more evidently than on *The Divine Miss M*. The first album's song sequencing was just about perfect, revealing Midler's singing and acting skills in a mix of genres and moods across its entirety. The new album took a bifurcated approach, placing ballads and character songs on side one, with period numbers and up tempos on the second side. The approach itself felt like a novelty, but the album's breadth of material and Midler's continuing evolution as a song interpreter made it work.

It's just Midler and Manilow's piano on *Bette Midler*'s first two cuts, each in a different emotional register. The many jazz and big-band singers who sang the wistful, questioning lyrics of "Skylark"

---

period sound, and it was this version that was released as a single and became Midler's first top ten hit. It's available as part of the 2016 expanded edition of *The Divine Miss M*.

("Can you tell me where my love may be?") did so with a certain decorum, as if they were afraid to disturb its gentle melody. Midler sings it with a delicacy that shades into a deeper desire. Her longing is palpable when she riffs on the final line, "Won't you lead me there?" and her straining for the notes makes it even more poignant. She claims this oft-covered standard as her own.

Midler must have first heard "Drinking Again" when Ben Gillespie introduced her to *Unforgettable*, Aretha Franklin's 1964 Dinah Washington tribute album. Franklin's youthful, ringing voice doesn't exactly convey a lonely woman drinking alone in a saloon. Midler sounds as if she's holding up the end of the bar. With a cigarette-scarred voice, she admits to "just being a fool" and "buying a round for total strangers," but her sardonic edge gradually evaporates, and she ends up "with just my memory," croaking out the final lines.

Ann Peebles took the soulful "Breaking Up Somebody's Home" at a steady beat, singing regretfully that loneliness might cause her to go after another woman's man. In contrast, Midler becomes the most flagrant of homewreckers, taking it in a rougher, rock direction and screaming out her furious desires in unexpected Janis Joplinesque style.

She hit a speed bump with Bertolt Brecht and Kurt Weill's "Surabaya Johnny." It's a first-person monologue delivered to a lover she now recognizes as a liar and a charlatan. As she catalogs his cruelties, her anger alternates with professions of love despite his failings. The best interpretations of "Surabaya Johnny" maintain a sense of Brecht's epic theater practice, appealing to an audience's reason rather than its emotions. Lotte Lenya (Weill's widow) mixed fury with a resignation that never spilled into pathos. Midler unfortunately wallows in the woman's degradation. Acquiescence replaces anger, with her wan vocal ending in a whimper. It's an odd miscalculation for a singer who more often found strength and resiliency in her song choices.

Curiously, following up this doormat characterization with "I Shall Be Released" makes the latter sound even more defiant. The raw power in Midler's live performance of what she called "my Woman Song,"[4] makes it difficult to capture on record. But starting with Manilow's plaintive piano underscoring and backed by a chorus of supportive voices, she sings with discipline, building in intensity until she explodes in righteous anger. "I Shall Be Released" comes as close as any of her recordings to conveying the impact of a Midler live performance.

The upbeat side two opens with Manilow's witty arrangement of the Munchkin-voiced "Optimistic Voices" from *The Wizard of Oz*, which leads into Midler's own Oz-like version of "Lullaby of Broadway." She's her own backup trio on this close-harmony take on the 1930s hit, giving it plenty of husky-voiced hubba-hubba. It's another example of Midler ironizing nostalgia: she honors the original songs while delivering a performance that sounds as if it's occurring within air quotes.

But it's only a warm-up to the album's vocal tour de force, a freewheeling adaptation of "In the Mood," the classic big-band swing number popularized by Glenn Miller and his orchestra. She and Manilow add new lyrics that Midlerize the staid originals ("Don't be rude!" "I'm hot now!"), and Midler again triple-tracks her vocals. After listening to "Boogie Woogie Bugle Boy" for a year, it was great to hear a new Andrews Sisters–style outing, this time with a more complex vocal and musical arrangement.

She reinvigorates another batch of 1960s girl-group hits with a medley of "Uptown" (the Crystals), "Don't Say Nothin' Bad (about My Baby)" (the Cookies), and "Da Do Ron Ron" (the Crystals again), veering from warm and womanly on "Uptown" to tough and overheated on "Da Do Ron Ron." Annie Ross's jazz novelty, "Twisted," was a deadpan sendup of psychoanalysis and split personalities, sung by Ross with consummate intonation and jazz phrasing. Midler doesn't have Ross's cool precision but instead makes it a conniption-fit comedy song, with characters bursting in and out.

"(Your Love Keeps Lifting Me) Higher and Higher" was a 1967 hit for Jackie Wilson, his swooping falsetto punctuating what the British call a "rhythm number" that started in high gear and kept going. Manilow's arrangement slows the tempo and adds a stentorian vocal chorale. Midler starts off kittenish but grows more assertive as the track gathers force. Midway through, the tempo doubles, the congas kick in, and Midler and the singers take it to church. The result is not exactly gospel, not exactly R&B, but a propulsive rave-up that builds higher and higher, then pulls back before reaching even more frenzied heights. Midler rides the rhythms and fronts the chorus like the star choir soloist. Side two of *Bette Midler* is nothing but a party, and "Higher and Higher" is its fervent climax.

Bette Midler, with another cover drawing of the diva by Amsel, was her second hit. With her first two albums, Midler had successfully transferred the "gay show-biz sensibility" to the general record-buying public, proving that it would respond to the camp elements, musical daring, and jubilant role play of the Divine Miss M as keenly as her concert audiences. These recordings also established a loose formula: songs from across eras and genres unified by settings that showcased Midler's skill at musical characterization.

When the Formula Breaks Down I

Manilow was already recording on his own when he produced *Bette Midler*, and he soon departed, leaving Midler adrift without the person who had helped craft her musical profile both onstage and on record. It would be more than two years before she released her next album—a lifetime in pop music. In the meantime, she recorded the gospel-ish "Gone at Last" with Paul Simon, but when it was released, Simon's Columbia Records mate Phoebe Snow was on the track instead of Midler. There were sessions for a Motown album with Hal Davis, one of the company's star producers, but the project was abandoned. Instead, Midler began working with Moogy Klingman, the co-writer of "Friends," who had his own recording studio. Together they recorded a slew of songs for an album eventually called *Songs for the New Depression.*

Midler took a hands-on approach to her first album without Manilow. She co-wrote two songs, co-produced two others, and was even listed as assistant engineer in the credits. She was also a perfectionist who insisted on reworking songs over and over, resulting in an album that sounds fussed over and flat. Worse, Midler's vocals are tamped down, as if she is trying to rid herself of its distinctive edge. It sounds as if she is aiming for a smooth pop-singer sound, a tendency she would continue to indulge at times. There are lots of pop singers but only one Bette Midler, and she only rarely appears on *Songs for the New Depression.*

A disco version of "Strangers in the Night" wasn't a bad idea, given the burgeoning new genre, but it isn't clear whether it's a spoof or a serious attempt at a new sound. Phoebe Snow's quirky, stream-of-consciousness "I Don't Want the Night to End" recast as an R&B slow groove was another good idea, but Midler sounds muffled and lost in the mix. It's the first time a Midler cover suffered in comparison with the original. Klingman's masochistic torch ballad, "Let Me Just Follow Behind," is a downer, with Midler all too convincingly submissive. It was dispiriting to hear the woman who sang a powerful "I Shall Be Released" sound so pallid.

Midler took two songs from *The Divine Miss M* sessions, both Dorn productions, and reworked them with mixed results. She improved the Patti Page hit "Old Cape Cod" by punching up the triple-tracked vocals. Dorn's take on "Marahuana" was capable of providing a contact high, its atmosphere and sonics conjuring a 1930s opium den, with Midler striking just the right note of Gertrude Niesen contralto camp. But she rerecorded her vocal, for some reason deciding that a straightforward account of the silly lyrics was more appropriate. The results were nowhere—not camp and nothing the listener could take seriously.[†] The album's most bewildering cut is a duet with Bob Dylan on his "Buckets of Rain." For Midler, a longtime fan, it was a coup to get Dylan into the recording studio, but their voices don't blend, both sound detached, and the track meanders. Curiously, a YouTube sound clip of the two riffing in the studio as they prepare to record brims with flirty, musical energy entirely missing from the finished cut.

There were a few bright spots. Having grown up on an island in the middle of the Pacific Ocean, Midler had a natural affinity for Tom Waits's gentle ode to the mysteries of the sea, "Shiver Me Timbers." Her sensitive reading and the gentle string and accordion arrangement made it an instant fan favorite and a concert staple. "Shiver Me Timbers" segues into the album's most delightful surprise, a new song by Midler and Klingman, "Samedi et Vendredi" ("Saturday and Friday"), sung entirely in French. Midler, singing all the voices, sounds like a nursery full of precocious children dropping a veritable United Nations of familiar names who appear in their dreams ("Pacino et Tricia et Spiro / Jackson Cinq et Simone Signoret / Zizi Jeanmaire, Mamie Eisenhower / Ursula Andress, Carmen McRae"). They sing "Bienvenus à mes cauchemars" ("Welcome to my nightmares") as the song fades, but the mood is anything but frightening. "Samedi et Vendredi" bursts with witty wordplay and infectious rhythms, and its sequencing with "Shiver Me Timbers" makes the odd medley the album's highlight.

For better or worse, Midler's first two efforts had set the bar high. She wasn't the kind of singer who could just put ten or twelve songs together and call it an album. *Songs for the New Depression* had the framework of what we had come to expect from a Midler album, but a sense of fun and theatrical flair was missing. She just didn't show it to us, and the album was a letdown when it was finally released in

---

[†] Joel Dorn's early productions of "Old Cape Cod" and "Marahuana" can be heard on the 2016 expanded edition of *The Divine Miss M*.

early 1976. Worse, it kicked off a depressing run of Midler albums that stalled on the charts and produced no hit singles.

"Did I Sing the Ballad Yet?"

The next year, Atlantic finally got around to releasing an album that presented Midler in her natural habitat. *Live at Last* was the soundtrack to Midler's HBO special that captured the Cleveland stop on her *Depression Tour*. For those without HBO or who had never seen Midler in concert, *Live at Last* was a revelation. It was *Judy at Carnegie Hall* for the Stonewall generation, with Midler in all her glory. "Boogie Woogie Bugle Boy" and "Delta Dawn" and "Hello in There," already Midler standards, were electrifying in live performance. It was as much a comedy album as a vocal showcase. Vicki Eydie and Soph and Ernie were never funnier than the first time they were introduced. She could dish Neil Young ("so mellow, so laid back") then give his "Birds" a shattering, driving reading. It was the first time we heard her recurring, dense diva joke, "Did I sing the ballad yet? Was it wonderful?" It was also the first time we got one of her extended song riffs, in this case a decimation of the recent Paul Anka cheese-fest, "(You're) Having My Baby."

Live at Last contains music that wasn't available live or on the HBO special. The propulsive "Bang, You're Dead," written and produced by Nick Ashford and Valerie Simpson, was inserted with applause and cheers added. It was a curious addition that nevertheless reconfirmed Midler's affinity for R&B and managed to fit perfectly with the show's song list.[‡]

The album also had an intermission, with a studio recording inserted at the end of the first disc. "You're Moving Out Today," one

---

[‡] According to Midler biographer Mark Bego, Ashford and Simpson gave Atlantic an ultimatum: the song would go to another artist unless Midler's recording, produced prior to *Songs for the New Depression*, was finally released. See Bego, *Bette Midler: Still Divine* (New York: Cooper Square Press, 2002), 121.

of a series of songs Midler co-wrote during this period with Carole Bayer Sager and Bruce Roberts, is a catchy pop novelty listing all the personal items Midler's freeloading friend must pack up when she throws him out ("Pack up your dirty looks / Your songs that have no hooks / Your stacks of *Modern Screen* / Your portrait of the Queen").

Visuals were beside the point. Midler's humor, audience interplay, and vocal dynamism leaped from the speakers. By the time she got to the inevitable "Friends," there was no doubt that there had never been anyone like Midler. *Live at Last* didn't sell as expected, but for many fans, it's still the Bette Midler desert island disc.

When the Formula Breaks Down II

Midler's previous studio albums had all been recorded in New York, but *Broken Blossom* was a product of her relocation to Los Angeles. Everything about it had a shiny, buffed sheen that extended to its burnished cover image of Midler photographed by legendary glamour photographer George Hurrell. Producer Brooks Arthur had just overseen Peter Allen's *Taught by Experts*, a successful transfer of Allen's New York cabaret singer-songwriter style to a bright, accessible pop setting. Surely he could do the same for Midler.

Arthur was known for getting the best out of vocalists, and *Broken Blossom* featured Midler's strongest, most assured singing to date, and in an even wider range of material than before. Each cut was orchestrated and played with authenticity regardless of style or genre. It was as meticulous an album as Midler had made.

So why is *Broken Blossom* so forgettable? Nearly every song appears chosen to check off a box on a list drawn up to demonstrate Midler's versatility: rock ("Red"), raunchy blues ("Empty Bed Blues," finally getting recorded years after Midler first sang it at the Continental Baths), country-blues (the old Ray Charles hit "You

Don't Know Me"), Phil Spector "Wall of Sound" pop ("Paradise," "Say Goodbye to Hollywood"), chanteuse torch ("La Vie en Rose"), doo-wop ("Make Yourself Comfortable"), character sketch (Midler and Tom Waits as a couple of flirty barflies on his "I Never Talk to Strangers"). The album sounds like a string of eleven singles rather than a fully realized whole. There's no overarching musical point of view; it doesn't build or establish a mood or tone, as her first two albums did.

There are two musical highlights. "Yellow Beach Umbrella," a singsong ode to the delights of anonymity on Southern beaches, appeared on a Three Dog Night album the previous year. Providing her own backing vocals, Midler sings it as both a gleeful escape to the sand and a poignant tale of dropping out. Arthur's bouncing production carries an undercurrent of anxiety that complements Midler's vocals as they strain to sound carefree. "Yellow Beach Umbrella" doesn't fit into a neat song category, and that's what makes it stand out on *Broken Blossom*.

"Storybook Children" is solid, middle-of-the-road pop, with a catchy hook and a big orchestra and chorus backing Midler's smoothest, most conventional vocals yet. It should have been at least a modest hit, but just like her other singles and the *Broken Blossom* album, it stalled on the charts.

Midler was sensitive about her lack of record sales. When she mentioned *Broken Blossom* during her club tour, she was greeted with appreciative sounds from the crowd. "Don't whistle at me, just go buy the damn thing," she retorted. She was well aware that her former collaborators were outpacing her. As soon as he and Midler parted ways, Manilow began turning out a string of million-selling singles and albums in his easy-listening style. Erstwhile Harlette Melissa Manchester had hits with big-voiced ballads she co-wrote and was selling more albums that her former boss.

Midler was a victim of her own versatility; she didn't fit neatly into any one music format. As listenable as it is, "Storybook Children" doesn't sound like it came from the same singer who made "Friends" or "Boogie Woogie Bugle Boy," and *Broken Blossom* was nearly impossible to categorize. She made fun of her problem with a riff on visiting Tower Records and moving her records from the Female Vocalists section to the Pop section. "I'll be a son of a bitch if I'm going to sit there and rot with Liza Minnelli!" she said to uproarious applause and laughter. But the joke pointed to a growing frustration about her inability to break through to record buyers in big numbers.

Black Leather, Married Men, and Rose

By 1979, the disco craze was in full swing, with everyone from the Rolling Stones to Dolly Parton jumping on the thump-thump bandwagon. Midler joined them by releasing what fans call her "disco album," *Thighs and Whispers.*

While more than half its songs are variations on the disco genre, Midler wrings a remarkable range of vocal characterization and emotion from them. From the boisterous big-band sound of "Big Noise from Winnetka" to the orchestral R&B of "Hang On in There Baby" to the Village People camp of "My Knight in Black Leather" she never lets the extravagant arrangements overwhelm her. She would later trash "My Knight in Black Leather," but it's as much a part of the camp continuum as "Leader of the Pack." If disco had been around in her Continental days, she would have made the song a bathhouse showstopper.

"Married Men" has all the trappings of high disco, including the four-on-the-floor beat and "whoo! whoo!" seagull chirps from the background singers. But Midler admonishes her female listeners ("Don't trust 'em!") with the same throat-ripping passion she brought to the rock anthems in *The Rose.* It's not surprising that "Married Men" didn't go very far when it was released as a single. It's too rough, too in-your-face compared with the smoothed-out sound of the biggest disco hits.

She offers a beaten-down yet lyrical reading of James Taylor's "Millworker" that calls to mind Sally Field's textile worker in *Norma Rae*, the performance that would best Midler's Rose later in the Oscar race. The album's real winner is "Cradle Days," a slab of redneck soul that may be Midler's best all-time vocal performance. Cushioned by creamy background vocals led by Luther Vandross, Midler runs the emotional gamut from resignation to defiance as she alternately pleads with and excoriates a faithless longtime lover. When she cries, "You took my darlin' babies from me / You really broke my heart in two / God in heaven knows that I loved you / And in your heart you know it's true," she summons the primal force of a modern-day Medea. The ferocity she brings to "Cradle Days" is at least the equal of her more celebrated rip-your-guts-out performances of "Delta Dawn" and "Stay with Me."§

The album's title, spoofing Ingmar Bergman's ultra-serious film *Cries and Whispers*, makes it seem as if it's going to be a lark, a drive-by sampling of the sound that had practically eaten the music business—and would soon face a furious backlash. But *Thighs and Whispers* mines the disco genre for variety and features some of Midler's most spirited singing. It's ironic that a genre so reviled by the rock world would dominate what turned out to be her most satisfying—and fun—studio album in years.

The best of Midler's albums feature a gallery of characters bounding forth in a variety of musical settings. In *The Rose*, she was limited to singing as one character, a driven, destructive rock singer suggested by Janis Joplin on a downward spiral she's unable to stop. Rock material had been part of Midler's diverse repertoire since the beginning, but like everything she sang, it was mined for character. The songs on *The Rose* were straight-up rock, demanding an ability to ride over a banging band with unrelenting lung power and stamina.

§ Oddly, Midler has never added "Cradle Days" to any of her live shows.

Musical supervisor Paul A. Rothchild knew the terrain, having produced the Doors, the Paul Butterfield Blues Band, and, appropriately, Joplin's final, posthumously released album, *Pearl*. He picked most of the songs for the film, with Midler contributing two others, both '60s soul ballads: the Percy Sledge hit, "When a Man Loves a Woman," and "Stay with Me," introduced by Lorraine Ellison. Midler knew her R&B and recognized that both songs powerfully evoked the soulful spirit of classic Joplin songs like "Cry Baby" and "Piece of My Heart."

"When a Man Loves a Woman," powerful and wrenching, is a highlight in the film, and "Stay with Me," delivered in the final moments of Rose's life, is as devastating a performance as Midler ever gave. But the songs on the soundtrack album have to stand on Midler's vocal performances alone, and in song after song, she pushes her voice to its limits and beyond, screaming for notes she doesn't possess. Straight rockers like "Keep On Rockin'" and "Sold My Soul to Rock 'n' Roll" become monotonous shouters. By the time she gets to "Stay with Me," the listener could be forgiven for wanting to brew her a cup of chamomile tea and give her a throat lozenge. What's powerful on-screen is too often painful to listen to when divorced from the film's visuals.

When Midler sings "Some say love," the first words in Amanda McBroom's "The Rose," it's like a soothing salve applied to a deep wound. The hushed power of her voice captures Rose's "endless aching need" for love and acceptance before resolving with a cleansing image of a rose emerging from a winter snow. The simplicity of Midler's singing was itself purifying after the raucous vocal workout she'd just put herself through.

With *The Rose* and "The Rose," Midler got not only a hit album but a career-defining, Grammy Award–winning signature song. "When a Man Loves a Woman" barely made the top forty as the soundtrack's first single. Like nearly every single she released, it was too big, too emotional for radio programmers and listeners. Starting with "The Rose," Midler's biggest hits sanded off her rough edges and her flamboyance for unthreatening, reassuring, hymn-like balladry.

The Rose soundtrack is a mixed bag vocally. So is her next album, another soundtrack, this one for her 1980 concert film, *Divine Madness*. It plays more like *The Rose 2*, eliminating Midler's comedy and warmth for hard-edged renditions of "I Shall Be Released," "Stay with Me," and "Paradise." Midler herself hadn't quite shaken off *The Rose*, and her singing here is rough and rock-inflected, even on old favorites like "Shiver Me Timbers" and "Boogie Woogie Bugle Boy." *Divine Madness* carries a general air of obligation and is her least compelling record release.

Why Bother?

Around the time Midler won a Grammy Award for "The Rose," she told *Billboard* magazine she would now focus on "straight-ahead rock 'n' roll and rock ballads."[5] She mostly made good on that plan with *No Frills* (1983), her first studio album in four years. It was rock and roll but with a then-current new wave edge, driven by guitars and synthesizers. Working with Chuck Plotkin, who had produced albums for Bruce Springsteen and Bob Dylan, Midler indeed played it straight ahead, singing with swagger if not personality.

There is plenty of radio-friendly rock, like Marshall Crenshaw's "Favorite Waste of Time," which sounds like an updated girl-group song, and the car-as-metaphor-for-sex "Let Me Drive" ("Let me behind the wheel / I wanna know how your hot rod feels"). But most of it is formulaic, with Midler coming off like a Pat Benatar wannabe. "It just doesn't sound like a Bette Midler album," a friend, another Midler fan, complained.

There were compensations that inched it closer to what might be expected of a Midler album, including a deceptively festive-sounding tale of a Cuban immigrant, "Only in Miami," and "Soda and a Souvenir," a charming 1950s throwback with background vocals from the latest Harlettes. On "All I Need to Know," a mature reflection on a longtime love, Midler's vocals are strong, her emotional range undiminished. But the album is all about establishing her rock bona fides with pedestrian material.

"Beast of Burden" is one Midler recording that very nearly matches the force of her live performance. She jumped into the new world of MTV with an elaborate video of the song bracketed by spoofing vignettes of a tabloid romance with Mick Jagger himself. Before going onstage, Midler begs him to stay for her performance of the song, bragging, "I sing it better than anybody." "Well, almost anybody," he responds. Jagger joins her onstage, vamping and trading dance moves. Midler looks terrific, humping the floor (as she liked to say) and playing to the crowd. She not only outdanced her costar, but she was funnier in their brief dialogue. It was an auspicious entry into the new music-video realm.

"Beast of Burden" was released as a single, and Midler was all over TV promoting it. But while "Beast of Burden" was nominated for Best Female Video at the first MTV Music Video Awards (it lost to Cyndi Lauper's "Girls Just Want to Have Fun"), it made no impression on the charts. Neither did "All I Need to Know." Apparently, no one wanted to hear Midler sing it as a character study, but Linda Ronstadt and Aaron Neville's dreamy duet (known as "Don't Know Much") made it a hit a few years later.

Midler worked on *No Frills* for nearly a year and was bitterly disappointed that both it and its singles were received with a collective shoulder shrug. At her husband's urging, she leaned in on her ability to be funny for *Mud Will Be Flung Tonight!*, a comedy album recorded live at the Improv in Los Angeles, run by the same Budd Friedman whose club in New York City had been Midler's pre-Continental home base.

Midler wrote the stand-up act, along with Jerry Blatt, Bruce Vilanch, Marc Shaiman (a young musician who first worked with her on *Thighs and Whispers* and was now very much a part of Team Midler), and several others. "More Hebrews worked on this act than built the pyramids," she quipped. With its knowing, insider slant on celebrity and pop culture, *Mud Will Be Flung Tonight!* shows just how thoroughly the "gay show-biz sensibility" circa 1985 had penetrated the mainstream.

As expected, the set includes a thorough skewering of celebrities, from Bruce Springsteen ("I remember when his arms were as skimpy as his chord changes") to Sally Field, Meryl Streep to Madonna ("The only thing that girl will ever do like a virgin is have a baby in a stable. By an unknown father"). Her ongoing interest in the female breast occupies significant play time. "Everyone has their field of expertise," she reasons. "Mine just happen to be tits. Do they dump on the pope 'cause all he ever talks about is God?" The size of her own endowments led her to weigh them on a postal scale. "I won't tell you how much they weigh," she says, "but it cost $87.50 to send them to Brazil. Third class. . . . If I was a guy and had this much extra flesh, I'd have a dick down to my ankles." Inevitably, jokes lead to songs, in this case "Otto Titsling," a deliriously wacky comic fable about the inventor of the modern foundation garment who was ultimately bested by one Phillipe de Brassiere.

Midler's comedy was intertwined with her singing; each talent enhanced and deepened the other. It was difficult for her to keep away from music, even in stand-up comedy, and *Mud Will Be Flung Tonight!* is regularly punctuated with song. Vicki Eydie returns for a Mermanesque "I'm Singing Broadway," and Midler laments her weight problems in the torchy "Fat as I Am" ("Fat as I am / Who wants to see a diva fat as I am / I get mistaken now for Lainie Kazan / How is it that I'm fat as I am?").

The album's high point is "Why Bother?" To Shaiman's existential piano doodlings, Midler confronts the contradictions of contemporary society, from art ("Modern painting is supposed to be the panacea for all the ills of modern life. And yet everybody still buys the painting that matches the couch. Why bother?") to celebrity ("I have a star named after me on Hollywood Boulevard. It's under a fire hydrant. Why bother?"). Designer labels inspire tedium

("Calvin Klein wears his own jeans, his own underwear, his own co-logne. I still wouldn't fuck him. I said, 'Calvin, why bother?'"). Sex isn't worth the trouble ("Halley's Comet comes once every seventy-six years. So do I. Why bother?"). Self-improvement is doomed ("I fasted for twenty-five days. I took a high colonic every day. I lost three pounds. My enemist said, 'Why bother?'"). At last, she seeks refuge in literature ("Is this what T. S. Eliot meant by 'the hollow men,' 'the stuffed men'? Or did he only mean, 'Why bother?'"), only to be left with more questions than answers. "Why Bother?" is smart, sophisticated writing and performing, as astute an examina-tion of modern life as George Carlin or Lily Tomlin at their best.**

Hollywood Hitmaking

Mud Will Be Flung Tonight! sold even worse than Midler's other re-cent albums and effectively marked the end of the first phase of her recording career. By the time it was released, Midler had completed *Down and Out in Beverly Hills*, her first film in three years. Its suc-cess and a string of hit comedies for Disney put her recording ca-reer on hold. The nine Midler vocals on the soundtrack album for her 1988 film *Beaches* were her first music recordings in five years.

Beaches is a sleek, smoothed-out Hollywood take on the template of her earlier, successful albums. There's the updated oldie, "Under the Boardwalk," with a voluptuous vocal from Midler; a cabaret-pop version of Cole Porter's "I've Still Got My Health"; Randy Newman's introspective "I Think It's Going to Rain Today"; a left-field lullaby, "Baby Mine," from Disney's 1941 *Dumbo*; a repurposed period ballad, "The Glory of Love"; the Brechtian-techno "Oh Industry";

** "Why Bother?" was produced as a short film titled "Angst on a Shoestring," set in a desolate 1950s coffeehouse and filmed in smoky black-and-white. It was a highlight of *David Letterman's Holiday Film Festival*, a TV special made up of shorts. Midler, in black wig, thick eyeliner, and alligator coat, is the epitome of Beat Generation ennui and manages a rainbow's worth of shadings out of the title question.

an adult contemporary romantic duet (with David Pack), "I Know You By Heart"; and the Broadway burlesque of "Otto Titsling," recycled from *Mud Will Be Flung Tonight!*

But the song that made *Beaches* the biggest-selling album of Midler's career wasn't one she initially chose. Shaiman, the film's music supervisor, suggested the syrupy "Wind beneath My Wings," already recorded by everyone from Gladys Knight and the Pips to Perry Como. It served its purpose as a voice-over during the film's climactic friendship-through-tears-and-death montage—and surprised everyone by becoming a breakout hit single.

"Wind beneath My Wings," with its greeting-card lyrics about flying like an eagle and a beautiful face hiding its pain, was the kind of song Midler would have spoofed as Vicki Eydie or Delores DeLago. Instead, she sings it straight, taking it soaring to the top of her register, backed by a bombastic *echt*-1980s orchestration. It's as shameless as it is effective, and the fans who couldn't believe our ears that the Divine Miss M was singing this musical mush were powerless to fight it. "Wind beneath My Wings" was a monster hit, Midler's first and only record to go to number one, and another Grammy winner for her. Even more than "The Rose," it became the song most identified with her, and in countless performances over the years, she gave it a healing warmth that transcended the treacle.

Midler followed *Beaches* with *Some People's Lives* in 1990, another hit album anchored by another hit single. Julie Gold's "From a Distance," with lyrics envisioning a world in which "There are no guns, no bombs, and no disease / No hungry mouths to feed," gets the grandiose, drum-machine-driven "Wind beneath My Wings" treatment. "From a Distance" benefited from timing, hitting the airwaves just as the United States was celebrating the successful expulsion of Iraqi troops from Kuwait in the Persian Gulf. It quickly became the unofficial anthem of Operation Desert Storm, its antiwar sentiments happily converging with this US victory.

After an early performance of *A Chorus Line* in 1975, Midler reportedly said to James Kirkwood, one of the show's book writers,

"It's such a pity. You almost had a hit. But that awful song—what was it? Something about what they did for love?—that threw it right down the toilet."[6] Midler had a nose, and an ear, for mawkishness. But that was then, and now "Wind beneath My Wings" and "From a Distance" unleashed a streak of sentimentality that had always been lurking in Midler's work but was tempered by ribald humor and irony. There was nothing ironic in these full-throated secular hymns that positioned her as a Hollywood earth mother, sage and all-knowing.[††]

The songs in *Some People's Lives* weren't as varied as those in *Beaches*. Most were adult contemporary ballads and mid-tempos, but a few stand out. The cabaret standard "Spring Can Really Hang You Up the Most" is a rarity, a sober, clear-eyed torch song that Midler delivers with admirable astringency, demonstrating that she hadn't fully given in to tearjerking. The album's highlight is a swinging version of Cole Porter's "Miss Otis Regrets." The morbid tale of a lady who shoots and kills an unfaithful lover and is then hanged in the public square was usually taken at a dirge-like tempo. Midler gives it the tight Andrews Sisters treatment and makes it a rollicking lark. Its small-combo orchestration is a refreshing change from the album's otherwise synth-heavy backing tracks.

Her next album, the soundtrack from 1991's *For the Boys*, followed Midler's Dixie Leonard character from World War II to Vietnam and allowed Midler to perform the kind of material for which she'd always felt a kinship. Skewed toward the 1940s, the musical selections are impeccably curated, featuring forgotten gems and new discoveries. Midler unearthed a never-heard Hoagy Carmichael song, the rhythmic "Billy-a-Dick," which kicks the

---

[††] Irony and gay camp humor, as practiced by the 1970s Midler, were out of step by the late 1980s. The AIDS epidemic was nothing to laugh about for gay men who were busy taking care of, or burying, their loved ones and fighting an unresponsive government for effective drug treatments. Aside from the fact that her old ironic approach to musical nostalgia wouldn't have fit the period songs in unironic weepies like *Beaches* or, later, *For the Boys*, Midler's music of this period reflected a general cultural desire (including among many gay men) for sincerity and uplift rather than caustic wit.

album off in vintage 1940s style. "Stuff Like That There," a Betty Hutton novelty, gets plenty of hubba-hubba. The Johnny Mercer–Gordon Jenkins "P.S. I Love You" perfectly captures the yearning tone of wartime correspondence.

When Midler's costar James Caan sings and banters with her on "I Remember You" and "Baby, It's Cold Outside," he sounds like he's having more fun than he did singing with Barbra Streisand in *Funny Lady*, and Midler's interjected comic put-downs couldn't be bettered. The Lennon-McCartney "In My Life" is perfect as a Christmastime lullaby for the troops in Vietnam, and Midler's middle-aged Dixie sings it with just the right mix of sugar and vinegar.

Apparently, even period musicals require a new theme song, and *For the Boys* obliged with "Every Road Leads Back to You," a nonperiod ballad straight off the busy Diane Warren songwriting assembly line. It's the first in a line of songs tailored to repeat the success of "Wind beneath My Wings" and, in this case, to qualify for a Best Song Oscar nomination. It failed in both instances.

Trouble comes when Midler tackles rangy ballads like "Come Rain or Come Shine" and "For All We Know." Without the benefit of character context and with no option for riffing or relying on her rhythmic sense, her voice comes across as thin and strained. ("Come Rain or Come Shine," arriving at a highly emotional moment in the film, plays much better there than on record.) Her performances aren't disastrous, just ordinary, when her singing otherwise is filled with so much color and character.

When Midler sings these mid-century American song-book ballads "straight," it brings to mind a double meaning. Her "straight" singing cleans up the dramatic messiness that makes her such a compelling vocalist. It recalls the early headshots intended to make her look like other girls but which only obscured what made her unique. Midler was never going to have the big, velvety voice of a Linda Ronstadt or a k. d. lang, and when she aims for that sound, when she "straightens" her singing, it feels boxed in, closeted. It robs her of the bold, bawdy effervescence and the warmth and emotional empathy that first blossomed in her singing at the Continental Baths. She doesn't show it to us.

More Roses and Bathhouses

The problems Midler had with the ballads in *For the Boys* are apparent on the soundtrack album for her 1993 TV production of *Gypsy*. As Rose, the ultimate myopic stage mother, Midler has plenty of character to play, and she digs in with gusto. But the songs by Jule Styne and Stephen Sondheim require her to adhere to their rhythms and cadences, to sing them as written. The listener can sense her itching to cut loose from the confines of the songs' structures. Partly, that's because the songs push her to the top of her vocal range and leave her sounding tinny, particularly on quiet ballads like "You'll Never Get Away from Me." She never sounds more like a pop singer than when she's singing this classic musical-theater role.

Still, her "Everything's Coming Up Roses" and "Some People" are ferocious. On the latter, when she spits out, "Well, they can stay and rot!" about people like her father who are too complacent to escape their dull lives, she chillingly conveys a lifetime of thwarted ambitions. No one has ever been quite as funny or taken as much joy in the wordplay in "Mr. Goldstone." And she rips into the climactic "Rose's Turn," the Mount Everest of musical mental breakdowns. She's resentful, introspective, and brazen all at once, and her final "For me!" gets an added roar of defiance.

So the Midler *Gypsy* ends with a split decision. It became part of a growing shelf full of recordings of the oft-revived musical. How does she compare with other recorded Roses? Midler doesn't have the leather lungs of Ethel Merman, the role's originator in 1959, or the warmth of Angela Lansbury (1974 revival). Imelda Staunton (2015 London revival) has a gentler way with the ballads. But

Midler is more consistent and listenable than Bernadette Peters (2003 revival) and Patti LuPone (2008 revival), each with her own vocal eccentricities. And she's miles ahead of the vocally challenged Tyne Daly (1989 revival) or the down-in-the-cellar combo of Rosalind Russell (for the low, talky notes) and Lisa Kirk (dubbing in the higher tones) in the 1962 feature film.

Unlike those of many pop singers, Midler's voice improved as she got older, a result of her attention to vocal study and coaching. The vocal work she did as she prepared for *Gypsy* paid off on the cloyingly titled *Bette of Roses* (1995), a collection of contemporary pop ballads that features at least half a dozen would-be "Wind beneath My Wings." (That's not counting "God Help the Outcasts," yet another inspirational ballad she recorded for the soundtrack of the Disney animated film *The Hunchback of Notre Dame*.)

Midler sounds robust and secure, with a voice that now connects fully from warm chest tones to a surprisingly strong falsetto. She emotes up a storm on the baroque, masochistic "To Deserve You," and she's jazzy on the late-night "To Comfort You." But midway through, the songs all start to sound alike, and musical sludge sets in. There's no faulting Midler's singing, but she checked her sense of fun and frivolity at the recording-studio door. It's too bad her new vocal prowess was squandered on an album with all the impact of mid-career Rita Coolidge.

Bathhouse Betty (1998) is not only a loving salute to a generation of fans, many now gone, who first championed Midler at the Continental but a refreshing return to the eclecticism that marked her earliest recordings. Arif Mardin had produced all her recent albums, but this time, Midler mixed it up by inviting several other producers to contribute to what became her most enjoyably diverse recording in some time.

She reclaims the Divine Miss M's spirit in "I'm Beautiful," an earlier dance hit for New York City–based duo Uncanny Alliance. Midler revamps this insistent rap tribute to the beauty of the individual, adding lyrics about gays to those targeted for abuse because

Figure 1. How do you sum up a half-century superstar career in just twenty images? Start with Midler's star entrance in her *Clams on the Half Shell Revue* (1975), then circle back to her New York City debut a decade earlier.

Figure 2. Midler graduates from one of the "assorted virgins" to the title role in Tom Eyen's *Miss Nefertiti Regrets* (1966), at La MaMa. Here Midler's cherubic Nefertiti is preyed upon by Marvin Peisner as Caesar.
James D. Gossage/La MaMa Experimental Theatre Club Archive

Figure 3. Midler's expression carries a double meaning. As Tzeitel, Tevye's oldest daughter, she appears to be mulling the offer of a dance from her new husband, Motel (David Garfield). As an actor unable to get another job after three years in *Fiddler on the Roof*, she's losing patience with the theater.
Photofest

Figure 4. By 1972, clothed women and men were crowding in alongside the towel-clad regulars to see the Belle of the Continental Baths.

Fairchild Archive/Penske Media via Getty Images

Figure 5. Barry Manilow at the piano and Midler at the mic. "Two ambitious Jews," she called them, but their musical alchemy resulted in timeless performances. Here they turn it out on *The Tonight Show* in 1973. NBC

Figure 6. Who's Fay Wray? Midler looks right at home singing "Lullabye of Broadway" from King Kong's palm during her *Clams on the Half Shell Revue.*

Figure 7. Midler enjoyed an even more copacetic teaming in her *Clams on the Half Shell Revue* with the Harlettes (from left, Robin Grean, Sharon Redd, and Charlotte Crossley).

Figure 8. It's her best film and her finest performance, so it's worth examining Midler's emotional range in *The Rose* (1979). Her 1960s rock star is exultantly in charge onstage but self-destructive off.
Photo 12/Alamy Stock Photo

Figure 9. The film's happiest sequence and a rare moment of intimacy for Rose with Frederic Forrest as Huston.
United Archives GmbH/Alamy Stock Photo

Figure 10. After driving Huston away, Rose is an angry, helpless speck on the ground as she makes her final descent. A massive drug overdose and one final, galvanizing performance are all that remain.
Twentieth Century-Fox

Figure 11. Delores DeLago is elevated to icon status in an image used to promote *Divine Madness* (1980).

AJ Pics/Alamy Stock Photo.

Figure 12. *Outrageous Down and Out Ruthless People in Big Business Beverly Hills.* Her money-making Disney comedies most often featured Midler as a braying wild woman, as in this scene from *Ruthless People* (1986).
Touchstone

Figure 13. *Beaches* went gold early on, but it ultimately sold triple platinum, or more than 3 million records, making it Midler's biggest hit and driving a resurgence in her recording career.
Atlantic Records

Figure 14. She wears the costumes, the costumes don't wear her. Midler previewed the conservation work she would undertake with her New York Restoration Project when she played none other than Mother Earth, who is made sick by the condition humans have left her in during *The Earth Day Special* (1990).
ABC

Figure 15. The epic-sized *For the Boys* (1991, with James Caan) was the purest distillation of the star's image and aesthetic. The movie's failure was a crushing blow to Midler.

Photofest

Figure 16. Everyone who didn't go see *For the Boys* tuned in a few months later to see Midler say, and sing, farewell to Johnny Carson–– not just for herself but for all of America. There wasn't a dry eye across the country.

NBC

Figure 17. Midler barely broke a sweat as the dowdy member of the divorced trio, along with Goldie Hawn and Diane Keaton, in *The First Wives Club* (1996), her biggest film hit.
Photofest

Figure 18. But she brought nuances of maternal regret to *Then She Found Me* (2007), costarring and directed by Helen Hunt. It's Midler's best latter-day film performance.
Photofest

Figure 19. She's still got it. Midler and the 2015 edition of the Harlettes don fine feathers to deliver some vintage Soph jokes in *Divine Intervention*.
Vidura Luis Barrios/Alamy Stock Photo

Figure 20. And she keeps rolling. Midler finally comes to Broadway in her first book musical since *Fiddler on the Roof*, breaking box-office records and winning a Tony Award in a much-loved revival of *Hello, Dolly!* in 2017.

Noam Galai/Getty Images

Figure 21. One more for good measure: Midler and costars Sarah Jessica Parker and Kathy Najimy loom over the Sunset Strip in Los Angeles ballyhooing *Hocus Pocus 2*, their Halloween 2022 streaming success on Disney+.

of their weight or color. When the star arrives to exclaim, "This is the Divine Miss M and I'm here to share with you some rare and stimulating insight into my cosmic fabulosity!" the extravagant rap/R&B cut becomes a delicious return to old-school form.

The spirit of Sophie Tucker is updated in two wildly different keys. The old Big Maybelle hit "One Monkey Don't Stop No Show" is a natural for Midler's vamping as she lays down the law to any man who doesn't do his duty ("There's a million men who can fill his shoes"). The album's biggest surprise is an original, full-on hip-hop number, "Big Socks," chock full of single and double entendres expressing skepticism of a man's bragged-about endowment. Midler delivers dense run-on lyrics like "Full figured in a place that can deliver? / Ha ha, not from what I've seen / I can't trace what's below your waist / There's too much space to be inside those jeans" with hip-hop swagger and just a touch of camp.

Despite its number of producers, *Bathhouse Betty* has a creative consistency derived from Midler's commitment to a dizzying variety of songs and styles. The gentle "Ukulele Lady" is a warm embrace of her Hawaiian youth; the Kurt Weill–ish "Boxing" is Midler-as-Lotte-Lenya; "I'm Hip," a comically jazzy tale of staying au courant, gets an appropriately cool and trippy vocal.

The girl-group hit "I Sold My Heart to the Junkman" was part of *The Depression Tour* back in 1976, but here Midler gives it the torchy treatment, finding surprisingly adult resonance in this teenybopper saga. Producer Marc Shaiman gives "Laughing Matters," from *Howard Crabtree's When Pigs Fly*, a ravishing orchestral backing for Midler's wry and reassuring vocal. This is the inspirational ballad that should have become a Midler standard.

Bathos was kept in check on ballads like "Lullaby in Blue." For a change, Midler holds back on the emotion, and her restraint makes this tender remembrance of a teenage pregnancy deeply affecting. *Bathhouse Betty*'s only dud is "My One True Friend," another would-be tearjerker that evokes God and/or prayer in the "Wind beneath My Wings"/"From a Distance" mold. ("I smell a

'Wind beneath My Wings,'" Midler crowed to Rosie O'Donnell about the new song's hit potential. Uh, no.) It was the theme song, sung by Midler under the closing credits, for *One True Thing*, a 1998 Meryl Streep drama in which her character loves Midler's records. The film included bits of "Do You Want to Dance?" and "Friends." The connection between songs from *The Divine Miss M* and the new album was apt. *Bathhouse Betty* turned out to be one of the most consistent and satisfying albums of her recording career.

Midler promoted *Bathhouse Betty* with a series of shows at gay dance clubs around the country, where she performed a short set of songs to backing tracks. A highlight of her appearances was "I'm Beautiful," which got umpteen dance remixes and ended up going to number one on *Billboard*'s Dance Club Song chart. Dance remixes of "To Deserve You" had done almost as well a few years earlier. After forays into disco failed to yield any chart hits in the 1970s, Midler now found herself enjoying surprising dance diva status.

When the Formula Breaks Down III

Bette arrived two years later, timed to drop just as her new TV sitcom of the same name debuted. The generic title and blandly pretty cover photo packaged the star in the mildest, most sitcom-like manner possible. Producer Don Was was a hot name, having produced hit albums for the Rolling Stones, Bonnie Raitt, the B-52s, and Garth Brooks, and he might have taken Midler in a Raitt-ish, guitar-driven, rock-R&B direction. Instead, he and Midler crafted an album that tried to replicate the diversity of material and moods on her best recordings—but it didn't.

The mix of songs is off kilter, with fully a third of *Bette* devoted to soul classics like Baby Washington's "That's How Heartaches Are Made," the Temptations' "Just My Imagination," and the

Manhattans' "Shining Star." These facsimile covers require none of Midler's special skills, and at times it's easy to forget exactly who is doing the singing. Only Teddy Pendergrass's "Love TKO," with its chorus urging her to "Let it go, Miss M.," shows any wit or stylistic flourish.

The other songs never capture the spirit of unity Midler can create from dissimilar material. Kirsty MacColl's "In These Shoes" should have been a hoot: over a killer Latin rhythm track, Midler passes up increasingly exotic assignations with panting men in order to protect her genteel footwear. But her voice is mixed too low, and the song is never as wildly funny as it thinks it is. Midler was singing better than ever in recent years, but she lacks the range to navigate Burt Bacharach and Elvis Costello's near-operatic "God Give Me Strength."

Since Midler had a club hit with "I'm Beautiful," *Bette* added another dance track, the machine-like "Bless You Child," an obvious copycat of Cher's recent hit, "Believe." "Nobody Else but You," written by Midler and Shaiman as the theme song for her new sitcom, is so generically perky that it sounds like a pastiche of every sitcom theme song ever written. Completely out of sync with the rest of the album, its inclusion is as blandly calculated as *Bette*'s title and cover art.

On the other hand, she sounds exquisite on the colorless "Color of Roses" and the more interesting "When Your Life Was Low." On this meandering Will Jennings–Joe Sample ballad, her voice carries years of weary experience as she reminds a friend who is now on top that it was she who helped him at his lowest. Best of all is her revamp of Patty Griffin's "Moses," a throw-up-your-hands cry for some mercy in an alienating world. Midler is all earthy, wry humor as she swoops up to her head voice and down to her chest tones, riding the song's hypnotic country-calypso rhythms. "In These Shoes" got the dance-remix treatment, but it's "Moses" that was a missed opportunity for a breakout single from the otherwise forgettable *Bette*.

Girl Singer

After *Bette of Roses*, Midler moved from Atlantic to Warner Brothers Records, thus staying under the Warners-Atlantic-Elektra umbrella. Of her Warners albums, *Bathhouse Betty* sold well, but *Bette* was a sales disappointment, and the label dropped her. At fifty-five, after nearly thirty years at a major label, Midler was now itinerant, no longer on the cutting edge, and—if she could get a record deal—definitely relegated to the easy listening/female vocalists category she once feared.

She was brought back to a major label by Barry Manilow, of all people, when he set up a project at Columbia Records in 2003. According to Manilow, he had a dream about reuniting with Midler for a tribute to the recently deceased Rosemary Clooney. *Bette Midler Sings the Rosemary Clooney Songbook* would be their first collaboration in thirty years.[‡‡] Clooney's song catalog, featuring her warm, open-hearted phrasing and undervalued sense of swing, was a good fit for Midler, and Manilow proved again that he was her best musical maestro. (He co-arranged nearly all the album's eleven songs and co-produced with Robbie Buchanan.)

Midler had always been her own auteur, overseeing every element of her recordings. But on the Clooney project, Manilow was in charge and she was the girl singer, showing up and recording her vocals in just two days. The results were some of her most graceful and spontaneous vocal performances.

Manilow's musical settings update and bring out new flavors in Clooney's Eisenhower-era novelty hits. "This Ole House" gets a spirited bluegrass makeover, with Midler heartily embodying a country matriarch. She's Ma Joad with a blowout. Midler and Manilow do a sexy, pulsating take on the otherwise annoying "Come On-a My House." "Mambo Italiano" is good-naturedly camped up, with a

---

[‡‡] Manilow co-wrote a song for Midler's character, a diva poodle named Georgette, in Disney's 1988 animated film *Oliver & Company*.

killer rhythm track. Clooney was never a fan of these songs, but it's hard to imagine she wouldn't have enjoyed Midler and Manilow's playful and musically adventurous way with them.

Manilow's arrangements nestle and support Midler in a way that allows her to be more vocally fluid and subtle. She has a nice, easy way with "Hey There," and "Memories of You" is stunning, with Midler's sensual croon backed by warm male voices. But it's the up-tempos that shine the brightest. Midler and Manilow spar their way through a swinging "On a Slow Boat to China" (Clooney recorded it with Bing Crosby), and she and Linda Ronstadt get pretend-catty on a pumped-up "Sisters." The album's highlight is "In the Cool, Cool, Cool of the Evening," with Midler at her good-humored best, bouncing through Johnny Mercer's dense, savory lyrics. Hearing Midler on *Bette Midler Sings the Rosemary Clooney Songbook* is like running into an old friend and remembering everything you always liked about her—humor, warmth, understanding, and a sense of the silly.

Bette Midler Sings the Rosemary Clooney Songbook sold well, so two years later, Manilow had another dream, resulting in *Bette Midler Sings the Peggy Lee Songbook*. Lee's icy precision was the opposite of Midler's volatile warmth, and the songs associated with her aren't a comfortable match for Midler. "Fever," "I'm a Woman," and "He's a Tramp" all sound perfunctory. "Big Spender" plays like a first run-through. The album is ballad-heavy, and Midler sounds pinched and nervous on "The Folks Who Live on the Hill" and "He Needs Me" (an extra on editions of the album purchased at Barnes and Noble stores). And what the hell was she doing singing a straight-faced "Mr. Wonderful," a big, steaming slab of cheese that under other circumstances she would have assigned to Delores DeLago for a swift evisceration?

There's no attempt to revisit and update Lee's excursions into Latin rhythms, which would have played to Midler's strengths. Only a few cuts stand out. She heats up the chilly "Is That All There Is?" She's good and tough on "Alright, Okay, You Win," and she and

Manilow once again swing winningly on "I Love Being Here with You." *Bette Midler Sings the Peggy Lee Songbook* was a nonstarter and quietly ended Midler's songbook series at Columbia.

It's a shame she and Manilow didn't investigate the Laura Nyro catalog. Nyro's output mixed Tin Pan Alley, R&B, and a womanly, urban perspective that would have made it a natural for Midler. Instead, in 2006, she returned to Columbia with another songbook, this time of Christmas songs.

The title track, Steve Allen's hipster "Cool Yule," hints that this could be a Christmas album in the swingin' Ella Fitzgerald style. But once again, there are too many stately ballads (including another version of "White Christmas," already covered on the Clooney set). One surprise exception is "From a Distance," reworked as a seasonal hymn. Divorced from the bombast of Midler's original version, it sounds like it was always meant as a Christmas song. It's surprising that it hasn't caught on as a Yuletide standard.

Midler is at her best on the gently swinging "I've Got My Love to Keep Me Warm" and the wistful, questioning "What Are You Doing New Year's Eve?" She's flirty as she harmonizes with Johnny Mathis on "Winter Wonderland" and "Let It Show! Let It Snow! Let It Snow!"

"Mele Kalikimaka," based on the Hawaiian derivation of the phrase "Merry Christmas," is an affectionate tribute to her home state sung more playfully than Bing Crosby and the Andrews Sisters on their original recording. *Cool Yule* could have used more holiday pep and less pomp.

Still Showing It to Us

And then that was it. There were no new recordings from Midler for a full eight years. What does a diva do when she's cut loose from a second major label? She might have gone the indie route and recorded a set of saloon songs with a small combo, or investigated the musical legacies of Mae West and Sophie Tucker, two of her stylistic forebears. Instead, in 2014, Midler was back with an album so inevitable that it's hard to believe she didn't think of it earlier.

It's the Girls! is a droll and loving salute to the girl groups that had informed her musical style from the beginning. She and producer-arranger-orchestrator Shaiman, who at last had charge of an entire Midler album, dug deeper than just the Andrews Sisters and the Shangri-Las for the album's whopping fifteen cuts. While their selections hovered most often near the late 1950s to early 1960s, they stretched back to the 1930s and up to the 1990s.

There's more variety than expected as Midler and Shaiman turn the Supremes' "You Can't Hurry Love" into guitar-and-banjo country swing. Other cuts are faithful to the youthful exuberance of the originals but with more oomph. The Marvelettes' "Too Many Fish in the Sea" is a brass-heavy blast, with the added kick of Midler's ad libs ("Oh look girls, it's Moby Dick!"). She's in full gay-icon glory singing the Shangri-Las' "Give Him a Great Big Kiss" as if to the boys at the baths, only the boys have grown old along with her. The song's "him" is now an alte kaker in ICU. "I've known him since the first time this record came out," she airily notes.

And enough with the stately ballads! Here Midler returns to the kind of easy-cadenced pop songs that allow her to inhabit a character while also finding nuances within the melody line. She unearths surprisingly adult themes in these cotton-candy tunes. She slows down the perky teen angst of Martha and the Vandellas' "Come and Get These Memories" and makes it an understated consideration of a middle-aged breakup. Her heartbreaking take on the Shirelles' "Will You Still Love Me Tomorrow?" carries the weight of years, as if she's afraid there won't be enough tomorrows. Her most audacious makeover is TLC's 1995 "Waterfalls," its hip-hop gait slowed to a halting, haunting whisper with Midler as a grieving mother who has lost her son to the streets. Her lived-in vocal lets the sorrow speak for itself and makes "Waterfalls" a latter-day classic to stand alongside "Hello in There."

The woman who re-popularized "Boogie Woogie Bugle Boy" naturally includes some choice self-harmonizing. Midler swings effortlessly, and authentically, on the Andrews Sisters' "Bei Mir Bist Du Schön" and the Boswell Sisters' "It's the Girl." Her tight, precise, and loving recreations of these three-part-harmony classics are among the album's highlights.

Midler, nearing seventy, showed it to us just like the old days. Her singing was equal parts muscular and meltingly emotional, some of the best of her forty-plus-year recording career. If this was to be the last Midler album, she was going out in peak form. (It's best to pass over the cast recording for her 2017 Broadway return in *Hello, Dolly!* The vocal diminishment that was apparent in the theater is even more pronounced on the recording.)

So what of Midler's legacy as a recording artist? It's been a volatile series of hits and misses, and her best work is often forgotten. Her most frequently downloaded and streamed songs continue to be the "big three" ballads, "The Rose," "Wind beneath My Wings," and "From a Distance." These days, one of her most recognized songs is "I Put a Spell on You" from *Hocus Pocus*, the 1993 Disney witch comedy that's become a Halloween staple.

Like most long-timers, Midler has had several greatest-hits packages, including *Experience the Divine* (1993) and *Jackpot! The Best Bette* (2008), each highlighting the eclecticism of her recorded output at the time of their release. The two most recent packages stress Midler as a middle-of-the-road balladeer, not her strongest suit. *Memories of You*, a 2010 UK-only release, leans heavily on the least persuasive ballads from *For the Boys* and the Peggy Lee set. *The Gift of Love* (2015) is only a bit more varied but includes nearly half of the *Bette of Roses* album. If Martians arrived on earth and listened to these ballad-centric compilations, they'd have no idea what made Midler so special. Her most incisive ballad performances are skipped over—there's no "Hello in There," no "Superstar," no "Skylark," no "Cradle Days." These repackagings reduce Midler to a just another girl singer.

Midler deserves a career-spanning collection that reminds listeners of the full scope of her remarkable singing talents. *The Divine Miss M* got a stingy expanded edition in 2016, with some single versions and alternate takes of already-released songs and only two new discoveries. The unused cuts by Dorn and Manilow for that first album and those produced by Klingman for *Songs for the New Depression* are a good starting point for a career retrospective.

Joni Mitchell's "For Free" remains unreleased from the first album, and Midler oozes so much warmth and sensuality on a live 1971 recording of "River" that it's a pity she never fully explored Mitchell's songbook. She and Manilow gave Melissa Manchester's and Carole Bayer Sager's "Easy" a sultry workout that didn't make it onto her second album. The never-heard Hal Davis–produced Motown sessions could reveal Midler in all her R&B glory.

A handful of Midler movie songs, mostly played over the end credits, have never been released, including a brassy "You Do Something to Me" from *Scenes from a Mall*, the stiff-upper-lip "One More Cheer" from *Stella*, and the catchy "No Jinx" from *Jinxed* (not to mention that film's Vegas-y renditions of "A Cowgirl's Dream" and "Papa Loves Mambo"). The standard "Somewhere along the Way" from *That Old Feeling* would fit in nicely, and why not include the girl-power "You Don't Own Me" from *The First Wives Club* and the witch-power doubleheader of "I Put a Spell on You" and "One Way or Another" from *Hocus Pocus 2*?

Midler live is the sweet spot, and there's an endless number of live performances that have never been officially released but are available on YouTube. Tom Waits's "Martha" gets an emotionally raw rendition from Midler on *Saturday Night Live* in 1979. She's blistering on the soul shouter "It Should Have Been Me" from *De Tour*. Her 1972 Carnegie Hall concert includes a beseeching performance of the Howard Dietz–Arthur Schwartz standard "Something to Remember You By," with one of Manilow's gently supportive piano arrangements. Midler is of good cheer and in great voice in a 1995 performance of "The Hostess with the Mostes' on the Ball," with some Midler zingers thrown in. She had to wait until 2011 to do "Pirate Jenny" at a Carnegie Hall gala. Her spine-tingling performance is a reminder of the power Midler could have displayed in fully staged productions of Brecht.

A large-scale retrospective of Midler's recordings would be a much-needed reminder that she's not just the Queen of the Inspirational Ballad or Miss Trash with Flash. In all her musical guises, she's been a friend, a confessor, a confidante. She makes you feel heard even as she's been showing it to us in song for five decades.

3

"I'll Show You a Pair of Golden Globes!"

Bette Midler's Television

For those who don't live in the big (or medium-sized) cities that hosted her tours or don't go to the movies much or aren't avid consumers of recordings, the small screen has been the gateway to getting to know Bette Midler. Over the past fifty years, she has been a near-constant presence, trading earthy, informed, quote-worthy chat with everyone from Oprah Winfrey to Graham Norton. She's shaken up staid awards shows as both presenter and honoree, memorably guested on variety specials, and packaged her stage shows as HBO event programming. She's been on telethons and reality shows and was immortalized as a cartoon figure on *The Simpsons*. She even (briefly) had her own sitcom. Lately she's turned up in choice character parts in series and specials available on streaming platforms. Midler has been so ubiquitous for so long that it's revelatory to revisit her many appearances on YouTube and other social-media sites—not only to experience the raw vitality of those early performances but also to find that the more she's changed, the more she's stayed the same.

New York–based talk shows in the 1970s offered plentiful opportunities for quirky young talents like Midler to sing a song or two and maybe kibitz with the host, regardless of whether they had a Broadway show or film or new record to promote. Midler had none of these when her manager Budd Friedman got her booked on Merv Griffin's and David Frost's shows in early 1970, just before she landed at the Continental Baths.

These early appearances showed her already to be a remarkably poised and fearless song interpreter. On her first *David Frost Show* appearance, on April 7, 1970, she sang "Am I Blue?" and followed it up with an old Mae West song, "Come Up and See Me Sometime," delivered with robust Westian innuendo and ending with a wailing roar—to the delight of the studio audience. A few months later, she was back belting out the old blues number "C.C. Rider" and interpolating a monologue on discovering the truth about a faithless lover. "He told me he was single with a future. He was married with a past," she dished with Divine Miss M–in–training attitude. Clearly, she was already finding her take-no-prisoners style and vocal delivery, if not yet her look. With her straight, shoulder-length dark brown hair and long dress, she looked like an attractive young secretary commuting in from Long Island for a night in the city.

Draped in a shawl, she channeled Laura Nyro on her next *Frost* appearance, singing the mostly forgotten "Remember My Forgotten Man," from *Gold Diggers of 1933*. Her intensely dramatic interpretation of this plea for a World War I soldier now neglected by society brimmed with pathos and righteous fury that found common cause with the disregard now facing many returning Vietnam veterans.

When Midler traveled to Philadelphia for *The Mike Douglas Show* a year later, her versatility was on full view with a tender and beaten-down "Ten Cents a Dance" followed by a brazen "Great Balls of Fire." These afternoon talk shows seemed barely able to contain her. She was almost too boisterous, too sexual, for the likes of Douglas and Frost, with their polite studio audiences of housewives and retirees. (She was apparently too much for Lawrence Welk, who refused to dance with Midler or even touch her during one of her *Douglas* appearances.)

Here's Johnny!

It was a nighttime talk show that provided Midler a national launching pad, as well as an early champion. Her booking on *The Tonight Show* just weeks after starting at the Continental, and her immediate chemistry with Johnny Carson, led to a string of appearances that allowed television audiences to experience both her bawdy humor and her genuine comic wit. Midler's brash boundary-pushing in these early television appearances synced up with the comedy trends in the 1970s toward political, taboo-busting comedy embodied by Richard Pryor, Lily Tomlin, and George Carlin. In chat-show parlance, she was a "good talker," always prepared with a zany story. She told about singing for a group of towel-clad men at a Turkish bath (skipping over their sexuality), working in a pineapple factory, and the personalities of her plants (including a Venus flytrap that she insisted was Jewish), all to Carson's vast amusement.

Carson's on-screen interactions with attractive young women in the 1970s can look like leering from today's perspective. But Midler was a match for him, volleying quips back and forth while maintaining a good-natured, flirty energy. Midler had a similar bantering chemistry with Phil Donahue during her 1980s appearances on his show. She also had a knack for warmly connecting with hosts across generations. When she appeared on Dinah Shore's afternoon talk show in 1977, the two chatted like old friends, despite the thirty-year age difference. In her numerous appearances on Rosie O'Donnell's daytime show in the 1990s, Midler was a cool older sister to the younger woman. With the cross-generational hosts of *The View*, Midler was a smart and funny BFF.

In the early *Tonight Show* appearances, Midler is still finding her voice, working the outrageous, but occasionally revealing the strain. A story about a burglar coming in through a window in her apartment and robbing her while she was in bed is unpleasant rather than sexy, especially with a final punctuation, "It was fabulous!" But after an affecting "Hello in There" and a turbocharged "Chattanooga Choo Choo," Carson is left to marvel, "You're going to be a big star in this business because you're unique and you're different." "I can't wait," says the happy star-to-be. "Well, you'll have to," comes the surprisingly paternal response.

Carson's flirtatious/fatherly chemistry with Midler continued during her frequent returns to his show over the next twenty years. Her appearances offer snapshots of the state of her career—not to mention her hairstyles. In 1973, now a bestselling recording artist and concert star, Midler made a triumphant return in all her curly red-haired glory. The entire Midler troupe gave a mini-concert, with the Harlettes' "Optimistic Voices" leading into Midler's grand entrance for "Lullaby of Broadway" and a sizzling "Boogie Woogie Bugle Boy." They were a sight: Midler in her "baked potato" dress, stone martens, and platform shoes and the Harlettes in vintage tie-and-tails harmonized and danced their stylized 1940s moves like contemporary women giddily discovering a new/old musical world. Barry Manilow and the band in their 1970s shaggy hair and street clothes jammed expertly on this World War II rocker. If any single performance exemplified the musical and sartorial fun of the early-1970s nostalgia trend, it was surely this one.

In a 1980 *Tonight Show* appearance, publicizing her new book, *A View from a Broad*, Midler looked remarkably subdued, wearing what she might sardonically call a "tasteful" ensemble of slacks, jacket, and high-necked blouse, with her now-blond tresses pulled back behind her ears. Her conservative look is in sharp contrast to Carson's observation that she used to dress "like a stolen car," but she's as vivid a conversationalist as ever. When Carson asks if she ever imagined she would be as big a star as she has become, her answer is a straightforward, sincere "Yes." But she's quick to point out that her early view of stardom was superficial. "I didn't realize that the one thing that's worse than not being looked at is being looked at," she says, before launching into a comic riff on being followed in the grocery store by fans who judge her food choices. "I can only go to the fancy food section now." It was a perfect Midlerian anecdote: outlandishly funny, told with mock horror, but with an underlying seriousness that made it entirely plausible.

Carson introduced Midler in 1983 as having first appeared on Broadway in *I Can Get It for You Wholesale* (no, that was Barbra), but otherwise her appearance was stellar. She's first seen on the floor, crouching like a caged animal as she launches into a savage "Beast of Burden." Her tight, spaghetti-strapped cocktail dress and spike heels don't inhibit her from dropping to her knees and "humping the floor," as she liked to call it. The performance practically blows up the television screen, ending with a full round of microphone swinging that threatens to destroy the set. Midler made the television rounds pushing "Beast of Burden," mostly in lip-sync performances; this live rendition is easily the most riveting. As if any more proof were needed, the highly stylized and carefully staged song performance, followed later by a complete turnaround with the wistful "Come Back, Jimmy Dean" from her current *No Frills* album, marked her as a theatrical artist and actor par excellence, quite apart from other popular vocalists. The topper is her ad lib as she takes her seat next to Carson: "And she writes books, too!"

Midler was referring to her latest literary effort, *The Saga of Baby Divine*, a lavishly illustrated children's book. (With bits of fabric woven through her tightly curled hair, she looked like she was wearing an elaborate new wave headdress. "Every authoress should wear a hat," she announced with jokey hauteur.) By now, her easy camaraderie with Carson allowed her to "go there" with a knowing joke about his many wives, all with similar names, and costly divorce settlements. Noting that his first wife was named Joan, his second Joanne, and his third Joanna, she linked him to *Citizen Kane*'s Rosebud: "You must have had a sled named Joanne when you were a kid."

Midler had just turned forty when she returned to *The Tonight Show* at the end of 1985, and unlike so many other women in show business, she wasn't afraid to joke about getting older and trying to stay in shape. She was a bit more zaftig than usual, evidenced by the plunging neckline of her dress (a miniature poinsettia appeared to be growing from her décolletage). Ruing her love of food, she launched into "Fat as I Am" while seated between Carson and his sidekick, Ed McMahon ("I've never sung from this position before. I've sung from others, but never sitting up"), and proceeded to take over the set, lounging on Carson's desk, kicking off her shoes, and pulling every laugh out of the comic torch song. It was one of her funniest, most uninhibited comic performances. She then turned around and offered a heart-stopping "Skylark" that surpassed her recording from the 1970s.

Midler wasn't exactly at a low career ebb during those two most recent Carson shows, but her record sales were in a slump, and her film career hadn't recovered from the disastrous *Jinxed*. By her next appearance at the end of 1988, she was one of the most successful and highest-paid women in films following a string of hit Disney comedies. She was there to promote her latest film, the dramatic musical *Beaches*, and was very much the regal film star, complete with an opulent mane of auburn hair cascading to her shoulders. Midler got a full band and backing singers for "Under the Boardwalk," from the film's soundtrack album. ("Wind beneath My Wings" hadn't yet been identified as its breakout single.) She was more subdued than usual, chatting earnestly about her marriage and her young daughter. "I Think It's Going to Rain Today," also from *Beaches*, was beautifully sung—and just a touch great-ladyish.

She was on another upswing when she returned to *The Tonight Show* just as *For the Boys* was opening in November 1991. The expensive and ambitious movie musical had good buzz, and Midler, coming off big record and film hits, was in high spirits and looking splendid, her hair now a short, bouncy blond bob. It seemed more like *The Bette Midler Show* than *The Tonight Show*, with the star showcased in three songs from the film: the boogie-woogie "Stuff Like That There," the power ballad "Every Road Leads Back to You," and an emotional "In My Life." In between, Midler did another impromptu (but not really) comedy number from her guest chair, making "Otto Titsling" a hellzapoppin' history lesson about brassieres that even for her was wildly, comically flamboyant. At moments, Carson appeared to be overwhelmed, as if watching a talented daughter come gloriously into her own. It was by any measure a triumphant appearance.

For the Boys was a high-profile failure for Midler, and she lay low for months, finally reappearing, at Carson's request, on his penultimate episode as host of *The Tonight Show*. After nearly thirty years, Carson was retiring from the show that had come to define late-night television. His last guests were Midler and Robin Williams, on May 21, 1992. It was an emotional and nostalgic evening, with Midler first performing the driving "Miss Otis Regrets" like it was 1973 all over again (veteran Harlettes Charlotte Crossley and Jenifer Lewis were her backups). Her attire, a tunic made of flowered panels over leggings, was "the last one out of Frederick's of Hollywood before they torched it." (Midler was referring to the recent Los Angeles riots that broke out after four white police officers were acquitted of beating Rodney King, a Black man.)

It was rare for Williams to be relegated to the role of second banana, but that night Midler left him in the dust. There were old stories and reminiscences, like the one about Midler being slapped with a cease-and-desist order by Mae West after singing "Come Up and See Me Sometime" on the show. (Apparently, it was fine with West for drag queens to sing the song but not a cisgender woman.) She pulled off one more sitting-on-the-chair song—this one for the television history books—with a specially tailored version of "You Made Me Love You" and its introductory "Dear Mr. Gable" first performed by Judy Garland to movie heartthrob Clark. "Dear Mr. Carson" and "You Made Me Watch You," with new lyrics co-written by Midler, Marc Shaiman, and Bruce Vilanch, hit all the comic bases, from Carson's personal life ("I watched your hair turn slowly from dark to white / And when I can't sleep I count your wives at night") to jokes about McMahon and even Carson's longtime producer Fred de Cordova ("Before you bid adieu / Don't be cheap / Put De Cordova to sleep"). Once again commandeering Carson's desk, Midler paused the merriment to tenderly stroke his face ("you sexy thing") and extol "your charm, your wit, your civility," before a bravura conclusion ("How I'll miss the social intercourse so varied / Now I'll have to have it with the guy I married / You know I'd rather watch you!")

Midler was known for her razorlike timing, but here every slow take, grimace, and pause was comic perfection, deepened by her genuine affection for and gratitude to Carson. That affection was palpable when the two launched into an unprompted duet of Carson's favorite song, "Here's That Rainy Day," and ended with a gentle kiss, a deeply moving moment of friendship and intimacy.

It felt like the emotional climax of the evening. But after returning from a commercial, Midler sang Carson one last song. On a stool in the center of the soundstage, she delivered Johnny Mercer and Harold Arlen's "One for My Baby (and One More for the Road)," first out to the audience and then, midway through, directly to Carson. She turned this boozy barroom standard into a final, loving tribute, as if standing in for the millions who had watched him over the years. Midler could sometimes overdo the pathos, but here her smiling warmth was even more affecting because it kept the tears at bay. It was Carson who grew increasingly misty-eyed as the camera captured him over Midler's shoulder while she bade him farewell on "that long, long road."

The moment was instantly iconic, a prime example of live television at its best. The night was as much a milestone for Midler as it was for Carson. The eager, anxious-to-outrage young chanteuse had matured into an evergreen entertainer who could effortlessly toggle between uproarious comedy and deep emotion. All her Carson appearances had been notable, but this night it was impossible to imagine anyone in show business other than Midler creating this final moment for him.

"Shut That Crap Off!"

Midler won an Emmy Award for this last Carson show, and her appearances on televised awards shows over five decades—both as presenter and as winner—injected a jolt of the "gay show-biz sensibility" into many a long, grandiose broadcast. The pomp and posturing of show-business awards shows made them a perfect target for Midler's unbridled impudence.

She seemed to turn up at the Grammy Awards every other year back in the 1970s, tweaking the sensibilities of the self-important and verbally challenged music-industry insiders. When she won as Best New Artist in 1974, the award was presented by Karen Carpenter, whose squeaky-clean image had made her a target for some of Midler's most withering putdowns. The irony was not lost on Midler, who cackled, "I'm surprised she didn't hit me over the head with it!"

Long before stylists began dictating awards-show looks, Midler mocked the fashion pretensions of the rock crowd by turning up in 1977 wearing a gown with a humongous, thirty-foot train. Presenting the Album of the Year award in 1975, she wore a 45-rpm record plastered to the side of her head. It was "Come Go with Me" by the Del Vikings, "a great record, but a better hat," she said. Her brief remarks brought roars from the audience. Acknowledging her recent lack of activity, she noted that Carpenter had presented her with the Best New Artist award the previous year, "and if that ain't the kiss of death, honey, I don't know what is!" She even managed to work some laughs into Stevie Wonder's acceptance speech. Wonder referred to the man who escorted him to the stage as his father but seemed stymied for anything else to say. "And this is your mother, honey!" Midler helpfully offered.

MTV audiences were equally in thrall to Midler's sense of humor, as if they had never experienced verbal wit. She and Dan Aykroyd hosted the first annual MTV Video Music Awards in 1984, rising from the stage of Radio City Music Hall in silver spacesuits, an homage to the network's animated logo of an astronaut planting the MTV flag on the moon. As Aykroyd solemnly intoned that this awards show would be an event of "galactic proportions," Midler removed her space helmet and vamped across the stage. "What about *my* galactic proportions? . . . Here I am standing in front of the hippest crowd in the history of the world, and I look exactly like a baked potato."

She injected some much-needed levity into the long evening by donning a series of outlandish costumes and headpieces. To introduce the award for special effects, she appeared in a Rube Goldberg–style hat dripping marabou streamers around her neck and topped by a garden patch of flowers rotating above her head which she vividly referred to as "Turd Curls from Outer Space." Over the years, Midler has never gotten lost in any of the outrageous costumes, hats, or wigs she's donned. She wears them, they don't wear her.

At her very first film awards presentation in 1980, just after the release of *The Rose*, Midler rocked the Golden Globes with not one but two acceptance speeches. The Globes audience, enjoying dinner and plentiful drinks, is famously uninhibited, and Midler took full advantage of the vibe. Winning first for New Female Star–Motion Picture, she quoted Joan Crawford's supposed exclamation when she won the award: "I'll show you a pair of Golden Globes!" As the audience erupted in laughter, Midler insisted she had reformed her risqué ways, even as she briefly performed mock-fellatio on her award statuette.

The jokes were fun, but when she returned to accept the award for Best Motion Picture Actress–Comedy or Musical, she got surprisingly emotional, thanking her "Ma" and, after a long, hesitant pause, "Pa." It was a rare public glimpse of Midler's connection to her parents, one of whom had never seen her perform.

Her next win at the Golden Globes was in 1992 for *For the Boys*, in the same category for musical or comedy film actress. Still smarting from the film's box-office failure, Midler wore her heart on her sleeve, at times holding back tears as she thanked the Globes for recognizing "our work when the American public dismissed us."

For viewers who don't follow box-office tallies or movie news, the speech carried a bitter aftertaste. Afterward, in the press room, Midler was more candid, expressing resignation and bewilderment at the film's lack of success. Her good humor momentarily abandoned her in this interview, which was later edited into small bites. When asked what was getting her through this failure, she snapped, "What makes you think I'm through it?" Did winning the award ease some of her pain? "Not even remotely." When asked about making movies versus making art, she fixed the questioner with a steely glare. "When I do my art, I'll do art. When I make movies, that's another story." No one got a pass; asked if she'd like to do another film with Nick Nolte, her costar in the hit *Down and Out in Beverly Hills*, she sniffed, "No, not particularly." It was an uncharacteristically down-and-out moment for Midler.

The Academy Awards have sometimes been called the "Gay Super Bowl," but more often than not, they're a deadly serious affair with precious little fabulosity. Midler was the funniest presenter in memory when she flounced onto the stage in 1982 in a massive metallic gold dress with swatches of fabric hanging from one shoulder as if she were the grand marshal at a gay pride parade. "I guess you didn't think it was possible for anyone to overdress for this affair," she joked, before launching into what sounded like a loosely improvised spiel that took aim at the stately proceedings. "So this is what it actually feels like to be up here. . . . I've been waiting for two years for the Academy to call me up and tell me they made a mistake," she said, referencing her loss as Best Actress two years earlier for *The Rose* to Sally Field for *Norma Rae*.

The live audience sounded like it was just waiting for Midler to give the broadcast a goose, and she didn't disappoint. "Don't you just hate it when presenters come out here and use this moment for their own personal aggrandizement?" she teased. The laughter came in waves as she continued, "This is the Oscars. We have to be . . . as dignified as humanly possible. That is why I have decided to rise [giving a theatrical lift to her ample bosom] to the occasion and give the nominees for the Best Original Song all the respect I feel they deserve." She proceeded to throw in pithy and pointed comments as she listed the nominees. "'Endless Love' from the endless movie *Endless Love*" was written by "the extremely rich Lionel Richie." For the obligatory nomination for a James Bond title song, "For Your Eyes Only," she added, "and they weren't kidding, I couldn't watch a single frame!"

Forty years later, Midler's digs sound tame. It was the deadpan sarcasm of her delivery that had the audience doubled over, most likely because they agreed with her. (These days, this kind of unbridled ribbing from a presenter might be met with an onstage slap.) Her flair for playfully poking a hole in the Oscars' self-importance has been picked up by later Oscar hosts from Billy Crystal to Amy Schumer and Wanda Sykes—and makes it regrettable that she has never hosted the televised broadcast, or any other awards show.

Midler could cut the joking when she felt a particular kinship with the honoree. When she inducted Laura Nyro into the Rock and Roll Hall of Fame in 2012, her ten-minute appreciation of the late singer-songwriter was practically a TED Talk. Midler's passionate, heartfelt tribute displayed an intimate familiarity with and love of Nyro's work, linking her vividly with New York City in the 1960s and '70s and underscoring the social consciousness at play in so much of her work. "She wrote her name on the blues," Midler concluded. It was an eloquent homage from one artist to another.

And she keeps rolling. When she won the Tony Award for *Hello, Dolly!* in 2017, she riffed on the over-the-top praise she had received ("I can't remember the last time I had so much smoke blown up my ass. But there is no more room. So thank you") and thanked both her current colleagues and those who had come before her in the role of Dolly Levi. The two-minute limit on acceptance speeches led to the orchestra attempting to play her off, but Midler would have none of it. "Shut that crap off!" she demanded, as she went on to sing the praises of the show she was starring in: "This thing has the ability to lift your spirits in these terrible, terrible times." (*Hello, Dolly!* opened just months after Donald Trump's inauguration, and Midler, a devout progressive and longtime critic of the new president, had wasted no time in blasting him to her one million Twitter followers.) Her speech, a four-minute ramble that managed to be both sincere and ironic at the same time, was pure, unfiltered Midler. After all this time, she was still one of the best things an awards show could offer.

Dropping Her Dress for Israel

Midler came to prominence in the days when musical-variety specials were a staple of television programming. She did a select number of memorable guest shots on other people's specials while also taking advantage of the new cable television landscape to present her work free of network censors. On a Burt Bacharach special in 1973—her first big prime time guest shot—her performance of "Superstar" was less a song than an interior monologue filled with deep sexual longing. Seated on the floor against a bare wall, illuminated only by light streaming from a window, she was filmed in a series of long takes that revealed her to be an uncommonly subtle and camera-ready singing actor.

Her other spot on the show featured Midler in triplicate, singing Manilow's reworked arrangement of "Boogie Woogie Bugle Boy." Dressed in contrasting blouses and hairstyles, she filmed the routine three times, with the performances then spliced together to provide a seamless Midler Sisters act. Her mother, watching from Hawaii and knowing nothing of the technical wizardry, marveled, "Gee, that's terrific. They found two girls who look just like Bette."[1]

Midler ended her 1974 disappearing act when she appeared on the inaugural episode of Cher's new television variety show in early 1975, joining a starry guest list that included Elton John and Flip Wilson. The show had all the hallmarks of mid-'70s variety series: thrown-together musical medleys and not-so-funny comedy sketches with plenty of canned laughter.

Midler and Cher did an extended, awkwardly staged "Trashy Ladies" medley of songs like "Sweet Georgia Brown" and "Put the Blame on Mame," dressed in corsets, stockings, and garters and brandishing feather boas. (Midler never looked so svelte, even next to the beanpole Cher.)

Midler, Cher, and John were all known for their outré fashion sense. Their styles were amped up for an R&B medley, with the trio in dazzling spangled Bob Mackie costumes amid a stage full of balloons. Midler was used to being the most overdressed person onstage, but not in this company. (She had been promised a solo during the show, which never happened. But she did make off with her glittering gown, which was recycled perfectly for Vicki Eydie.)

A comedy sketch sent the star and her guests fifty years into the future. It was 2025, and they were all residents of Final Curtain, a rest home for aged rockers, decked out as exaggerated, ancient versions of themselves. What laughs there were came from the sight of the stars made up to be in their late seventies and still working their same images. Midler was in Mae West mode, sporting oversized breasts and butt, a steel-gray wig, and glasses courtesy of Picasso. "Anybody want to hear a few of my old records?" she vamped. "Well, I was arrested for drunk driving in '68! Assault with a deadly weapon in '74!"

It's fascinating to view this sketch, and the entire show, from the perspective of almost fifty years, with Midler, Cher, and John still going strong in the twenty-first century and even alternating their shows on the giant stage at Caesars Palace. Even as styles change and entertainment eras pass, they continue to thrive, each in their own lane—hardly the decrepit retirees portrayed for laughs. (Cher's trademark long, straight hair, seen as snowy white in the sketch, is scarily on point with her look today.)

During the Broadway run of *Clams on the Half Shell* in 1975, Midler took part in the United Jewish Appeal telethon. After a close-harmony "Sentimental Journey" and a boisterous "Boogie Woogie Bugle Boy" with the Harlettes ("three prime examples of non-kosher meat," she helpfully explained), she launched a comic riff for the ages. "Sunday night at the UJA. What could be more wonderful? My first telethon, and in the Ed Sullivan Theater," she announced breathlessly. "The great, the near great, and the lame have played here. Some as recently as this evening." All the telethon participants asked for money, but Midler put a special spin on her appeal, offering "for the pledge of a mere five thousand dollars, to drop my dress for Israel."

She played the studio audience like a fine violin, pausing for laughs and applause, letting the bawdy fun of the moment sink in before introducing "a little song about survival, that's what we're all here for." In seconds, she moved into the pathos of "Hello in There," giving it a special resonance for the hometown crowd of mostly Jewish New Yorkers. She wasn't in fine voice that evening, but she sang as if she were addressing each audience member individually. The contrast between her dishy high-spirits moments earlier and her moving dramatic performance was almost too much for this audience—not the hippest—to take in. As the applause continued, individuals slowly began standing until nearly the entire crowd was on its feet—at a time before standing ovations were considered de rigueur.

"Well, the question in everyone's mind is, did I get my pledge?" she asked. Of course she did, and the announcement sent her into a strip routine worthy of the most practiced burlesque queen. She teased and strutted as she slowly removed her evening dress to reveal a short lace-trimmed slip. Sensing some disappointment, she quipped, "I hope you all weren't expecting to see the whole thing. You're going to have to pay a lot more than five grand to see the whole thing." With the Harlettes back, she launched into the inevitable "Friends," quietly noting, "this is what it's all about." When she sashayed off the stage, she took the entire show with her. It was the full Midler experience in just a quarter of an hour.

Midler had zero chemistry with the chipper Neil Sedaka on his 1976 special, and on *Rolling Stone* magazine's tenth anniversary celebration in 1977, she and Jerry Lee Lewis performed "Whole Lotta Shakin' Goin' On" as if in parallel performing universes. More interesting than the special was CBS's memo regarding Midler's appearance, in which it decreed "no tit holding, no crotch playing, no pulling up her dress at end to expose crotch . . . no 'Thanks for coming, thanks for showing up too' . . . no Jesus Christ reference, no 'Fucking Helen Reddy' . . . no God damn's [*sic*]." The network did allow her to say "rat's ass" and to tell her Sonny Bono "bazoom" joke.[2] (Midler insisted that Bono, recently divorced from Cher, kept eyeing her from the audience because "he's never been with a woman with bazooms before.")

Much better was her appearance the same year on one of Bing Crosby's last specials. Midler appeared from the audience as a shy usherette called to the stage, who proceeds to harmonize to period-perfect effect with the star on "Accentuate the Positive." She was delightful, playfully bantering with Crosby, then reappearing as a turn-of-the-century prima donna to sing "Glow Worm" with the Mills Brothers. Midler was as charmingly at home with these senior citizens as she was with her peers, proving once again that she was wonderful company.

"Try to Remain Vertical, Girls, at Least through the First Commercial"

The Depression Tour was taped in Cleveland and broadcast on HBO in June 1976 as *The Bette Midler Show*. Midler had never been presented as fully (or unedited) as in the HBO special. By the time she appeared as the Statue of Liberty in a tribute to the bicentennial to sing "Friends," a nationwide audience (or at least those with HBO) had seen a full Midler stage show. Early Betamax home tapings of the special soon became staples of gay bars around the country, further expanding the show's reach.

When she finally got around to doing her own network special for NBC in 1977, the results felt recycled and scrubbed up. *Ol' Red Hair Is Back* (a spoof on Frank Sinatra's *Ol' Blue Eyes Is Back* special from a few years earlier) was mostly Midler's greatest hits sequenced between commercials. It kicked off in gleeful camp mode with a revamp of her opening from *Clams on the Half Shell.* A bejeweled Midler emerged from a giant clam, singing and dancing to "Oklahoma!" with a group of Hawaiian natives, before doing her expert poi ball demonstration.

Most of the special took place before a studio audience on a soundstage set oddly dressed as an urban tenement. In between songs, she got in a few comic bullseyes, many of which must have pushed up against the network's censors. Addressing all the "box watchers," she insisted that her special would be "devoted to the twin deities of truth and beauty," carefully pointing to each of her breasts. After a taxing number, she dramatically reclined on the floor, wondering, "Oh, Lord, how does Marie Osmond do it? You mean Marie Osmond doesn't do it? I heard she did." As for the Harlettes, they were instructed by their boss, "Try to remain vertical, girls, at least through the first commercial."

Midler could easily fill an hour all by herself, but the special nonetheless boasted guest stars. Emmett Kelly was on hand for some sad clown moments during "Friends" and "Hello in There." But Midler didn't need him; she was fully capable of creating her own pathos. On a set featuring large Gustav Klimt images (Midler resembled many of his lush, strong-featured models), Dustin Hoffman accompanied her as she sang "Let's Shoot the Breeze," a musical collaboration between the two stars. Midler's lyrics sketched a woman's plaintive reflection on the past with an old friend. Hoffman's minor-key, meandering melody got a sumptuous arrangement by Peter Matz, and Midler gave it a touching, chin-up performance. It was the special's musical highlight.

Ol' Red Hair Is Back didn't have the conceptual daring of Barbra Streisand's 1960s specials or of Midler's stage shows. And it paled in comparison with her full-length HBO show. But if it was mostly "smorgasbord leftovers," as she put it, it was spicier and more satisfying than other musical-variety specials. Even tamped down for television, Midler was funnier and more audacious than anything else in prime time.

Ol' Red Hair Is Back won the Emmy Award for Outstanding Special–Comedy, Variety, or Music, but it was Midler's last broadcast network special. She was more comfortable with the freewheeling HBO, and she repackaged several of her stage shows as specials for the pay network. *De Tour* was carved into the ninety-minute *Art or Bust* (1984), a slightly updated *Experience the Divine* became *Diva Las Vegas* (1997), and *The Showgirl Must Go On* was edited down to just over an hour when the final show of her two-year residency was broadcast in 2010.

The most unusual of her HBO specials was 1988's *The Mondo Beyondo Show*, a takeoff on late-night cable-access shows hosted by self-important non-celebrity hosts. Mondo Beyondo, a creation of Midler and Jerry Blatt, is a Eurotrash Lady Bountiful with mountains of red hair and an overflowing bodice who speaks in pidgin Italian. (It's hard to imagine Midler getting away with this character or accent today.)

Midler as Mondo offered introductions to a cross section of 1980s performance artists who appear by way of short-form films and videos (though Midler did offer a brief performance as one Eudora P. Quickly, a gray-haired and bespectacled, tone-challenged soprano). The special's climactic act featured Midler's husband, Martin von Haselberg, as one half of the Kipper Kids, an act he had been performing since the 1970s. The flatulent duo, wearing little more than inner tubes around their waists, performed rituals of cartoony violence such as setting off firecrackers on their heads and spraying each other with food. *The Mondo Beyondo Show* had the look of a quirky family affair featuring a very game Midler.

Rose's Turn

As early as the 1970s, *Gypsy* had been mentioned as a potential Midler vehicle. The celebrated 1959 musical about the early vaudeville days of stripper Gypsy Rose Lee focused on Rose, the mother of all stage mothers, whose maniacal efforts to make her daughters stars ultimately push them away. Midler would have been the world's youngest Rose at the time, but in 1993, when she was announced as the star of a new television adaptation, it was as if the role had finally caught up to her.

Gypsy had already made it to the big screen in 1962, with Rosalind Russell as Rose. It was generally considered a disappointment, particularly by its creators, librettist Arthur Laurents, composer Jule Styne, lyricist Stephen Sondheim, and original director-choreographer Jerome Robbins. They had resisted all further attempts until they were assured that the show's text and songs would be filmed exactly as written, with no alterations or cuts. This new Midler *Gypsy*, positioned as prestige television, would be a permanent filmed record of the show.

By television standards, it was a lavish production, complete with luxury casting in even the tiniest of roles and directed by Emile Ardolino, who had had big hits with the movies *Dirty Dancing* (1987) and *Sister Act* (1992). *Gypsy* got a tremendous amount of advance press and praise, with Midler appearing on the cover of *TV Guide* and television critics giving it near-unanimous rave reviews prior to its CBS broadcast on December 12, 1993.

Rose *was* an ideal role for Midler. She had no trouble conveying the pushy, sweaty desperation of a woman whose need to be noticed is trained on her daughters. Early on, when singing "Some People," her excitement at the show-business world awaiting her (and her girls) is contagious. She's predictably over-the-top funny when she learns the act has been booked on the Orpheum circuit in "Mr. Goldstone." When she first meets Herbie, played by Peter Riegert, she has a nice, easy way about her that makes it clear why he's attracted to her. In "Rose's Turn," she's every bit the showstopper while also revealing shades of regret and confusion and defiance.

The problem with the performance, on which the entire enterprise rests, is that much of it is played at the same emotional pitch. There's little modulation from scene to scene. She barrels her way through, too often relying on Midlerisms. She is done no favors by Ardolino's flat direction, which alternately feels rushed and static, or by the sometimes elongated editing. Moments are held too long, catching Midler in awkward transitions before cutting to another actor. Ardolino was in the last months of his battle with AIDS during filming and would die before the broadcast. It's possible that at full strength he could have guided Midler to a more consistent and nuanced performance.

Sometimes she's both chillingly controlled and bug-eyed broad all in the same scene. "Something's very funny here," she says with slow-dawning alarm when she learns that the boys in the act are leaving. When she reads the letter from her daughter June, the act's star, telling Rose that she's gotten married and is also leaving, it's with the shock of someone sure of her control now finding out she's been completely duped; Midler's placement of June's letter in her bra like a grudge she'll carry with her forever is genius. But her maniacal zeal during "Everything's Coming Up Roses" verges on the comical and isn't helped by her strained vocals.

The performance would have been more effective onstage than in the tight confines of the television screen. One byproduct of this new *Gypsy* was a reconsideration of the 1962 film. Russell was rightly criticized for her lack of vocal skills, and the lowering of the keys to accommodate her female baritone robbed Rose's music of its excitement. But Russell was a compelling, if rather grand,

Rose, and the widescreen Technicolor film had a more modulated pace, as well as a depth and expanse that the spatial limitations of the home screen couldn't match. Today the 1962 version stands in higher regard than the 1993 iteration.

Gypsy was a huge ratings winner, and Midler received some of the best reviews of her career, but by the time the Emmy Awards rolled around nine months after it aired, the mood had shifted. After opening the awards broadcast with a rock-star-worthy "Rose's Turn," she watched from the audience as *Gypsy* lost nearly all of its twelve nominations, including her own to Kirstie Alley in the TV film *David's Mother*.

"Don't Do a Sitcom"

It was around this time that she began morphing from Bette Midler into BETTE MIDLER, not just a diva but a DIVA. Was it in response to the failure of *For the Boys*? Or because *Gypsy* wasn't quite the triumph she had hoped for? Did she lean into the lowest common denominator of the Divine Miss M because she thought her acting career had dropped off?

Midler began appearing more frequently on television sitcoms, often playing a cartoony version of herself. She was literally cartoony in a 1993 episode of *The Simpsons*, spoofing her Adopt-a-Highway cleanup activities in California. She goes full action hero on carloads of litterers, chasing them down and knocking them out. Later in the episode, she guests on Krusty the Klown's television show, singing "Wind beneath My Wings" to the host while sitting on his desk, in an obvious nod to her recent Johnny Carson appearance.

On a 1995 episode of *Seinfeld*, she was Bette Midler, Broadway Star, who can't go anywhere without an entourage, even to play in a baseball game. When she's injured on the field, she grandly holds court in a hospital room draped in a marabou-trimmed bed gown and ordering around a surprisingly devoted Kramer. When she meets Fran Drescher's Fran Fine on *The Nanny*, Midler gushes, "I love your accent." When Fran says, "Thanks, I owe it all to Queens," Midler snaps back, "Same with me and my career!" She was now joking about her legions of gay fans in a way she hadn't done earlier. It was a trope that soon grew tired.

Midler didn't play herself on the final episode of *Murphy Brown* in 1998. Instead, as Caprice Feldman, an entitled mantrap, she was the last in a long line of wacky secretaries Candice Bergen as Murphy had to cope with for ten seasons. With her exaggerated accent, mincing walk, and sexual voracity, Caprice was a nightmare version of the Divine Miss M.

When Rosie O'Donnell ended her daytime talk show in 2002, Midler's serenade to her was similar to her tribute to Carson on his last show. Singing special lyrics to "How about You?" she issued four words of advice to the departing O'Donnell: "Don't do a sitcom." It was a reference to one of the biggest debacles of Midler's career and the pinnacle of her I-AM-BETTE-MIDLER period.

"Who'd want a future on TV?" Midler said back in 1977, when her NBC special aired. "Television is a medium that eats you alive. You can't keep turning out good material week after week!"[3] Since her view of the medium hadn't changed in the intervening years, her new CBS sitcom *Bette*, which debuted with much fanfare in the fall of 2000, smacked of a calculated career move rather than an artistic choice.

Midler rejected formats that cast her as a real estate agent or a school principal. Instead, she would play a heightened, comic version of herself. The TV "Bette" (she was never referred to by her last name) would be surrounded by stand-ins for important people in her real life: Bonnie Bruckheimer, Midler's friend and partner in her production company, would now be Connie; her husband, Martin, would be not an outrageous performance artist but a college professor named Roy; Midler's pianist and musical director Marc Shaiman was now Oscar; and her daughter Sophie was now Rose.

Midler was on to something with this cheeky, insidery look at the life of a well-known show-business figure. Jack Benny and George Burns and Gracie Allen had all played themselves in their early-1950s sitcoms, frequently introducing episodes in front of a stage curtain which would then part, allowing them to enter the action. It was art imitating life imitating art, capitalizing on the well-known personalities of these much-loved comedy stars. More recently, Larry David's *Curb Your Enthusiasm* followed the life of the *Seinfeld* comedy writer in deadpan, mockumentary style. A show about the adventures of the Divine Miss M promised lots of comedy and songs and celebrities and show-biz fun.

Midler was never shy about puncturing her own image or dishing her various choices in movies and music, and *Bette* was loaded with one-liners and running jokes about her career. On the first episode, she ponders her weary visage in a mirror: "I look like the last twenty minutes of *For the Boys*." Her pretend feud with Sally Field, who bested her for the Oscar in 1980, was good for a weekly joke. (Trying to relax and watch television, "Bette" is confronted with a rerun of *Norma Rae*.) "Bette" thinks she's being honored by the American Film Institute, but it turns out to be a tribute from the Airline Film Invitational because her movies flop out in theaters quickly and go directly to in-flight programming.

There were prime zingers in just about every episode, but *Bette*'s biggest problem was "Bette." The contours of the Midler career were in place, but the person at the center of all the action was not the warmhearted bawd and witty raconteur. This "Bette" was a clueless narcissist with the attention span of a child with ADHD. Since Midler worshipped at the shrine of Lucille Ball, there were attempts to set her up in wacky stunts similar to those performed by the famous redhead. Each episode revolved around "Bette" getting into wild shenanigans—doing Shakespeare for the first time, bluffing her way through a discussion on Oprah's Book Club, faking a nervous breakdown for publicity—resulting in slapstick antics and, presumably, laughs.

But *I Love Lucy*'s chocolate factory and grape stomping and Vitameatavegamin were all grounded in real situations encountered by real people, albeit hyped for comedy. In *Bette*, the star's clowning felt pasted on, less a natural extension of character than the desperate machinations of the writing staff. "Bette" is afraid of getting older, so suddenly she's wrestling with a Pilates contraption. Guesting on Dolly Parton's show, "Bette" decides to pull focus by wearing her mermaid costume and wrecking the set. "Bette" insists that Oscar play piano for her on the next treadmill as she works out.

Midler wasn't content to be Lucy; she also wanted to be Ricky and Ethel and Fred, both star comic and straight woman, leaving little for her costars to do but stand around and feed her lines. (Kevin Dunn, playing Roy, was disgruntled enough to leave after several episodes.) Worse, and most dismaying, the star turned out to be less adept than expected in the sitcom format. Her physical comedy was labored (and not helped by the mostly awkward direction), and her performance overall was manic and mugging. Midler had always been a welcome visitor to TV land because she was so real, so much herself. There was little recognizably human about this sitcom "Bette."

Unused to the fast pace of weekly television and generally unhappy with the experience, Midler began airing her upset. On David Letterman's show, she compared herself to "a dung beetle pushing this ball of dung up a mountain."[4] After debuting to good ratings, *Bette* quickly began losing viewers. Midway through the season, CBS pulled the plug, not even bothering to air two episodes that were already completed.

Lock Her Up

Ever the recycler, Midler contemplated writing a tell-all about her disastrous television experience, but it never happened. For the next several years, she mostly kept to guest shots on talk shows, where television's standards and practices had loosened enough for her to get away with the kind of jokes she told in her live shows—at least on late-night. She memorably left Conan O'Brien sputtering with laughter over her jokes about Viagra (the new FDA generic version: Mycocksafloppin or, alternately, Ibepokin).

It wasn't until after she ended her run in *Hello, Dolly!* that Midler got back in the television game, proving her mojo was intact. If her role as Bella Abzug in the Gloria Steinem biopic *The Glorias* broadcast on Hulu was mostly ceremonial, she was at her zestiest as Hadassah Gold, a veteran political operative on Ryan Murphy's *The Politician.* Maneuvering through ludicrous plot twists, including covering for her boss's throuple relationship by faking her own affair with a much younger man and discovering the joys of "spicy lube," she was a septuagenarian Divine Miss M, brassy and bumptious and the best thing in the misbegotten Netflix series.

And she keeps rolling. Midler's best work in some time came during the Covid-19 pandemic in Paul Rudnick's *Coastal Elites* on HBO, a series of monologues delivered to the camera via Zoom. In "Lock Her Up," Midler is Miriam Nessler, a retired New York City schoolteacher arrested for assault now pleading her case to an unseen police officer while in a holding room. She's an NPR tote bag–toting, *New York Times* (print only)–reading "liberal Jewish woman" who exchanges insults with a Trump supporter in a Starbucks before snatching his MAGA hat and seeking refuge in the sacred space of the Public Theater, only to have him file a police complaint against her.

Midler looks every bit the urban matron with her frizzled gray hair and "drugstore reading glasses," explaining the incident while venting her anger and despair over the state of Trump-era America.

She excels in delivering Rudnick's motormouthed verbiage—part stand-up, part partisan fury—and makes the twenty-three-minute monologue a tiny tour de force. This Divine Mrs. Nessler is ultimately unrepentant, celebrating the theater as a form of civic rebellion where "every ticket is a weapon." "I *am* the wall," she insists, as she commands the officer, "Lock me up." *Coastal Elites* is a reminder that beyond all the diva posturing, Midler has always been an actor.

In the latest installment of Ryan Murphy's FX horror series, *American Horror Story: NYC 1981*, Midler's presence looms over the period drama. Its story of an existential threat to New York's gay community sets key scenes in a gay bathhouse presided over by its resident singing diva, played by Patti LuPone. Never mind that Midler was long gone from the baths by 1981. A Midler doppelganger was mandatory for a period television story of New York City gay men and sex. Even as she continues to work and create, Midler's legend has become part of contemporary cultural history, on screens of all sizes.

4

"I've Been Kidnapped by Kmart!"

Bette Midler's Movies

Movie stardom in the twenty-first century isn't what it used to be for today's multiplatform divas. Hits such as *A Star Is Born* (2018) and *House of Gucci* (2021) don't loom as large for Lady Gaga as sold-out concerts, Vegas residencies, Super Bowl performances, philanthropy, and status as an all-around style maven. Beyoncé's decorative roles in *Austin Powers in Goldmember* (2002) and *Dreamgirls* (2006) are nothing compared with her form-shifting "visual albums" (some of which she has directed), billions of streams on music platforms, fashion lines, and pay-it-back-and-forward activism. She even created her own performing alter ego, Sasha Fierce, a younger, more ferocious descendent of the Divine Miss M.

Back when Bette Midler made her film debut in 1979's *The Rose*, success with recordings, live performances, and television appearances were one thing, but movies were the entertainment summit. And just like Judy Garland, Doris Day, Barbra Streisand, Liza Minnelli, and Diana Ross before her, Midler was a pop singer who proved a natural in her very first film. It just took forever to get her to the screen.

From the moment she burst onto the scene, Midler had been viewed as a potential movie star, but Aaron Russo took her "make me a legend" demand seriously. "I wanted her first film to be a role that only Bette Midler could play," he insisted.[1] It sounds like savvy career management, but Russo's game plan kept Midler off the screen until the very end of the 1970s, an exhilarating decade when filmmakers, given mostly free rein by the film studios, were flying high with risky, convention-busting films. It was the perfect climate for the risky, convention-busting Midler to begin her film career.

Instead, she (or Russo) turned down the role of Adrian in *Rocky* (1976), thereby robbing her of a franchise opportunity and awards consideration. (Talia Shire got the role and an Oscar nomination.) She could have had a big fat hit starring with Chevy Chase in *Foul Play* (1978), a Hitchcock-derived comedy that instead went to Goldie Hawn. She dodged a bullet when a meeting with director Mike Nichols didn't go well and she lost the role of a kidnapped heiress in his black comedy set in the 1920s, *The Fortune*. (Stockard Channing played the role in the 1975 flop.)

The real pity was her decision not to be part of the ensemble in Robert Altman's panoramic politics-and-music epic, *Nashville* (1975), in a role eventually played by Barbara Harris. Albuquerque, a bedraggled wannabe country-music star, turns up everywhere in the film, finally getting her chance to sing when she leads an im-promptu and ultimately stirring performance of the gospel-ish "It Don't Worry Me." It was a musically and dramatically compelling role in an acclaimed, high-profile film by a celebrated director—and it would have given Midler an early anthemic song hit as well.

The most intriguing Midler film that never got made was *Little Me*, the 1962 Broadway musical comedy featuring a leading lady whose prodigious endowment (her name, Belle Poitrine, means "beautiful chest" in French) leads to stardom and a string of marriages to increasingly rich men. During a meeting with pro-ducer Ross Hunter unrelated to *Little Me*, Russo mentioned that after he and Midler had seen Hunter's latest film, the widely reviled musical *Lost Horizon* (1973), filled with non-singing stars like Peter Finch and Liv Ullmann, they questioned his judgment. (The two referred to it as *Lost Her-Reason*.) Later, when Hunter learned that Russo and Midler were interested in *Little Me*, he bought the project as a vehicle for Goldie Hawn.[2] *Little Me* never got filmed, but at least the incident gave Midler one of her prime one-liners: "I never miss a Liv Ullmann musical!"

"Where's Everybody Going?"

It wasn't long after Janis Joplin died of a heroin overdose in October 1970 that rumors of film projects about her troubled life and career began making the rounds. "Everybody's Doing a Film on Janis," reported *Rolling Stone* in January 1974, the most outlandish being a proposed exploitation film by a porn producer starring Patty Duke as Joplin. In the same article, Russo said several Joplin projects had been pitched to Midler, including both a film and a Broadway musical. "It's obvious," he said. "'Cause she's probably the only person who could do it, and she's the biggest singer in the business."[3] On that point, Russo was right: Midler was as natural a fit for a Joplin-like character as Barbra Streisand was for Fanny Brice.

Midler originally rejected the script for *Pearl*, as the Joplin biopic was called, after her last, posthumous album. She thought the script "ghoulish"[4] and wasn't interested in doing an impersonation of a singer who had helped her liberate her own performances. But after coming up blank with a star vehicle, Midler revisited *Pearl* and agreed to sign on—if obvious Joplin biographical details were eliminated and she could create a new 1960s rock-star character.

As *Pearl* evolved into *The Rose*, it became less Janis Joplin and more Bette Midler. Rudge, Rose's controlling manager (played by Alan Bates), who appears to have no other clients but Rose, carries strong traces of Russo, who co-produced the film. A Florida concert promises a triumphant hometown return for Rose, just like Midler's stop in Hawaii in 1973, and, just as Midler's father didn't bother to attend, Rose's family also sits it out. Scenes were added referencing Midler's gay fans and her days at the Continental Baths. Rose's insistence that she needs to take a year off is reminiscent of Midler's own dropping out during 1974 just as her career was moving into high gear.

The script by Bill Kerby and Bo Goldman, developed with director Mark Rydell, gets a lot right about the rock scene circa 1969. It skips the early days of Mary Rose Foster, a junkie with a big voice from small-town Florida, and begins when Rose is already a superstar rocker, jetting to tour stops in a private plane and leading a circus of musicians and hangers-on. She should be riding high: she's rich, her records are bestsellers, her concerts are Dionysian affairs with massive crowds pouring on the unconditional love she craves. But she's also exhausted, afraid she's losing her voice, and worn down by the road. She may have kicked a heroin habit, but she's a hard and nonstop drinker, carrying a bottle with her at all times. She can't get laid, even as the guys in her band are surrounded by adoring groupies. It's a lonely, stressful life that she doesn't have the discipline or emotional strength to manage. When she meets Huston, an AWOL Army sergeant played by Frederic Forrest, she experiences a brief moment of contentment with a man who takes all her neediness and volatility in stride.

Rose is a big character—contradictory, out of control, dogged by secrets and unspoken traumas—and it requires a big talent like Midler's. Her Rose is violent yet fragile, destructive but delicate, often at the same time. It's a role tailor-made for the woman who once demanded, "Make me a legend!"

To play Rose, Midler changed the way she moved, the way she sang, her entire emotional register. Working with choreographer Toni Basil (the two would collaborate on movement for decades), she replaces her familiar mincing walk with big, aggressive strides. Rose gets on the floor as much as Midler, but here she's athletic, lunging and somersaulting. She's sexual in a way that Joplin wasn't, flaunting her body and engaging in sexual play with her musicians. Her voice takes on a throat-shredding ferocity that defies comprehension, coming as it does from her tiny body. Rose's hair is a brassy yellow that in the light forms a golden halo around her face.

Her wardrobe, both on and off the stage, is all pinks, purples, and vermilions, in sheer, filmy fabrics. In motion, she's like a cloud frantically floating through her own life. She's most at home in the nighttime or under stage lights; she looks oddly misplaced on the rare occasion she strays outside in daylight.

But the Midler style of drama is also present, particularly on "When a Man Loves a Woman" and its introductory monologue about the age-old differences between what men and women want from each other. Written by Midler and Jerry Blatt, it tiptoes into Divine Miss M territory before settling into the song's rugged R&B power. Director of photography Vilmos Zsigmond starts out from a distance but slowly draws the camera in tight. Midler appears to pull the song out of herself. As she enumerates all the sacrifices a man will make for a woman he loves, her bone-chilling intensity can't hide Rose's awareness that she has no man like this in her life.

Like all the concert performances, "When a Man Loves a Woman" is photographed in deep, saturated indigos and simmering magentas that capture the grubby, hothouse aroma of a 1969 hard-rock concert (complete with a period-perfect liquid light show on the back wall). It's the film's first thrilling musical performance, the moment when the woman who has to pump herself up backstage to face her audience reveals her emotional life through song.

The Rose is less persuasive as a cohesive narrative than as a series of bravura set pieces leading up to Rose's final concert appearance. The glue that holds it all together is Midler. In a two-minute scene that encapsulates much of the scorn directed at 1960s rockers by established artists, Billy Ray, a steely country star, one of whose songs Rose has covered, cuts her to the quick, directs her not to record any more of his songs, and dresses her down for her "trashy behavior" toward his son. (It doesn't help that she practically jumps this "fine young piece" when she enters.) It was another scene with a parallel to Midler's life. "Once I drove all the way out to Cherry Hill, N.J. to see Aretha Franklin, and it ended with great disappointment," she later said without elaborating. "I just idolized her. It hurt a lot."[5]

"Your hair's got a hard-on," Rose quips to a queen in a towering coiffure when she and Huston end up at a drag club in New York's meatpacking district, one that she used to live over and frequent. She's welcomed back like a favorite small-town girl made good. (This, not the big Florida concert, is Rose's real homecoming.) The sequence has clear connections to Midler's performing past and her gay audience, especially when four drag queens stage a special number for Rose. Out come Diana Ross, Barbra Streisand, and Mae West in full regalia along with—wait for it—Rose. "That drag queen's doin' me!" she screams in delight as she joins the quartet onstage, a tiny doll amid these towering Glamazons. It's the happiest stretch of the film, continuing with Rose and Huston back at her hotel in bed. His easygoing acceptance of her past, including a gang bang on the high school football field, and her insecurity about her looks offers a glimmer of hope that Rose may have at last found someone who will love her unconditionally.

Scenes pile up like a highlights reel, often with little purpose other than to reference a Midler or Joplin signpost. When Huston and Rose fight, he takes refuge in a (straight) bathhouse so she can barge in and be surrounded by men in towels and offer a few choice Divine Miss M observations ("Keep watering it, honey, it'll grow!"). A scene with Rose and a former girlfriend trading kisses happens for no other reason than to remind viewers of Joplin's bisexuality and provide an excuse for Huston to leave Rose.

Rose is a woman unraveling even as she keeps going, like a train wreck taking place in slow motion. The unraveling speeds up inexorably once she hits Florida for her hometown concert during what turns out to be the final day of her life. As the massive stadium show is set up and television crews assemble to record the event for worldwide broadcast, the chaos of Rose's life finally catches up with her in a series of contradictory scenes: Rudge walks out on her, then begs her to return for the concert; she decides to leave her career for good with the returned Huston, then frenziedly changes her mind.

At a roadhouse where she once sang and scored drugs, she's like a feral cat, demanding drinks, singing a raunchy blues ("Love Me with a Feeling"), and savagely attacking Huston when he drags her outside. When a former friend gives Rose some heroin and his own drug paraphernalia, it's a dead giveaway that Rose will make use of them.

Midler is quietly astonishing in a lengthy scene in a graffitied phone booth next to the same football field where she took on the team in high school. After calling Rudge to pick her up for the concert, she's tempted by the heroin but instead gobbles up several pills and washes them down with a slug from her ever-present bottle. She places a call to her parents, the ones whose house she avoided as she drove by it earlier. It's clear they have no intention of attending the concert, and she rationalizes their absence (too crowded, too much traffic) before heartbreakingly confiding in them her fatigue with the road. But what could they possibly say to comfort this daughter they hardly know anymore? And would she even hear it? The call ends, the lights from the football field turn off, and Rose is alone, a tiny, desolate figure in the phone booth. It's the first time she's been by herself the entire film. The camera pulls back to watch her from a distance as she matter-of-factly shoots up.

Midler brings a strange lyrical quality to these grungy, desperate moments. We're aware for the first time of her small, graceful hands. She's dainty as she sifts through coins for the phone. She handles the drug works with delicacy, and she experiences her high with a trembling stillness. When she takes a beaded dress from her bag, she treats it like a precious robe.

The fanfare that heralds Rose's arrival by helicopter to the concert stadium is both exultant and like a funeral march. Rudge says she needs to go to a hospital, but Rose shakes her head knowingly, smiles softly, and says, "No." She shrugs him off as she takes the stage, strutting for the last time as the ultimate rock goddess, basking in the crowd's adoration. "Mama's home," she boasts, before launching into a blistering "Stay with Me." The song may be about a departing lover, but Rose delivers it as a final plea to her loyal fans. Midler's not maudlin; her Rose is still a performer. She straddles and strokes the microphone like a tender lover. When she dashes off a jaunty, girlish twirl, it's a sudden, tender grace note. After this paroxysm of a performance, she's got nothing left to give. Midler shows the life slipping out of Rose as she wonders, "Where's everybody going?" When she crumples to the floor, the moment is as shattering as it is inevitable.

The Rose is grand in every sense: in color and spectacle (Zsigmond brought in an all-star team of cinematographers for the panoramic concert sequences, including Conrad Hall, Haskell Wexler, and Owen Roizman); in scale, with massive crowd scenes featuring real, not CGI, audiences and spot-on period detail; in drama and emotion and music—it's got sex, drugs, rock and roll, and death. And it's centered around a heroic performance that carries strands of Joplin but also of Jim Morrison and Billie Holiday and Judy Garland—lights that burned white-hot and flamed out spectacularly.

Midler thrived on the film's outsize emotional demands. Speaking about it twenty-five years later, she said, "I'm not like Mary J. [Blige]. I want more drama. . . . It was so much fun. For me, it was like, finally, this is the part I was meant to play."[6] The Rose was a big hit, and it looked like Russo had been right all along. This was the film to establish Midler as a major actor and movie star. The question was, what would she do for a follow-up? Her four fellow nominees for the Best Actress Oscar—Sally Field (the winner for Norma Rae), Jill Clayburgh, Jane Fonda, and Marsha Mason—all could have played one another's roles. But none of them could have played Rose. It was an outsize part that had to be played by an outsize talent, and how often do those two elements match up? "I don't know if I'll ever get a part like that again," Midler worried at the time of The Rose's release.[7] The sad, heartbreaking fact is that she never did.

Down and Out and Up

Midler punted on her next screen outing, a concert film of her latest stage show. At the time of its release in 1980, *Divine Madness* felt like a backward move following the highly dramatic *The Rose* and after her full-length HBO show that featured some of the same repertoire. Midler was battling pneumonia when the film was shot in a series of performances at the Pasadena Civic Auditorium, and even after rerecording some of her vocals, she sounds ragged at times. The film doesn't have the freewheeling warmth and festiveness of the HBO special. An element of strain and weariness hovers over it.

There are compensations that make *Divine Madness* more enjoyable today. Cinematographer William A. Fraker captures the theatrical flair of the show's stage lighting, framing Midler in some exquisite shots. She's exultantly thin, and her hair is a flattering honey color. His camera catches her looking both radiantly beautiful and plainly frumpy, often just moments apart. Midler sprinkles in some new songs such as "Fire Down Below," sung in *The Rose* by the four drag queens but here a scorching solo. A mash-up of "The E Street Shuffle," "Summer (The First Time)," and a punked-out "Leader of the Pack" is staged like a Jerome Robbins urban ballet for Midler and the Harlettes and filmed in swirling camera movements that reveal Midler's volatile physicality more intimately than onstage. She has never been more screamingly funny than in an extended comedy riff on her world travels, her timing and audience interplay sharper than ever.

Her aggressively heart-tugging bag lady could easily have been cut, and a final, overwrought "I Shall Be Released" looks like an attempt to end on a *Rose*-like note. Nevertheless, *Divine Madness* plays today like a beautifully photographed big-screen time capsule of 1970s Bette Midler.

After *The Rose*, the search for a follow-up screen vehicle seemed endless. (*Divine Madness* played like a placeholder, besides doing poorly at the box office.) The situation was not unlike Midler's trouble finding another stage job after *Fiddler on the Roof*—a sign that producers and film companies didn't find her easy to cast. It felt like a desperation move when, two years after *The Rose*, she signed on for the all-too-aptly-titled *Jinxed*. Midler and Russo had long since severed their ties, and she was now managing herself. If he had still been around, he surely would have steered her away from what turned out to be a career low and an emotional tsunami.

Jinxed was concocted by playwright Frank D. Gilroy as a *Double Indemnity*–*Postman Always Rings Twice*–derived black comedy about a blackjack dealer named Willie and Harold, a small-time gambler who cannot lose whenever Willie is dealing. Harold, accompanied by his beaten-down girlfriend Bonita, an itinerant lounge singer, keeps following Willie on the Vegas-Reno-Tahoe circuit, winning big against the house and costing Willie one job after another. When Bonita and Willie meet and become romantically involved, they plot to kill Harold, making it look like an accident in order to collect his insurance money. Bonita thinks better of it, but not before Harold commits suicide (don't ask), allowing them to go ahead with their plan to make his death look like an accident. But Harold has thrown one more kink into their plans. He stopped paying on his insurance but provided Bonita with clues that send her on a scavenger hunt to find a large stash he left for her after all. With Harold's jinx on Willie over, the couple head off to new gambling territories, in love and now flush with cash.

Midler later said, "[*Jinxed*] didn't know whether it was a comedy or a thriller, but I thought a good director could find the proper tone for it."[8] Midler had director approval and chose Don Siegel, best known for macho action films, including several Clint Eastwood vehicles. "I thought with Siegel being good at [action] and me being good at comedy, we'd have a good marriage," she said.[9]

The marriage was a mistake from the start. No one was happy with the script, and rewrites were constant. (Gilroy took his name off the finished film, using the pseudonym Bert Blessing.) Midler's career had always been self-directed, working with close collaborators to realize her artistic vision. She expected those she worked with to value her opinions and respect her input. On *The Rose*, she benefited from Mark Rydell's supportive, encouraging direction. Siegel clashed with Midler from the beginning, chafing at the dialogue she produced with Blatt (though Siegel contributed rewrites as well) and her observations on all aspects of the production. He wasn't shy about expressing his displeasure: "She comes on as an expert in every facet of the business. I've worked with many stars who are difficult, but she's really a rough customer."[10]

Siegel seldom worked with female stars. The actresses in his testosterone-fueled films were mostly cast (if at all) as "the girl" supporting Eastwood or Lee Marvin or Charles Bronson. His harsh observations about Midler echo his remarks about working with Shirley MacLaine on an earlier Eastwood film, *Two Mules for Sister Sara* (1970): "It's hard to feel any great warmth for her. . . . She's too . . . unfeminine. She has too much balls. She's very, very hard. You have the feeling that if you talk gently to her, she'll ridicule you."[11] Siegel's response to working with Midler and MacLaine sounds like old-fashioned male chauvinism, except that he was ungracious enough to go public with his bias.

One could almost see the logic in Midler's choice of Siegel, but her approval of Ken Wahl as Willie was baffling. Wahl was a rising young actor who bore a superficial resemblance to Frederic Forrest, who was so effective with her in *The Rose*. That may have tipped Midler in Wahl's favor, causing her to ignore the fact that Wahl was twelve years her junior and would not be a congenial costar. At their first meeting, according to Midler, Wahl walked in and announced, "I want you to know that I hate niggers and faggots."[12] Presumably, it was too late to recast the role. Their white-hot passion was supposed to drive the murder plot, but Midler had more chemistry with Bonita's beloved black cat than with Wahl's blankly handsome lug. The two looked as if they couldn't stand each other, which, in truth, they couldn't. Just like Siegel, Wahl was quick to trash Midler to the press: "It's been miserable with her and took all my concentration to get up and go to work in the morning. . . . When I did the amorous scenes, I just thought of somebody else."[13]

Even the film's producer, Herb Jaffe, piled on, telling reporters that *Jinxed* could be "the Jewish *Heaven's Gate*" and insisting that Midler was "driving people crazy."[14] Siegel, incensed at "those two women,"[15] United Artists executives Anthea Sylbert and Paula Weinstein, both defenders of Midler, gave interviews insisting that Midler demanded upward of twenty-five takes on her scenes. This prompted United Artists to take the extraordinary step of issuing a memo to the press refuting Siegel's claims and confirming that, in fact, Midler's scenes were usually done in fewer than four takes.[16]

Midler kept quiet, waiting until the film was about to be released to give a couple of high-profile interviews in which she called *Jinxed* "the worst working experience of my life. It drove me to a nervous breakdown."[17] She admitted her error in approving Siegel and Wahl and attributed much of their ire to her being a woman in a position of power on the film. The dynamic was nothing new: a man with a strong point of view is a visionary, a woman is difficult. Midler had managed to bypass this kind of toxic work situation, and when she finally experienced it, it devastated her.*

By the time *Jinxed* was released in the fall of 1982, all this tsuris overshadowed the film itself. What ended up on-screen was a disjointed mix of comedy/murder/slapstick/romance with little connective tissue. It was a downer seeing Midler play this doormat character, cowering in fear of Rip Torn's brutish Harold when she seemed so capable of taking care of herself. Scenes of him threatening to beat up or kill Bonita are queasy rather than menacing. Midler's new white-blond hair washed out her natural effervescence. She looked tired and listless, and indeed like an older woman playing love scenes with Wahl.

---

* Midler got a bit of revenge later in *Beaches*, when her C. C. Bloom is bullied on a movie set by an obnoxious director and promptly slugs him, breaking his jaw.

The best moments came when Midler was relieved of her costars. She was uproarious during a frenzied performance of the old Perry Como number "Papa Loves Mambo," dashing on- and offstage as she finalized plans for Harold's murder. Midler's sense of the ridiculous enlivened the film's last quarter, when Bonita frantically searches for clues to the money Harold has hidden.

"I was trying to make the best movie I could make, and I was resented for it," Midler explained.[18] In the end, it was hardly worth it. *Jinxed* got mostly poor reviews and quickly disappeared from theaters. Appearing so long after her triumph with *The Rose*, *Jinxed* gave the impression that Midler was a one-hit wonder of a movie star. The bad press on *Jinxed*, even if unearned, did her no favors. No offers were forthcoming, and the movie career that had started so sensationally appeared stalled.

When writer-director Paul Mazursky offered her a role in *Down and Out in Beverly Hills*, it had been three years since *Jinxed*. Mazursky's comedy of manners is an update of Jean Renoir's 1932 film *Boudu Saved from Drowning*, itself adapted from an earlier play about a homeless man who tries to kill himself and is taken in by a wealthy family who attempt to domesticate him but instead see their household upended. Mazursky set the story in Beverly Hills, in the opulent but oddly dissatisfied household of Dave and Barbara Whiteman, a wealthy, self-made clothes-hanger manufacturer and his wife. Jerry, the homeless man, tries to drown himself in the Whitemans' luxurious swimming pool, and when he's made a part of the family, he shakes them out of their bourgeois anxieties.

At the time, much was made of Mazursky hiring the not-exactly-in-demand trio of Midler as Barbara, Richard Dreyfuss as Dave, and Nick Nolte as Jerry. Midler had been labeled difficult, and Dreyfuss and Nolte had had their share of alcohol and drug meltdowns and rehab stays. The kicker was that *Down and Out in Beverly Hills* would be the first R-rated film to be released by the family-friendly Walt Disney Studios, through their new adult division, Touchstone Films.

Midler bravely leaned into a role that teeters on stereotype. This pampered matron lives in luxury but, like the dowagers played by Alice Brady and Mary Boland in 1930s screwball comedies, endlessly searches for something to give meaning to her life. She has both a swami *and* a yogi (the latter encourages the couple to shake off their inhibitions by walking on hot coals), hires a psychiatrist for the family's misbehaving dog, and shops endlessly. Midler physicalizes Barbara in witty fashion. She drives her Mercedes convertible without clutching the steering wheel, the better to protect her impeccably manicured nails. And Midler uses her own mincing, tippy-toe walk to convey Barbara's agitation whenever her perfect, peach-colored world is threatened.

Barbara hasn't had an orgasm in years and is sex-averse with Dave; she even hires a hot Latina housekeeper to keep him sexually attended to. She has no sympathy for Jerry when Dave fishes him out of their pool, terrified that this filthy bum will steal everything in the house and then kill them. (Midler's old friend Vito Russo somehow got Bette and Barbara mixed up when he criticized her for warning Dave, "You'll get AIDS!" as he performs CPR on Jerry. In fact, it's exactly the kind of remark this coddled creature would blurt out in panic.) Midler's funniest and most touching moments come when Jerry tries some ashram-worthy muscle realignment to relieve her headaches. She's genuinely frightened and confused, but when it leads to an earthquake-level sexual reawakening, she's voracious and then blissfully serene, dragging on a postcoital cigarette and softly singing "You Belong to Me."

Jerry's sex therapy reinvigorates Barbara's interest in her husband, and Midler and Dreyfuss share a natural, lived-in banter as a couple whose lives have overwhelmed their genuine love for each other. Like Mazursky's earlier *Bob and Carol and Ted and Alice*, *Down and Out in Beverly Hills* was a warmhearted satire of upscale Southern California trend-chasing. It was funny and unexpected, with a big ensemble cast led by three stars in surprising new roles, and it was an instant hit when it was released in early 1986. Just like that, Midler's film career was back on track.

Bette Midler for Dummies

By the time *Down and Out in Beverly Hills* was in theaters, Midler was already filming another Disney/Touchstone comedy, *Ruthless People*, a broad comedy riff on O. Henry's *The Ransom of Red Chief*, with Midler as an heiress who drives her kidnappers crazy (threatening them at one point with "chainsaw enemas"). It was a small-ish role that called for Midler to undergo a comic physical transformation. When Barbara Stone is first seen, tumbling down the stairs of her kidnappers' basement tied up in a burlap sack, she's a corpulent, wild-haired harridan. The kidnappers demand a ransom of half a million dollars from her husband, Sam, who is delighted with the prospect of getting rid of her. While she endures her basement incarceration, Barbara watches televised aerobics classes and begins maniacally working out. Midler wore fat padding and a wig from hell in the early scenes, but eventually, after Barbara's exercise regimen, she turns from "corpulent little toad" (Sam's description of her) to sleek, slimmed-down doyenne.

The directing team of Jim Abrahams and David and Jerry Zucker, creators of the jokey comedy hit *Airplane!*, made *Ruthless People* a mean, dirty-mouthed comedy packed with physical gags and quotable lines. Midler's biggest laugh arrives when Barbara learns that Sam still won't pay even after the kidnappers reduce her ransom to ten thousand dollars: "Do I understand this correctly? I'm being marked down? . . . I've been kidnapped by Kmart!"

In their one scene together, she and Danny DeVito as Sam are a riot as she beats the hell out of him and throws him off the Santa Monica Pier. *Ruthless People* was a huge summer hit in 1986, and Midler's good-sport performance was a key part of the fun. At the end of the year, *Ruthless People* and *Down and Out in Beverly Hills* were among the ten top-grossing films of 1986. Midler was not only back in the movies but a bona fide box-office draw.

She went right back to work on another Touchstone comedy, *Outrageous Fortune*, this one a female buddy film costarring Shelley Long. The original screenplay by Leslie Dixon followed the far-fetched efforts of two wildly opposite women—both actors—chasing after the man both are in love with. As the chase extends from New York City to the mountains of New Mexico, they get mixed up with a cartoon KGB agent and bumbling CIA operatives and learn that the man they both love is a murderous counterspy.

Midler and Long play easy variations on their established personas. As Sandy Brozinsky, Midler is a brash vulgarian who just filmed the soft-core-sounding *Ninja Vixens*. Long's Lauren Ames, prissy and self-important, bears a resemblance to Diane Chambers, her prissy and self-important *Cheers* character on television. Sandy and Lauren hate each other on sight, but through their shared experiences climbing through airline luggage chutes and scaling mountains to escape the bad guys, they become fast friends. That touch of sentimentality is just one of the film's odd shifts in tone, including some surprisingly bloody violence.

Outrageous Fortune is no more believable than *Silver Streak* with Richard Pryor and Gene Wilder or *The In-Laws* with Peter Falk and Alan Arkin, two other buddy action films by its director Arthur Hiller. Some of its female-centric moments are funny and endearing, as when the two rivals pause to compare just how badly they were taken advantage of by their shared lover. Others now look cringey. When Midler is nearly thrown off a cliff, she's more worried about breaking a nail than surviving the fall. The pair abruptly interrupt life-or-death strategy planning to shop. Trying to get information out of a source, Midler cuts to the chase by offering a two-for-one blow job.

Midler pushes through with Divine Miss M energy, overdoing the mincing walk and using a broad New Yawk accent that goes in and out. When the pair pretend to be Eastern European orphans awaiting their father or two rambunctious boys on their first visit to a frontier bordello, it's Long who leads the characterizations, with Midler tagging along. But *Outrageous Fortune* was another big hit, Midler's third in a row, and audiences loved this cartoon Midler. Maybe Long was more familiar to them through television; some audiences and critics appeared to be meeting Midler for the first time in this series of broadly drawn comedy roles.

Around the time *Outrageous Fortune* opened in early 1987, in a throwback to the old Hollywood studio system, Midler signed an exclusive three-picture contract with Disney. "Investing in the Bette Midler business," as studio head Jeffrey Katzenberg put it, meant not only developing films for her but serving as a home for her new production company, All Girl Productions.[19] Midler had started the company with her friend and former assistant Bonnie Bruckheimer and Margaret Jennings South. (Their irreverent motto: "We hold a grudge.") All Girl Productions would develop projects that Disney would have first option to greenlight. After three career-reviving hits in one year, Midler was grateful for Disney's commitment and for the stability of this new home base. "These people are the only ones in town who gave me a job," she matter-of-factly said. "Why shouldn't I be loyal to them?"[20]

The cartooning continued with *Big Business*, built around a plot as old as the Greeks. Two sets of twins are switched at birth, and years later they've grown up to be Midler and Lily Tomlin, each playing two different comic characters. City Bette is the ruthless co-chairman of the board of the mighty conglomerate Moramax, who wants to unload a rural furniture-manufacturing company to a foreign investor who will shut it down and strip-mine the land it's on. City Lily, her co-chair, is the opposite of her ambitious sister, a dreamy nature lover who yearns for a simpler life. Meanwhile, the take-charge Country Lily, an employee and staunch defender of the backwoods company, travels to New York City to prevent the sale and is accompanied by her sister Country Bette, who feels out of place in the country and dreams of living in a big city. When all four women check into the Plaza Hotel, mistaken identities and near misses keep the mismatched twins from discovering each other until the last reel.

Midler and Tomlin aren't convincing as one set of twins, let alone two, but their four comic characters are so distinctive that the sloppy plotting and slapdash execution don't much get in their way. (*Big Business* was directed by Jim Abrahams, from *Ruthless People*, here working solo.) Midler is on cruise control as City Bette, snapping orders and giving out with the drop-dead takes that movie audiences now anticipate. She gets a star entrance, preening as she steps off an elevator in glam 1980s businesswoman attire. Told that lab rats used for testing Moramax products keep dying, she demands, "Get tougher rats."

Midler's Country Bette is a genuinely original creation. A wide-eyed closet voluptuary who worships Joan Collins on *Dynasty*, she experiences New York as a wonderland of consumerism inhabited by colorful characters she never knew existed back in the sticks. When she happens upon a steel-drum player on Fifth Avenue and begins joyously yodeling along to these strange, exotic rhythms, it's the film's most surprising and delightful sequence.

Big Business builds to the moment when the two sets of twins finally meet in the ladies' room, with all of them discovering one another in the mirror. It's a funny visual gag only if you've never seen the Marx Brothers do the same routine with more precision in *Duck Soup*. Here the spatial placement is messy, and the special effects look muddy. The quick wrap-up, with Country Bette pretending to be City Bette in front of the Moramax shareholders and saving the furniture company, is barely believable.

Tomlin brings more thoughtful character touches and physical detail to her portrayals (her culotte-wearing country girl is devoted to making the rattling sign of the snake), but Midler's big-city corporate diva dominates the laughs. *Big Business* is never as funny or inventive as it wants to be, and when it was released in the summer of 1988, it didn't do quite as well as expected. It was perhaps a sign that the Bette Midler for Dummies series of broad comedies was running out of steam.

The Weepy Trilogy

Midler was now a certifiable box-office powerhouse and one of the highest-paid women in Hollywood. But after three braying comedies (*Down and Out in Beverly Hills* being the exception), Midler knew it was time for a change. "I shouldn't bite the hand that feeds me, but I feel that my work for Disney has been all of a piece," she said. "And I would like to try another piece, a different piece. I need a challenge."[21] After all, this was the woman capable of pulverizing audiences with a string of ribald jokes and then reducing them to tears with the emotive power of her singing. The large audiences flocking to her comedy hits were getting only one part—the most obvious part—of the Midler experience. If these comedies made her bankable and better positioned to do the more ambitious work she was capable of, it felt like a reasonable trade-off.

The first film developed by All Girl Productions was based on Iris Rainer Dart's novel *Beaches*, the soapy story of two very different women who meet as children and establish a friendship that endures over the decades. Dart patterned the character of a brassy, red-headed singer and actor on Midler. The role was almost too good a fit, too obviously tailored to Midler's public persona. Still, it gave her the opportunity to be serious as well as funny, with the added bonus of allowing her to sing.[†]

Midler was not only the star but a producer on *Beaches*, and she was responsible for the casting of the other starring role and for hiring the film's director. The results were much happier than on *Jinxed*. As Hillary Whitney, the buttoned-up daughter of a San

[†] Aside from her brief vocalizing in *Big Business*, Midler also sang in another 1988 Disney release, the animated *Oliver & Company*.

Francisco society family, Barbara Hershey, with her dark patrician beauty and elegant composure, was a good contrast for Midler's brash, big-haired C.C. Bloom. Director Garry Marshall was a mensch, an efficient traffic supervisor who got along with the stars and kept things moving.

When they meet on the Atlantic City boardwalk in the 1950s, Hillary is a timid little girl and C.C. is already a show-biz trouper belting out "The Glory of Love." Their friendship continues via letters over the years, until Hillary moves to New York City and she and C.C. become roommates. There are romantic rivalries, feuds, marriages and divorces (for both), and childbirth (for Hillary), and C.C.'s career goes through as many ups and downs as Midler's. When Hillary is diagnosed with a fatal illness, C.C. at last gets past her own self-involvement and cares for her friend until the end. Hillary's will directs her young daughter to live with C.C. As C.C. sings a drawn-out orchestral version of "The Glory of Love," she waves up to her departed friend and over to the little girl now waiting for her in the wings.

Beaches didn't just jerk tears, it yanked them. It was a schmaltzy throwback to the old "women's picture" era when female stars battled over men (John Heard was here in the thankless George Brent role) and misunderstandings were quickly resolved with tears and vows of forever friendship.

The old pictures may have been melodramatic, but they had an internal logic and emotional consistency. They were authentic to their time. *Beaches* was ersatz in every way, from its color-by-numbers screenplay by Mary Agnes Donoghue to the rat-a-tat sitcom pace of Marshall's direction. Midler and Hershey share a warm, friendly camaraderie, but they fight an uphill battle to make something meaningful out of the contrived plotting and disorienting shifts in tone. (And the dynamic between an uptight WASP and an uninhibited, full-of-life Jew is an ancient cliché.)

Midler isn't afraid to play C.C.'s selfishness and ego-driven ambition, and as usual, she's the funniest person on-screen. But it's a great-ladyish performance. Midler gets awfully noble when she's showing us the heart underneath C.C.'s bawdiness. The film's best performance comes from twelve year-old Mayim Bialik as young C.C. in the film's early scenes. In a red wig, she's a dead ringer for Midler both in looks and in mouthy attitude.

The most welcome aspect of *Beaches* is its music, with songs well chosen to reflect C.C.'s turbulent life and career. But the big onstage numbers, designed to showcase C.C. as both a bold dramatic star and a ribald showstopper, go off the rails. Her big off-Broadway break comes singing a techno anthem, "Oh Industry," dressed as a circus ringmaster in what looks like a musical version of Fritz Lang's *Metropolis*. It's hard to know which is more ridiculous, the number or an opening-night review comparing C.C. to Hannah Arendt.

"Otto Titsling" was a witty tour de force for Midler in her comedy act. But blown up as a Broadway production number for C.C., with cartoony villains, ginormous-breasted divas, and scampering Bavarian villagers—all in vivid Disney colors—it's like a smuttier "Springtime for Hitler." Much better is Midler's recording-studio performance of Randy Newman's "I Think It's Going to Rain Today" which conveys more honest, plain-spoken pathos than anything else in *Beaches*. But of course, it was the bombastic "Wind beneath My Wings," played during Hillary's final deathwatch and funeral, that became the film's mammoth hit.

Beaches got mostly terrible reviews but was another hit for Midler, helped along by the surprise success of the soundtrack album and the chart-topping "Wind beneath My Wings." Disney/ Touchstone went all in on an Oscar campaign, pushing Midler for Best Actress. She was confident enough about her chances to muse with Oprah Winfrey about who else might be nominated in the category. But when *Beaches* was mostly shut out of the nominations (it received just one nod for its art direction–set decoration), she pulled out of the 1989 Academy Awards telecast. In doing so, she missed being part of a legendary Oscar moment. Producer Allan

Carr's notorious opening number featuring Snow White and Rob Lowe wailing on "Proud Mary" was to climax with Midler emerging from a glittering replica of Grauman's Chinese Theatre. Instead, her *Big Business* costar, Tomlin, took the spot.[22] It's tempting to imagine the comic spin Midler might have added to this infamous number, one that looks not nearly as outrageous today.

Beaches almost immediately became the ultimate chick flick, a pejorative applied regardless of quality to any film with female stars and concerns.[‡] It was the opening joke in the *Seinfeld* episode in which Midler played herself, with Jerry flummoxed by how to console his date who is weeping through the final moments of the film. Paul Rudnick used it as code for gay identity in his 1997 *In & Out* screenplay. When Matt Dillon's Cameron Drake is shown in a clip from his Oscar-winning performance as a gay soldier, he is outed to his unit by a VHS copy of *Beaches* discovered in his locker.

Beaches has proven remarkably durable, spinning off a TV-movie remake and a stage musical adaptation. It's almost as much a perennial as *Stella Dallas*. Olive Higgins Prouty's 1923 novel of maternal sacrifice was adapted for the stage, was made into a silent film, and was a long-running radio series. But its place in popular culture was secured by its 1937 film version.

Stella Dallas was dated in 1937, but Barbara Stanwyck's clear-eyed performance made this tale of motherly devotion and sacrifice a classic weeper. Stella, daughter of a millworker, marries Stephen Dallas, a businessman above her station. A daughter is soon born, but Stella has a crude (though loving) way about her that hinders her from settling into Stephen's society life. They separate, and she raises the girl herself. As the girl grows up, Stella realizes that her

---

[‡] Regardless of its quality, *Beaches* does pass the Bechdel test, which measures the representation of women in film and other media. Named for cartoonist Alison Bechdel, who first coined the term in a comic strip, it requires that a film must have at least two women characters who talk to each other about something other than a man. While C.C. and Hillary have plenty of conflicts about men, they're supportive of each other's personal and career goals and are always present for each other—even when the circumstances are implausible.

own uncouth, uneducated ways will hold her daughter back, and she gives her up to her father and disappears from the girl's life.

Both *Stella Dallas* films were produced by Samuel Goldwyn. In the 1980s, his son, Samuel Goldwyn Jr., had the idea of updating the property and commissioned a new screenplay by Robert Getchell, author of female-centered films like *Alice Doesn't Live Here Anymore* and *Mommie Dearest*. It was this new take on old Stella that became the next starring vehicle for Midler, Disney's number one female star, who had recently signed another multipicture deal with the studio. (Goldwyn and Touchstone would co-produce the film.)

Midler's Stella is now a barmaid in industrial 1969 Watertown, New York, who gets pregnant during a brief fling with Stephen, a doctor completing an internship nearby. She's a good-natured, self-sufficient working-class woman with a great figure. (She first appears doing a mock striptease on top of the bar where she works.) She and the visiting doctor have fun together, and theirs is a believable short-term affair. When Stephen makes a halfhearted marriage proposal, she sends him away and has the baby on her own. While the earlier Stella lived in comfort as Mrs. Dallas, supported by a husband she didn't live with, Midler's Stella stubbornly refuses any monetary assistance and joins the ranks of single mothers, scraping by on minimum wage and commission jobs as the story moves into the 1980s. To reflect her new unmarried status, the film's title was shortened to *Stella*.

Despite the film's various updates, it includes all of *Stella Dallas*'s heart-tugging greatest hits: Stella's raucous public behavior causes all the school friends invited by her daughter, Jenny, to her birthday party to cancel at the last minute, leaving mother and daughter shattered. Stella makes a scene at a fancy resort, humiliating Jenny in front of her friends. Stella visits Stephen's new wife-to-be and offers to "give" Jenny to her and Stephen to raise as their own. And there's the final "money shot," with Stella standing gallantly outside in the rain watching Jenny get married, then walking off, never to be seen by her daughter again.

Some of these scenes have an undeniable emotional pull even when they don't make sense from a contemporary standpoint. (It's hard to imagine 1980s teenagers standing up a friend on her birthday because they've heard her mother is wild; if anything, they'd be intrigued.) *Stella* treats Jenny's two worlds—her mother's downscale Watertown and her father's New York–based Ivy League land of unlimited opportunity—as completely unbridgeable. But the rigid class differences that the plot hinges on aren't as fixed as they once were, making Stella's sacrifices for her daughter appear unhinged.

Though she looks a bit mature for the early scenes, Midler is good casting as Stella, and she has a number of affecting moments. Her characterization makes sense: a working-class woman content with her lot who instinctively understands that her way of life and all that goes with it are a dead end for a daughter with promise. (Jenny wants to study architecture in college and has a dreamboat boyfriend from a "good" family.) Whether softly harmonizing together or arguing and making up, Midler and Trini Alvarado as Jenny share a loving mother–daughter bond. But the old-lace-curtains plotting keeps leading Stella down dramatic cul-de-sacs. One minute she's a party girl with a mouth like Midler (she tells a snooty PTA parent, "I'll bet your legs have been together longer than the Lennon Sisters"), the next she's a domestic drudge sewing her daughter's clothes. She's either decked out like "Pee-wee Herman's wife," as someone says with a smirk, or she's playing the harpy (through tears) to force her daughter to leave.

Touchstone planned a fall 1989 release for *Stella*, positioning it for Academy Awards consideration, but when the studio pushed it back to early 1990, it was a sign they had lost faith in it. *Stella* was roundly panned and didn't come close to *Beaches'* box-office performance, though Midler's residual popularity meant that it did far better business than other female-driven dramas released at the same time, like Jessica Lange in *Men Don't Leave* and Jane Fonda with Robert De Niro in *Stanley and Iris*.

Stella is better paced and more caringly directed (by John Erman) than *Beaches*, but seeing the two films back to back is depressing. Were these retro weepies really the kinds of films Midler wanted to squander her dramatic gifts on? She shows enough range and sensitivity in them to make anyone familiar with her stage work or with *The Rose* wish she was doing tougher, more challenging material.

All Girl Productions had another film on its slate, a promising original musical drama starring Midler as a World War II entertainer. But first there was an intriguing reteaming with director Paul Mazursky. *Scenes from a Mall* paired Midler with Woody Allen as a professional couple living in the Hollywood Hills. Nick, a harddriving sports agent, and Deborah, a psychotherapist and author of a trendy new book on marriage, spend the day running errands at the upscale Beverly Center. As they stroll through this hermetically sealed cocoon of consumerism, each reveals affairs that lead to further confessions, secrets shared, and demands for divorce.

What was intended as a smart, satirical LA take on Ingmar Bergman's savage *Scenes from a Marriage* instead became a tedious exercise in high-end navel-gazing. The two shop, get drunk on margaritas, have sex in a movie theater, make up and break up repeatedly, and regularly cross paths with a winsome shopping-mall mime (Bill Irwin at his most irritating). Its eighty-seven minutes feel as long as *Gone with the Wind*. *Scenes from a Mall* didn't work as a riff on LA consumer culture, and it didn't work as a seriocomic teaming of two highly individual stars. Midler and Allen play off each other well enough that it's too bad they never appeared in another, better film, perhaps one of Allen's own productions (though he seemed to like his leading ladies younger and WASPier). *Scenes from a Mall* was forgotten as soon as it was released in early 1991.

For the Boys had been in development by All Girl Productions since the mid-1980s, but Disney wasn't interested. It was too ambitious and pricey for the budget-conscious studio. Instead, Midler and company set up the film at Twentieth Century-Fox and signed Mark Rydell, her simpatico director on *The Rose*, to helm the

$45 million era-spanning musical. When Rydell came aboard, he brought on Marshall Brickman, co-writer of Allen's *Annie Hall* and *Manhattan*, to revise the film's original story and screenplay by Neal Jimenez and Lindy Laub.

Girl singer Dixie Leonard is paired with established song-and-dance comic Eddie Sparks in 1942 for a USO tour at the height of America's war effort. The partnership lasts well into the next decade and makes them a beloved show-business duo. Dixie, a war widow and single mother of a young son, becomes disenchanted with the carnage of war, while Eddie drills deeper into jingoistic support for any and all US military action. Their final rift comes when her son, now an Army captain, is killed during a misguided Vietnam tour instigated by Eddie for television cameras. After twenty-five years of not speaking to him, Dixie reluctantly agrees to appear with Eddie one last time as he receives the Presidential Medal of Freedom during a George H. W. Bush–era patriotic television spectacular.

Midler's Dixie Leonard has some of the emotional heft and musical range of Garland's Esther Blodgett in *A Star Is Born*, Streisand's Fanny Brice in *Funny Girl*, and Midler's own *The Rose*. It's a complete star performance showcasing every aspect of the Midler mystique.

When Dixie sings the jivey "Stuff Like That There" in front of a hangar full of soldiers, it's with the same spirit of outrageous fun Midler had singing for the boys at the baths. When she's interrupted by a blackout, the soldiers hold up flashlights to light her way as she walks among them singing the fond, homesick "P.S. I Love You." In these two songs, Dixie reminds the boys of all the girls waiting for them back home. She's both the rowdy good-time girl and the tender sweetheart. And just as in countless backstage musicals when a performer is nervous before facing an audience, Dixie turns out to be a spectacular hit, bringing the boys cheering to their feet—as if anything less would ever be expected of the film's star.

This early sequence is Midler at her funny, touching, and good-hearted best. So is a much later scene in Vietnam where Dixie, now in her late fifties, quiets an edgy, near-violent squad of soldiers with motherly tough talk and a devastating version of the Beatles' "In My Life" that sums up both her life and the life of the country these men are ostensibly fighting to protect in a senseless war.

Looking at individual scenes and songs from *For the Boys* on YouTube, you might wonder why it failed at the box office and has largely been forgotten. It's a big, teeming film, confidently directed and performed, beautifully designed and photographed. And Midler is frankly wonderful in an expressly tailored role. But ultimately, *For the Boys* is flimsy, more an outline than a fully realized film. Scenes taking in World War II, the Korean War, early television, McCarthy-era witch hunts, and the Vietnam War play like bullet points dutifully hit, and a belabored framing device with a young production assistant sent to coax Dixie to attend the awards telecast only adds to the film's nearly two-and-a-half-hour running time.

A contemporary sensibility hovers over *For the Boys*, resulting in odd, anachronistic moments that pull the viewer out of the film. Dixie's blue rejoinders to Eddie during their first onstage meeting would never fly in the 1940s, even in front of a randy bunch of soldiers. Her sex jokes during their 1950s television series would make Belle Barth blush. The routine performed by the featured dancer in Eddie and Dixie's USO act is much too sexualized for the period. And did everyone in the 1940s and '50s really say "fuck" so freely and often?

Oh, James Caan is in the film, too. Since Dixie and Eddie don't much like each other, audience investment in their personal and professional relationship dwindles as *For the Boys* goes along, and Caan recedes from view. A one-night liaison between the two rings false. Their final confrontation over her rejection of his America First bromides just before going on television one last time is undercut by the distracting old-age makeup on Midler and Caan that makes them look like burn victims.

And the tears get jerked once again. The film's big emotional peak comes when a surprise raid during their Vietnam show kills everybody but Dixie and Eddie, and she watches as her son is slaughtered (in super-slow motion), then cradles him and calls for help (also in slow motion). Tearful goodbyes to children and best friends were now seemingly part of the Midler formula for drama.

Twentieth Century-Fox and Midler pulled out all the stops to promote the film ahead of its November 1991 debut. She was on the Johnny Carson and Arsenio Hall late-night shows. She did a prime-time interview with Barbara Walters and a full hour with Oprah Winfrey. *Vanity Fair* published a cover story on Midler and the movie, and the studio created a lavish eight-page advertisement for *People* magazine. Midler even got a tabloid-press boost when Geraldo Rivera published a memoir in which he claimed the two had a "torrid affair" back in the 1970s. Midler countered that it only amounted to him breaking poppers under her nose and groping her in the bathroom. The pair ended up on the cover of the *New York Daily News* under the headline "Geraldo Drugged Me for Sex."[23]

But no amount of ballyhoo could get people to see *For the Boys*. Just weeks after it opened nationally, the *New York Times* published a story about its "dismal performance" and quoted *Variety* describing the film as "the holiday's only turkey."[24] The postmortems suggested confusion about whether the film was a musical, a war drama, or a romance between Midler and Caan. It didn't appeal to young viewers, but even older audiences, including the women who made up the core of Midler's movie fandom, didn't show up. In the end, the elaborate, big-budget *For the Boys* made less at the US box office than the modest *Stella*.[§]

[§] To add legal insult to box-office injury, Martha Raye filed a $5 million lawsuit against Midler and just about everyone involved with *For the Boys*. Raye was known for her many overseas trips to entertain troops through several wars, and she claimed that the idea for the film came directly from her, especially after sharing a treatment for a film

A 2000 *New York Times* profile just prior to the debut of Midler's sitcom noted, "Strangely, Midler seems to be frustrated that she's not seen as a dramatic actress. She clearly enjoys being funny, but being relegated to the comedienne category seems to irk her. Throughout her career, Midler has gravitated toward nonhumorous roles. . . . Midler longs for the glamour and the respect of the serious."[25]

Yet when she is given the opportunity for dramatic roles, Midler's choices reveal a weakness for sudsy, old-fashioned weepers. During this period, she notably turned down the lead role in the film version of Stephen King's *Misery*, in which she would have played a disturbed woman who cuts off a man's feet (in the film, she breaks his ankles). The role was taken by Kathy Bates, who won an Oscar for it. "I was too afraid. I thought, 'What will the fans say?' " Midler admitted, then turned it into a joke, noting that audiences might rather see her cut off someone's balls.[26] Reluctance to challenge herself and fretting over her image got the better of her decision-making and led her to make safer but much less satisfying (and, ultimately, career-limiting) choices. Sentimental dramas like *Beaches*, *Stella*, and *For the Boys* mired her in treacle, and her innate good humor could only compensate so much.

The public's rejection of a passion project from her own production company left Midler devastated, and a Golden Globes win and an Oscar nomination didn't ease her upset. *For the Boys* essentially ended Midler's run as a Hollywood player, the kind who can get movies developed and made. Other ambitious musical dramas in development for Midler by All Girl Productions never got off the ground, including one about Ina Ray Hutton, the 1940s leader of an all-girl band, and, most regrettably, an ambitious biopic about Lotte Lenya. She would continue to work in films (and have her biggest hit with *The First Wives Club*) but on a sporadic basis, between the tours that became an increasingly important part of her career.

---

about her life with Midler some years earlier. The lawsuit dragged on for two years before being dismissed. Raye, already in ill health, died shortly afterward.

Sister Witches and First Wives

The drop-off in Midler's film career was also an indication of Hollywood's double standard for male and female stars. A few years earlier, Pauline Kael wrote, "The only fresh element in American movies of the eighties may be what Steve Martin, Bill Murray, Bette Midler, Richard Pryor, Robin Williams, and other comedians have brought to them."[27] All these men made their share of high-priced flops, including sentimental heart-tuggers, but there was always another star vehicle waiting for them. Women were forced to make the case for their box-office value with every film. Few second chances were offered. With three flops in a row, concluding with an especially high-profile failure, Midler was in a vulnerable position. After making eight films in five years, it would be two more years before she made another.

Midler's biggest hits had all been comedies with an adult edge, so it's puzzling why she turned down *Sister Act*, an original screenplay written for her by Paul Rudnick. The story of a nightclub singer who is placed by a witness-protection program in a convent and invigorates the nuns' choir with a new repertoire of pop and R&B songs, *Sister Act* was finally made with Whoopi Goldberg in the lead after Midler rejected it.** "My fans don't want to see me in a wimple" was Midler's nonsensical rationale for turning down a musical comedy that ended up making more money than any of her 1980s comedies.[28]

When she did return to films, it was in the kid-friendly comedy *Hocus Pocus*, released by Walt Disney Pictures rather than its adult-branded Touchstone division. Midler is Winifred Sanderson, the oldest of a trio of sisters who are hanged for practicing witchcraft on children in 1693 in Salem, Massachusetts. Three hundred years later, the Sanderson sisters are conjured back to life on Halloween

---

** By the time *Sister Act* made it to the screen, it had gone through so many rewrites that Rudnick chose to use a pseudonym in the credits, listing himself as "Joseph Howard."

1993 and continue their witchy ways, using young children as sacrifices to keep themselves young forever. Or something like that. *Hocus Pocus* was a tepid Disney comedy with some mildly scary special effects, peopled by blandly good-looking teens and adorable children and situated in an antiseptic, all-white suburb. Plus a talking black cat.

The best thing about the film is Midler, whose zesty comic performance outclasses everything around her. With her frizzy red wig, flowing gown and cape, and demented aristocratic accent, Midler looks something like Bette Davis playing Queen Elizabeth—if the royal monarch had protruding front teeth. Her two sisters, played by Sarah Jessica Parker and Kathy Najimy, function as clumsy Harlettes swatted and ordered about by their diva older sister.

Midler delivers even the flattest of supposed comic zingers with elan. On the rare occasion when she gets a funny line, she gives it a calculated camp edge. When the sisters crash a Halloween party and take over the stage, Winifred greets the audience with "Hello Salem, my name's Winifred. What's yours?" like a latter-day Rose from *Gypsy*, before rocking the crowd with a wicked Midleresque "I Put a Spell On You."

Hocus Pocus was a box-office disappointment when it arrived during the summer of 1993 in direct competition with *Jurassic Park* (though it still made twice what *For the Boys* brought in). Over the years, repeat broadcasts on the Disney Channel and other cable outlets during the run-up to Halloween turned *Hocus Pocus* into a holiday perennial with a fan base to rival *The Rocky Horror Picture Show*. Those who saw the movie as kids have now introduced their own children to the age-appropriate comedy. Today trick-or-treaters dress up as various Sanderson sisters.

At the height of the Covid-19 pandemic, *Hocus Pocus* was rereleased in twenty-five hundred theaters for the Halloween season and racked up another $5 million. In the surest sign of its ongoing popularity, a sequel starring Midler, Parker, and Najimy in their original roles was released on Disney+ in 2022. *Hocus Pocus 2*, even milder and more forgettable than its predecessor, immediately became the streaming service's most-watched program, with talk of a third film in the air.

Winifred Sanderson is now Midler's most iconic role. In a curious back-to-the-future twist, Midler's gay-icon status has been newly burnished by LGBTQ+ millennial and Gen Z audiences. The ripe-for-parody Sandersons—Parker's vampy horndog, Najimy's daffy sidekick, and especially Midler's fierce ruling diva—have been enthusiastically taken up by drag performers as deliciously camp theatrical characters.[††] The three stars' LGBTQ+ ally bona fides are also part of the attraction: Parker and Najimy as longtime advocates for the community and, of course, Midler as the queen mother of gay-friendly straights.

New fans who can't fathom her as a hard-driving rock star in *The Rose* or as the outrageous Divine Miss M, who never heard "Boogie Woogie Bugle Boy" or "Hello in There," love this buck-toothed, funny-scary Midler. Celebrity status ebbs and flows over time, and those who were there at the beginning can only shake our heads—while giving her credit for staying relevant to new generations—at the wide embrace of this camp, comic-strip Midler.

It was a surprise when Midler popped up in an unbilled cameo in *Get Shorty*, the 1995 film adaptation of Elmore Leonard's crime-comedy novel about gangsters and the movie business. Midler manages to make a splash in a couple of brief scenes as a sexed-up widow with a screenplay to sell. She looks terrific in full cougar mode, flashing Victoria's Secret lingerie beneath a fur coat and vamping good-looking policemen. She's so entertainingly over-ripe that she was named Funniest Supporting Actress in a Motion Picture by the American Comedy Awards for a role with less than five minutes of screen time. It was a relief to see Midler, even briefly,

---

[††] *Hocus Pocus 2* confirmed the Sandersons' status as drag favorites by casting Ginger Minj, Kahmora Hall, and Kornbread, three stars of *RuPaul's Drag Race*, as drag versions of the sisters in a Halloween-costume competition scene.

in a sharp, funny, adult comedy for the first time since *Down and Out in Beverly Hills.*

Olivia Goldsmith's best-seller *The First Wives Club* followed three college friends who reconnect following the suicide of another friend who killed herself when her husband left her for a much younger woman. The three discover that each of them has a similar marital history and join forces to seek revenge on their no-good ex-husbands.

The screenplay for *The First Wives Club* was by Robert Harling, whose play *Steel Magnolias* was a hit off-Broadway and an even bigger hit as an all-star film in 1989. Harling flattened out his eccentric Southern ensemble comedy into a glossy Hollywood tearjerker, every bit as emotionally manipulative as *Stella* or *Beaches*.

He did the same for *The First Wives Club.* He and director Hugh Wilson turn what had been a funny, but dark, revenge tale into an escapist farce built around three veteran female stars: Midler, Goldie Hawn, and Diane Keaton. Goldsmith's book included lots of steamy sex, financial chicanery, and truly despicable behavior by the husbands (one steals money from a trust fund for a daughter with Down syndrome). The film is nothing more than a romp, with the stars acting out Lucy-and-Ethel high jinks across a shiny, cleaned-up New York City in between sisterly sessions of truth sharing. The ex-husbands are comically defanged villains who don't know what hit them when the women begin exposing their financial irregularities.

All three leading characters are simplified and spruced up for the screen. Midler is Brenda, the Jewish girl who helped her husband Morty build his electronics business into a retail empire. But Morty gave her a raw deal during the divorce settlement, leaving her struggling while he lives in luxury with his new, much younger and skinnier girlfriend. In the book, Brenda is, by her own admission, "a middle-aged, divorced, fat lesbian."[29] Midler's Brenda is overweight-lite, dressed in baggy skirts and sweaters to suggest a heavy figure, until suddenly, without explanation, she's slim and wearing fitted dresses. The book's Brenda never really enjoyed sex with Morty and eventually finds love with another woman. The movie's Brenda is most definitely straight and ends the film in reconciliation with Morty, who realizes his error in leaving her.

You can practically feel Midler, in her mousy brown wig, itching to break out of this frumpy role, while the other stars play variations on their established screen images. Keaton does her dithering WASP routine, but Hawn is the funniest of the three, gleefully spoofing her own preternaturally youthful image as a plastic-surgery-addicted Hollywood star who helped her husband make his reputation by producing her hit films, only to be cast aside for a younger actress and mistress. (In a final insult, she is offered a career lifeline playing the younger woman's mother.)

For every funny scene, like one where the three sneak into Morty's penthouse and escape using a painter's platform that farcically plunges them downward, there are more that miss any kind of comic vivacity, even after a last-minute script polish by Paul Rudnick. The trio's drunken reunion after their friend's funeral isn't nearly as witty or sparkling as it thinks it is. The daughter with Down syndrome is here turned into a lesbian, presumably to give the three wives a reason to visit a lesbian bar.

A ginned-up conflict leads to a slapping match—yes, the three stars actually whack each other across the face—followed by a power-ballad-driven montage of regret and reconciliation, which in turn, leads to the film's final act and the biggest switch from its source material. Not content with bringing down their exes, the women open a vaguely defined "women's crisis center" named for their late friend in a palatial downtown building conveniently owned by Hawn's character. Cue the inevitable "Sisters Are Doin' It for Themselves" montage of the three bustling amid the construction. (They read blueprints upside down until a man helpfully turns them around.)

The center's gala opening is a tribute to corporate feminism, with a who's who of New Yorkers, including Ed Koch, Gloria Steinem, and Kathie Lee Gifford, drinking champagne and congratulating the uptown trio. Ivana Trump, apparently the patron saint of divorcées, imparts her final words of wisdom: "Don't get mad, get everything!" With that, the three first wives, in luxurious all-white outfits and matching coats, do an eleven o'clock song-and-dance number. "You Don't Own Me" was a radical statement of identity from a seventeen-year-old Lesley Gore in 1963. For these upper-middle-class (and above) matrons, it's a smug declaration of unlimited choices made possible by the privilege of money and class. When they dance out into the dark downtown Manhattan street, they don't even bother locking the door.

It doesn't make much sense, but, to paraphrase Midler herself, "Who gives a rat's ass? They look good!" Midler, Hawn, and Keaton looking fabulous as they riff off one another and dance down the street is its own pleasure. Despite her chemistry with Frederic Forrest and Richard Dreyfuss, Midler's most congenial pairings on-screen were with women: Shelley Long, Lily Tomlin, Barbara Hershey, Trini Alvarado, Sarah Jessica Parker, Kathy Najimy. She and Hawn and Keaton have a genuine camaraderie that helps smooth over plot inconsistencies and makes the film more enjoyable than it deserves to be.

The First Wives Club's go-girl revenge comedy swathed in glamorous star power made it a hit when it was released in the fall of 1996, taking in more than $180 million worldwide. The three stars landed on the cover of *Time Magazine* and made the talk show rounds basking in the film's success and celebrating their show business longevity. (All three were fifty when the film was released.)

Midler, Hawn, and Keaton were eager to reunite for a sequel, and audiences clearly enjoyed seeing them together. Successful action comedies with male stars like *Lethal Weapon* and *Beverly Hills Cop* get multiple sequels, but by Hollywood's brutal calculus, female-led hits are flukes, despite ample evidence to the contrary. The commitment—and the budget—for a reteaming of the three stars never happened, despite numerous false starts. Since 2020, a pre-production project variously titled *Family Jewels* and *A Childhood History Plan* has sat on the IMDB pages of Midler, Hawn, and Keaton, its synopsis describing the three now as grandmothers who were each once married to the same man. In today's movie market, with niche comedies like *80 for Brady*, *Queen Bees*, and the *Book Club* series starring septuagenarian (and older) female stars, surely the first wives deserve another outing.

Why Bother?

The success of *The First Wives Club* gave Midler's film career a brief bump. There were all kinds of projects announced for her, from a big-screen version of the 1960s sitcom *Green Acres* (with Midler in the Eva Gabor role) to *Show Business Kills*, based on a novel about four women in the movie business by *Beaches* author Iris Rainer Dart. More intriguing was a film biopic of the 1920s speakeasy hostess and entertainer Texas Guinan to be directed by Martin Scorsese. Ultimately, none of these projects happened. The Texas Guinan film joined the now-abandoned Lotte Lenya project as another sadly missed opportunity for Midler to stretch herself to an extent she hadn't since *The Rose*.

Instead, her next film was *That Old Feeling*, an All Girl Production for Universal that she had already filmed by the time *The First Wives Club* opened. The comedy by Leslie Dixon, who had previously written *Outrageous Fortune*, was about an acrimoniously divorced couple who reunite for their daughter's wedding. When their animosity erupts into renewed passion, they run away together, upending their current marriages as well as that of their daughter. Despite her above-the-title billing, Midler was part of an ensemble cast that included Dennis Farina as her ex-husband. As Lilly, a flashy actor only a few degrees removed from her own public persona, Midler shared an authentic spark of attraction with Farina that was both funny and believable. His sexy hangdog vibe played well against her feisty flamboyance, and he turned out to be one of her most copacetic leading men.

That Old Feeling, smoothly directed by Carl Reiner, was a throwback to romantic comedies of another era. The cast was solid, it looked sumptuous (with Midler blond, trim, and glam), and there were some funny lines. *That Old Feeling* was perfectly . . . okay. The first fifteen minutes, when Midler and Farina's nasty bickering turns to uncontrollable lust, is genuinely funny, but there's no sense of urgency to any of the various marital shufflings that follow, and the final pairings are telescoped a mile away. *That Old Feeling* played like a middling assembly-line product and disappeared quickly when it was released in early 1997.

The late 1990s saw a resurgence of interest in Jacqueline Susann, the ballsy author of potboilers like *Valley of the Dolls* (1966) and *The Love Machine* (1969), who died of cancer in 1974. It may have all started in 1995 with "Wasn't She Great?," a profile of Susann in *The New Yorker*. Writer Michael Korda, who in the late 1960s was an editor at Simon & Schuster, which published *The Love Machine*, wrote a remembrance of Susann and her press agent–promoter–producer husband Irving Mansfield that was both appallingly funny and warmly sympathetic to the show-biz couple. (The title paraphrased Mansfield's constant rhetorical affirmation of his wife: "Isn't she great?" Mansfield died in 1988.)

Seemingly overnight, Susann's novels, long-running bestsellers of their time, were given glossy reissues; screenings of the camp-classic film version of *Valley of the Dolls* were hits on the gay film-festival circuit; a stage version of the film was presented in Los Angeles and New York City; and Barbara Seaman's 1987 biography, *Lovely Me: The Life of Jacqueline Susann*, was reissued and served as the basis for a TV movie starring Michele Lee.

Korda's article was quickly optioned for film with Andrew Bergman as director, Paul Rudnick as screenwriter, and Midler as Susann. The participation of Rudnick at first seemed inspired. In his plays (*Jeffrey*, *The Most Fabulous Story Ever Told*), films (*In & Out*,

Addams Family Values), novels, and magazine pieces, including his hilarious alter ego Libby Gelman-Waxner, a Manhattan housewife and mother who reviews movies with the same passion she reserves for shopping and decorating, Rudnick injected the "gay show-biz sensibility" into sitcom plots, family comedies, and satires on contemporary life. Who better to cast a comic eye on the camp/kitsch world of Susann?

There was more than enough drama in Susann's life to make a compelling film. Not only was she a fixture of a bustling era in New York entertainment and nightlife, but she battled personal hardships that she kept out of sight, not wanting to diminish her glamourous, can-do image. The Mansfields had an autistic son at a time when little was known about the condition. Susann was diagnosed with malignant breast cancer in 1962 and underwent a mastectomy; a decade later, the cancer spread to her lungs and ultimately killed her.

With all these ingredients to work with, *Isn't She Great* (the title now back to Mansfield's original exclamation) should have been the movie equivalent of one of Susann's delicious page-turners. Instead, it's a lumpy cyclorama of Susann's later life, stitched together by nearly nonstop narration by Nathan Lane as Mansfield. In Rudnick's script, Susann is no longer a striver determined to make it as a novelist with the clock ticking on her life but a zany who bounces from one failed career to another, finally stumbling into writing. Midler and Lane come across as a couple of Damon Runyon kibitzers, not the leathery, deal-making sharks the Mansfields were in real life. The steely dragon lady who appeared on talk shows to relentlessly promote her books is nothing like the cuddly, smart-mouthed Susann that Midler plays. (Truman Capote once called Susann "a truck driver in drag," then apologized—to truck drivers.).

Midler could have played a tougher, more nuanced Susann, but Rudnick's script and Bergman's flaccid direction let her down. It was a performance on autopilot, with Midler giving audiences the raucous Bette they were used to. There's the Divine Jackie bawdily greeting the drivers who will deliver her new novel to bookstores! There's the Divine Jackie shocking her uptight editor! There's the Divine Jackie at a party celebrating her book sales and stealing the stage from Steve and Eydie! (Who knew Jackie Susann could sing like Bette Midler?)

Since everything is played at the same glossed-over pace, the true tragedies in Susann's life barely register. Though largely set in New York City, the film has a vague "nowhere" look to it, with bland period decor, costumes that make everyone look like they're headed to a '60s mod dress-up party, and a generic "groovy" score by Burt Bacharach.

Isn't She Great (the producers wisely removed the question mark from the title, perhaps not wishing to tempt responses) was completed in mid-1998 but held back until January 2000. Universal Pictures tried for counter-programming when they released it on Super Bowl weekend, hoping to get women and gay men into the theaters. But *Isn't She Great*, with terrible reviews and a budget approaching that of *For the Boys*, returned a pitiful $3 million. At the end of the year, Midler was nominated for a Golden Raspberry, or "Razzie," Award for Worst Actress. (She lost to Madonna.)

Isn't She Great was the last feature film Midler would headline. With a few exceptions, her roles in films would now run to cameos and sidekicks. Midler, in her mid-fifties, had entered a crowded demographic of established female stars who were vital and great-looking—and all seeking work in an increasingly youth-oriented film market. Anyone whose name wasn't Meryl Streep was left to vie for fewer and fewer age-appropriate roles.

If Midler coasted with *That Old Feeling* and *Isn't She Great*, she left it all on the floor in *Drowning Mona*, a low-budget black comedy in which she was killed off before the credits ended. As the title character, Midler went full-on white trash as the mother of a dysfunctional brood in backwoods Verplanck, New York. She mostly appears in flashbacks, as police chief Danny DeVito tries to determine how and why the brakes in Mona's car were stripped, sending her over a cliff and into a lake. Audiences who were expecting Midler and DeVito to be reunited in a *Ruthless People*–style farce instead got a combo platter of gross-out comedy from the Farrelly brothers playbook (*There's Something about Mary*, *Dumb and Dumber*) and deadpan violence similar to that in Coen brothers films like *Fargo*.

No one is sorry to see Mona dead, everyone has a motive (including her family), and the flashbacks reveal why: she's the wicked witch of Verplanck, a violent, foul-mouthed harridan. Seeing Midler throw herself into this hateful, one-note role—walloping her husband across the face with a frying pan and chopping off her son's hand—was dismal, and *Drowning Mona* mercifully came and went in theaters in mid-2000. ‡‡

All these movie misfires brought to mind Midler's own question, "Why bother?" She must have been asking herself this, too. As a parting shot just before starting work on her 2000 sitcom, Midler summed up her frustrations with the movie business both as an actor and as a producer who had tried to get ambitious films with meaty roles for herself off the ground: "You're in development for 15 years, and then you wait for a 25-year-old to give you the green light. When they learn how to make movies again, I'll be back."[30]

"I Wanted a Life More Than I Wanted You"

The sitcom didn't turn out the way anyone wanted, but Midler was busy making records, doing her stage shows, and heading up her New York Restoration Project to recapture green spaces in New York City. Movies didn't loom as large for her, and it was four

---

‡‡ Midler wasn't the only star to appear in downmarket gross-out comedies around this time. Her erstwhile Oscar rival, Sally Field, appeared in the ghastly *Say It Isn't So!* (2001) as a conniving low-rent wife and mother who ends up a stroke victim. The nadir of Field's career has to be a scene in which, responding to a request for lots of salt on a sandwich, she rubs the bread under her armpits.

years before she made another. When Joan Cusack dropped out of the big-budget remake of *The Stepford Wives*, Midler replaced her as Bobbie Markowitz, a celebrated writer whose family are the only Jews in the sterile WASP enclave of Stepford, Connecticut. (Bobbie's latest bestseller? A book about her mother: *I Love You, but Please Die*.)

Paul Rudnick's screenplay updated Ira Levin's science-fiction novel about fear of feminism in which the men in an idyllic suburb kill their wives and replace them with docile and submissive robots. A 1975 film version played the story for low-key horror, but Rudnick went for laughs, slathering on a heavy layer of the "gay show-biz sensibility," with on-target jabs at consumer culture, gay Republicans, reality TV, McMansion suburbia, and have-it-all superwomen. It's equal-opportunity Stepfordizing in 2004 as the town welcomes gay male and Jewish couples (but no Blacks or lesbians) and happily turns the female-identified partners into robots. (The femme half of the gay male couple, played by Roger Bart, goes from fabulous fashionista to a family-values politician.)

Midler is mostly along for the ride as Bobbie, first schlubby with a long, stringy dark wig and baggy clothes, then blond and beatific after being Stepfordized. She and Bart and Nicole Kidman, the town's newest and most skeptical resident, scamper around Stepford spying on their husbands, just like the three first wives in New York City. Midler's best scenes were cut from the brief, ninety-minute film, including an extended CGI demonstration of her cleaning skills (her arm becomes a long-stemmed vacuum cleaner) and her always-ready availability for sex with her husband. (She instantly becomes a moist, yielding supplicant, cooing in pure Rudnickese, "Oh Dave, you big bear, give it to me! I need it—all four inches!") Her lower extremities then turn into a lawn mower, and she's last seen cutting the grass. Midler is hilariously funny, hitting Rudnick's dialogue with just the right tone of camp knowingness. Losing these scenes meant she never got the loony, bravura

moments that made Glenn Close's performance as Stepford's ma-
levolent matriarch a stylized hoot.§§

Stepford Wives landed with a thud at the box office and did
nothing for Midler's stock in films. She never got a chance to star
in one of Nancy Meyers's middle-age comedy-romances like
Diane Keaton did in *Something's Gotta Give* or Meryl Streep in *It's
Complicated*. She was probably too funny, too formidable—and
maybe not WASPy enough—for these smooth wish-fulfillment
fantasies. It's just as well: when Midler showed up in an unbilled,
one-scene cameo as a psychiatrist in the Meyers-directed Mel
Gibson comedy *What Women Want* (2000), she was so tamped
down she was almost unrecognizable.

The success of the Oscar-winning movie version of the Broadway
musical *Chicago* (2002) led to a mini-revival of screen musicals, a
natural genre for Midler. But the timing was off, and she never took
part in the movie-musical renaissance. (Decades earlier, she had
turned down the role of Miss Hannigan in the 1982 film version of
Annie.) She was perfect for the Sophie Tucker–ish prison matron
in *Chicago*, but that role went to the younger Queen Latifah, who
brought with her a wider audience demographic. Midler would
have been a marvelously villainous Velma von Tussle in *Hairspray*
(2007), but that was taken by the younger Michelle Pfeiffer. If
Mamma Mia! had existed as a property twenty years earlier, Midler,
by dint of performance history and temperament, would have been
the logical choice to play the starring role of the one-time leader of
a girl group named Donna and the Dynamos. By 2008, she wasn't
even considered, and the role went to Meryl Streep.

Midler could easily have played Barbra Streisand's role as mother
to Ben Stiller and wife to Dustin Hoffman in the intergenerational
Fockers comedies. Instead, she was Billy Crystal's wife in *Parental
Guidance*, another multigeneration comedy. Midler and Crystal

§§ Midler's excised scenes can be seen as part of the special features on the film's DVD
release.

were a comfortable fit as grandparents tasked with looking after the grandkids while their parents are away, but *Parental Guidance* was essentially a Crystal vehicle, and Midler was frequently on the sidelines. The mild comedy was a surprise hit when it was released during the 2012 Christmas season and was Midler's highest-grossing film in some time.

And there were more cameos. In 2008, writer-director Diane English (creator of TV's *Murphy Brown*) updated *The Women*, Clare Boothe Luce's all-female society comedy best known for its celebrated MGM film, starring Norma Shearer, Joan Crawford, Rosalind Russell, and practically every actress in Hollywood. Midler was part of another all-star cast (including Meg Ryan, Annette Bening, and Candice Bergen) in a role equivalent to one played in the first film by Mary Boland. In 1939, the Countess de Lave was an uproarious, much-married dowager. In 2008, Midler played a much-married legendary talent agent referred to as the Countess, whose pot-smoking and truth-telling appear modeled on super-agent Sue Mengers. English's take on the material lacked the delicious dishiness of the 1939 film, and Midler's brief scene had her spouting earnest observations about love—all while wearing the world's ugliest wig.

Midler played Muv, the boozy, Auntie Mame–ish mother of a gender-nonconforming son forced to transfer to a school in red state MAGA territory in *Freak Show*, based on a popular YA novel by former club kid James St. James. In her few scenes, Midler was both smotheringly maternal and drunkenly out of it, demonstrating that her son was well rid of her when she exited his life. The low-budget film directed by Trudie Styler was barely released in early 2018.

Like many stars, Midler hopped on the gravy train with voice work on animated films. She vamped pleasantly as Kitty Galore, a hairless, PG-rated spoof on James Bond girl Pussy Galore, in *Cats and Dogs: The Revenge of Kitty Galore* (2010). She was a demented Grandmama Addams in two *Addams Family* movies (2019 and 2021), sporting a nearly indecipherable Eastern European accent in a starry cast that included Oscar Isaac, Charlize Theron, and Snoop Dogg.

The only film in the last twenty-plus years that gave Midler a chance to play a complicated, intriguing character was *Then She Found Me*, based on a novel by Elinor Lipman and directed and co-written by Helen Hunt. Hunt starred as April Epner, a thirty-nine-year-old schoolteacher whose adoptive parents are both dead. Not long after April's husband leaves her, she meets her birth mother, a local New York City TV host played by Midler. Bernice Graves is an Oprah-like personality—glib, performatively empathetic, and quick to share. "I'm very verbal during sex," she offers during their first meeting. She's also a serial fabulist, who lies about April's birth father and the circumstances of her adoption. (She first claims that April was conceived during a one-night stand with movie star Steve McQueen.)

While Bernice is over-the-top, Midler doesn't play her that way. Bernice tries to push forward with this new mother–daughter relationship, while April is wary and keeps her at arm's length, forcing Bernice to pull back and proceed at April's wary pace. Their growing bond, particularly as April works through issues with men and ultimately tries to have a child, is played with sensitivity and nuance by both Midler and Hunt.

Midler's Bernice reveals a TV personality when the cameras are off. She's used to having people do her bidding, and she's flummoxed when April doesn't respond to her too-quick attempts at intimacy. You can sense Midler's relief in playing a character who isn't a cliché, whose fabrications mask a difficult past. When Bernice is finally confronted with her lies and forced to admit, "I wanted a life more than I wanted you," Midler is quietly shattering.

Then She Found Me doesn't fit neatly into any genre. It isn't an all-girls comedy or a romcom or a tearjerker. It's a small-scale, low-key contemporary story with difficult, sometimes irrational adults muddling through unexpected situations, and it reveals Hunt as a fine-tuned director of actors. *Then She Found Me* made the film-festival rounds in 2007 and opened in fewer than one hundred theaters in early 2008. Its very limited release never allowed it to catch on with audiences; if it had, Midler's performance, some of her most subtle and understated work, would have earned the recognition it deserved.

Some have speculated that if Midler (or Liza Minnelli or Cher or Lady Gaga) had been around in an earlier, busier era of movies, she would have starred in one musical after another, alternating with comedy and dramatic roles, and would have enjoyed a more varied and impressive filmography. But the female stars of the 1930s or '40s or '50s, especially those who built careers in musicals, were mostly beauties with small, creamy features that could be lovingly caressed in close-up. Women with larger, less traditionally "pretty" faces—and the energy and humor to go with them—were relegated to subordinate roles.

Martha Raye, the woman who slapped Midler with a lawsuit over *For the Boys*, is a useful analogy. Like Midler, she was a well-endowed woman of diminutive stature with a big personality to go with her features (she was nicknamed the "Big Mouth" for the obvious reason). A fine singer and skilled comedic actor (she even stole scenes from Charlie Chaplin in *Monsieur Verdoux*), Raye never got a chance to show any kind of sensitivity or display her dramatic chops, though she was given more latitude to do so in her later theater work. She was almost always the comic relief alongside beauties like Betty Grable and Ann Sheridan.

In those days, Midler might have had a career like Raye's; or like that of Nancy Walker, alternating stage roles with occasional secondary movie parts; or like that of Joan Davis, a sidekick in A-pictures and the star of quickly produced B-comedies. By the 1970s, at least partly thanks to Streisand's success, there was a greater openness to casting women in leading roles who didn't fit the standard expectations of what a movie star should look like. Even given the problems she had in finding suitable film roles, Midler may have come along at just the right time. It's hard to imagine her string of raucous, R-rated 1980s comedies getting made twenty or thirty years earlier. No one in the old studio system would have done *The Rose* with the same grit. If the movies (and she herself, in some cases) let her down, she wasn't the only woman of her generation to be stymied by Hollywood's shortsightedness.

Midler's legacy in films—two dozen appearances over forty-plus years—is mixed: a brilliant musical and dramatic debut, a string of box-office comedy hits, wonderful moments in mediocre (or worse) films, a number of outright mishaps, and a small jewel of a performance in a film no one saw. But films are only one aspect of the Midler career, and the medium itself doesn't occupy the same position of supremacy it once held.

What is a movie today? A $200 million piece of Marvel Cinematic Universe IP? The umpteenth entry in an animation franchise? A niche comedy featuring legacy stars that plays in theaters a few weeks and disappears? The 2023 *Sitting in Bars with Cake* (another Midler cameo) streaming anytime on Amazon Prime Video? As the distinctions between movies and television continue to blur, what does a film legacy even mean to a multiplatform artist? Midler's movies stand alongside her accomplishments in other media to form a joyous, colorful assemblage of comedy and song and emotion that has proven truly divine for more than half a century.

Notes

"Any Day Now . . ."

1. Craig Zadan, "Bette's Back!" *New York*, April 14, 1975, 63.
2. Will, "Night Club Reviews: Sahara, Las Vegas: Johnny Carson, Bette Midler," *Variety*, April 26, 1972, 62.
3. Lisa Robinson, "My Life Story: Bette Midler," *Interview*, October 1972, 53.
4. Paul Gardner, "Divine Miss M. Is Set for a Tacky Gala," *New York Times*, December 29, 1972.
5. William S. Wells, "Midler: Nothing Divine in Her Film Non-Debut," *Rolling Stone*, July 4, 1974, 20.
6. Charles Champlin, "Lord Olivier: Just a Working Actor," *Asbury Park Press*, January 25, 1976.
7. Tom Eyen, as confessed to Zarko Kalmic, "The Many Mad Women in Tom Eyen's Life," *After Dark*, December 1974, 31.
8. Ron Pennington, "Pryor Tirade Mars Hollywood Bowl Benefit for Gays," *Hollywood Reporter*, September 20, 1977, 1, 23.
9. Richard Corliss, "Bette Steals Hollywood," *Time Magazine*, March 2, 1987, 66.
10. Stephen Schiff, "Winning Bette," *Vanity Fair*, December 1987, 191.
11. Michael Schiavi, *Celluloid Activist: The Life and Times of Vito Russo* (Madison: University of Wisconsin Press, 2011), 242.
12. Kevin Sessums, "La Belle Bette," *Vanity Fair*, December 1991, 206, 254.
13. https://www.youtube.com/watch?v=SrITcBUq09o&t=236s.
14. https://www.youtube.com/watch?v=2791ih71QSA.

Introduction

1. Bette Midler, *A View from a Broad* (New York: Fireside, 1980), 39.
2. Neil Appelbaum, "Bette, You Is My Woman Now," *After Dark*, May 1971, 32.
3. Jan Hodenfield, "Divine Miss Superstar," *New York Post*, December 30, 1972.

4. Ibid.
5. Ed McCormack, "The Gold Lamé Dream of Bette Midler: 'Puh-leez Honey,'" *Rolling Stone*, February 15, 1973, 39.
6. Appelbaum, "Bette, You Is My Woman Now," 32.
7. May Okon, "Today's Best Bette," *New York Sunday News*, October 28, 1973.
8. Tom Eyen, as confessed to Zarko Kalmic, "The Many Mad Women in Tom Eyen's Life," *After Dark*, December 1974, 31.
9. Ibid., 32.
10. Lisa Robinson, "My Life Story: Bette Midler," *Interview*, October 1972, 17.
11. Calvin Tomkins, "Ridiculous," *The New Yorker*, November 15, 1976, 60.
12. "Legit Bits," *Variety*, November 9, 1966, 75.
13. *Inside the Actors Studio*, June 6, 2004, https://www.youtube.com/watch?v=GKMtTXAPfKI.
14. Robinson, "My Life Story," 17.
15. Loraine Alterman, "Bette Midler: A Now Woman," *Record World*, May 19, 1973; reprinted in *Ms.*, August 1973, 49.
16. Al Rudis, "Bette Comes on Strong and Some Can't Take the Heat," *Chicago Sun-Times*, July 25, 1971.
17. "Andy Warhol Interviews Bette Midler Interviews Andy Warhol," *Interview*, November 1974, 6.
18. Nancy Collins, "Bette Midler: The Cheese-Bomb American Crapola Dream," *Rolling Stone*, December 9, 1982, 18.
19. Charles Michener, "Bette Midler," *Newsweek*, December 17, 1973, 63.
20. See Peter Ogren, "Doin' the Continental," *Gay*, July 6, 1970, 11.
21. See John P. LeRoy, "Rub a Dub Dub, 3,000 Men in a Tub: New York: Bath Capital of the World," *Gay*, February 7, 1972, 4–5, 19; John P. LeRoy, "Le Continental: C'est Moi: An Interview with Steve Ostrow," *Gay*, June 18, 1973, 5, 15; Barry Lester, "The Continental Miracle," *Gay*, December 21, 1970, 11; and Ogren, "Doin' the Continental," 11, for discussions of the Continental's physical space and amenities.
22. Grace Lichtenstein, "Steve Ostrow's Satyricon," *Saturday Review*, April 1973, 14.
23. "Continental Bath and Health Club" advertisement, *Gay*, July 6, 1970, 18.
24. See Dick Leitsch, "The Whole World's a Bath!," *Gay*, October 26, 1970, 16.
25. Charles Michener, "The Divine Miss M," *Newsweek*, May 22, 1972, 76.
26. James Spada, *The Divine Bette Midler* (New York: Collier, 1984), 22.
27. Susan Sontag, "Notes on Camp," in *Camp: Queer Aesthetics and the Performing Subject: A Reader*, ed. Fabio Cleto (Ann Arbor: University of Michigan Press, 1999), 53–65.

28. Jack Babuscio, "Camp and the Gay Sensibility," in *Camp Grounds: Style and Homosexuality*, ed. David Bergman (Amherst: University of Massachusetts Press, 1993), 19.
29. Ibid., 20.
30. Michener, "Bette Midler," 63.
31. John P. LeRoy, "The Bath Scene," *Gay*, February 1, 1971, 2.
32. Robinson, "My Life Story," 17.
33. Babuscio, "Camp and the Gay Sensibility," 21.
34. Bruce Vilanch, "Best Bette," *The Advocate*, November 10, 1998, 43.
35. Alan L. Gansberg, "'Tacky' Places and Future Plans Top Divine Miss M Talk," *Herald News* (Passaic, NJ), August 10, 1973.
36. Robinson, "My Life Story," 17.
37. Vito Russo, "I'll Take Manhattan: Butley, Bette & Bijou," *Gay*, December 11, 1972, 10.
38. McCormack, "The Gold Lamé Dream," 37.
39. Gregg Kilday, "Bette Midler Collides with Her Image," *Los Angeles Times*, March 19, 1973.
40. "Why Bette Midler?," *Ms.*, August 1973, 51.
41. "Andy Warhol Interviews Bette Midler," 6.
42. Richard Goldstein, "The Dark Side of Bette Midler," *Village Voice*, April 21, 1975, 127.

Chapter 1

1. Michael Shurtleff, *Audition: Everything an Actor Needs to Know to Get the Part* (New York: Walker, 1978), 170.
2. "Seattle Opera's *Tommy* 'As Warm as Dry Ice,'" *Puget Sound Trail*, May 14, 1971, https://bootlegbetty.com/2019/03/16/betteback-may-14-1971-seat tle-operas-tommy-starring-bette-midler-and-steve-curry-rare-photo/.
3. Paul Anderson, "Bette Midler Gives Extraordinary Performance in *Tommy*," *Arizona Republic*, May 3, 1971, https://bootlegbetty.com/2015/10/24/betteback-review-may-3-1971-bette-midler-gives-extraordinary-performance-in-tommy/.
4. Kevin Sessums, "La Belle Bette," *Vanity Fair*, December 1991, 264.
5. Abe Peck, "Bruce Vilanch: Miss M's Divine Gag Writer," *Rolling Stone*, March 23, 1978, 30.
6. Barry Manilow, *Sweet Life: Adventures on the Way to Paradise* (New York: McGraw-Hill, 1987), 246.

7. Claudia Driefus, "Bette Midler: The Outcast Who's Finally 'In,'" *Playgirl*, September 1975, 105.
8. Gerald Clarke, "Midler: 'Make Me a Legend!'" *Time*, December 31, 1979, 69.
9. *The Phil Donahue Show*, ca. 1983, https://www.youtube.com/watch?v=xG_B77oMBTo.
10. Dan Aquilante, "A Good Bette," *New York Post*, January 2, 2004.
11. Ian Dove, "Stage: Miss M. Divine," *New York Times*, December 4, 1973.
12. Robb Baker, *Bette Midler* (New York: Popular Library, 1975), 80.
13. Neil Appelbaum, "Bette, You Is My Woman Now," *After Dark*, May 1971, 34.
14. "Rolling Stone Music Awards '73," *Rolling Stone*, January 17, 1974, 11.
15. Dennis Hunt, "Bad Is Better with Millie Jackson," *Los Angeles Times*, August 14, 1979.
16. "Midler Hottest Aussie Import in Long Time," *Variety*, October 11, 1978, 174.
17. See James Spada, *The Divine Bette Midler* (New York: Collier, 1984), 145.
18. See Bette Midler, *A View from a Broad* (New York: Fireside, 1980), 102–103.
19. Lynn Hirschberg, "Meta-Midler," *New York Times*, October 8, 2000.
20. Robert Christgau, *Village Voice*, October 5, 1993, 71, 86; in Bette Midler clipping file, Billy Rose Theatre Division, New York Public Library for the Performing Arts.
21. Andrew Goldman, "A Showgirl of a Certain Age," *New York*, March 24, 2008, 33.
22. "Divine Intervention" had lyrics by Marc Shaiman, Scott Wittman, and Midler, with music by Shaiman.
23. Patrick Healy, "After Years of Playing Bette, Another Role," *New York Times*, April 10, 2013.
24. Neil Appelbaum, "Bette, You Is My Woman Now," *After Dark*, May 1971, 32.
25. All dialogue from John Logan, *I'll Eat You Last: A Chat with Sue Mengers*, in *Plays One* (London: Oberon, 2016), 135–188.
26. Michael Paulson, "Bette Midler, Glowin', Crowin', Goin' Strong and Ready for 'Hello, Dolly!'" *New York Times*, January 20, 2016.

Chapter 2

1. Dick Leitsch, "The Whole World's a Bath!," *Gay*, October 26, 1970, 9.

2. See Barry Manilow, *Sweet Life: Adventures on the Way to Paradise* (New York: McGraw-Hill, 1987), 114–117, 121–124.

3. Lisa Robinson, "My Life Story: Bette Midler," *Interview*, October 1972, 51.

4. Claudia Driefus, "Bette Midler: The Outcast Who's Finally 'In,'" *Playgirl*, September 1975, 106.

5. Paul Grein, "A Rejected 'Rose' Blooms for Midler, Enhancing Credibility," *Billboard*, February 14, 1981, 6.

6. James Kirkwood, quoted in Mark Steyn, *Broadway Babies Say Goodnight: Musicals Then and Now* (London: Faber and Faber, 1997), 192.

Chapter 3

1. "Andy Warhol Interviews Bette Midler Interviews Andy Warhol," *Interview*, November 1974, 6.

2. "'The Tenth Anniversary': Rolling Stone on TV," *Rolling Stone*, November 3, 1977, 20.

3. Gerrit Henry, "What's a Nice Girl Like Bette Midler Doing on the Home Screen?" *New York Times*, December 4, 1977.

4. Paul Brownfield, "For TV Shows, Success Isn't Always in the Stars," *Los Angeles Times*, December 15, 2000.

Chapter 4

1. Warren Hoge, "Bette Midler Goes Hollywood," *New York Times*, December 10, 1978.

2. See Craig Zadan, "Bette's Back!," *New York*, April 14, 1975, 64.

3. Ben Fong-Torres, "Everybody's Doing a Film on Janis," *Rolling Stone*, January 3, 1974, 14.

4. https://www.youtube.com/watch?v=iKlPxr9_t_Y&t=281s.

5. Judy Klemesrud, "I Don't Know If I'll Ever Get a Part Like This Again," *New York Times*, November 11, 1979.

6. https://www.youtube.com/watch?v=GKMtTXAPfKI&t=1682s.

7. Klemesrud, "I Don't Know If I'll Ever Get a Part Like This Again."

8. Nancy Collins, "The Cheese-Bomb American Crapola Dream," *Rolling Stone*, December 9, 1982, 16.

9. Ibid.

10. Lee Grant, "Midler: In the Hubbub of 'Jinxed,'" *Los Angeles Times*, September 15, 1982.

11. Don Siegel quoted in Patrick McGilligan, *Clint: The Life and Legend* (New York: St. Martin's Press, 1999), 182.

12. Collins, "The Cheese-Bomb American Crapola Dream," 16.

13. Lee Grant, "Trouble on the Set of 'Jinxed'? You Can Bette on It," *Los Angeles Times*, September 27, 1981.

14. "Jaffe: You Better, You Bette," *Rolling Stone*, October 1, 1981, 79.

15. Grant, "Midler: In the Hubbub of 'Jinxed.'"

16. See Grant, "Trouble on the Set of 'Jinxed'? You Can Bette on It."

17. Collins, "The Cheese-Bomb American Crapola Dream," 15.

18. Armistead Maupin, "Bette Midler," *Interview*, September 1982, 34.

19. Aljean Harmetz, "Bette Midler and Disney Sign Three-Picture Deal," *New York Times*, February 5, 1987.

20. Ibid.

21. Stephen Schiff, "Winning Bette," *Vanity Fair*, December 1987, 145.

22. See Robert Hofler, *Party Animals: A Hollywood Tale of Sex, Drugs, and Rock 'n' Roll Starring the Fabulous Allan Carr* (Cambridge, MA: Da Capo Press, 2010), 220.

23. "Geraldo Drugged Me for Sex," *New York Daily News*, November 2, 1991.

24. Bernard Weinraub, "'Boys' Film Leaves Studio Wondering," *New York Times*, December 5, 1991.

25. Lynn Hirschberg, "Meta-Midler," *New York Times*, October 8, 2000.

26. *The Arsenio Hall Show*, December 6, 1991, https://www.youtube.com/watch?v=0tlxv9mxkYA.

27. Pauline Kael, "Fakers," *The New Yorker*, January 11, 1988, 78.

28. Paul Rudnick, "Fun with Nuns," *The New Yorker*, July 20, 2009, 38.

29. Olivia Goldsmith, *The First Wives Club* (New York: Pocket Books, 1992), 439.

30. Cynthia Littleton, "Midler Takes Parting Shot at Film Biz," *Hollywood Reporter*, July 24, 2000, 29.

"Now Write This Down!"

A Selected Bibliography

Bette Midler has been the subject of several biographies over the course of a career that is now into its seventh decade. The best are by those who followed her career from the beginning, offering the context and perspective of true believers who aren't afraid to call out the occasional missteps and blunders.

Robb Baker's paperback *Bette Midler* (New York: Popular Library, 1975) appeared awfully early—it takes the Midler career only up through her Palace Theatre triumph and the first two albums. But Baker, a rock critic and journalist—and a Midler fan—is especially good at getting members of the Midler troupe to discuss the excitement and turbulence surrounding her early breakthrough. There are lengthy interviews with Billy Cunningham, the Continental Baths' accompanist when Midler arrived; Bill Hennessy, the mastermind behind the Divine Miss M; Bruce Vilanch; André De Shields, her early "boogie master"; and even Rosalie Marks, the singer who preceded Midler at Continental. The first wave of Harlettes chime in with astute observations about the theater and music business at the time and how sharing the stage with Midler was both a challenge and a rare opportunity for the kind of creative work unavailable elsewhere. Baker's book is a fascinating Midler origin story.

James Spada's coffee-table-sized *The Divine Bette Midler* (New York: Collier, 1984) takes the story up through the *Jinxed* debacle and *De Tour*. It's a well-organized and thorough chronology drawing from many published sources (not always cited) and select interviews. Marta Heflin, Midler's *Fiddler on the Roof* castmate who first got her to try singing in clubs, and Paul Aaron, the director of *Salvation*, an off-Broadway musical in which Midler replaced Heflin, fill in some blanks on the pre-Continental days. Spada is upbeat and supportive of his subject but doesn't shy away from reporting the low points. Linda Hart discusses the suit she and two other Harlettes filed against Midler when they were dismissed with no reason just before the filming of *Divine Madness* in 1980. (Midler later hired Hart for another tour, introducing her as "Linda [I Sued and Won] Hart.") *The Divine Bette Midler* is copiously illustrated, and many of its early photos were a revelation in 1984. Chockablock with details on every facet of Midler's career, it's a bit TMI for the casual observer. Of course, who but a serious fan would be reading it?

Baker and Spada are true fans passionately documenting the Midler career. Ace Collins's *Bette Midler* (New York: St. Martin's Press, 1989) gives the impression he'd never heard of her until he got the assignment to turn out this brief, error-filled book that carries all the passion of a college term paper. Collins, the author of more than eighty books, including crime and suspense novels, stories behind beloved Christmas songs, and "devotional books," characterizes Midler as a madcap zany, prone to "cussing," who finally settles down to a "normal life" when she becomes a wife and mother. Collins gets just about everything wrong, starting with her birthdate. Timelines are scrambled, and he conveys no sense of what made Midler so unique onstage. (She did not do "takeoffs" on Judy Garland, Tallulah Bankhead, and Bette Davis.) Collins describes the Continental Baths as if he's afraid of getting his fingers dirty while typing. This "hot spot for the New York homosexual crowd" could be an ice cream parlor in Collins's decorous telling, though he insists that Midler's performances were so wild that the men "asked her to make love to them." Skip it.

George Mair is another bustling author of books on everyone from the Reverend Rick Warren to Paris Hilton. His *Bette: An Intimate Biography of Bette Midler* (New York: Birch Lane, 1995) is a once-over-lightly tome that gets most of the facts correct but doesn't convey any real engagement with its subject. It's notable for a couple of detours from the standard Midler story. Mair found a number of former friends from Midler's high school and college days in Hawaii who go on the record with notably harsh assessments of her behavior both during her school years and after and dispute her sometimes grim descriptions of her family's financial hardships and her life on the island. Elsewhere, a former executive with Midler's All Girl Productions reflects on the difficulty Midler had in getting projects greenlighted by Disney Studios, even as she was their biggest and highest-paid star. The studio wanted simplistic, easy-to-shoot stories, while Midler and her team pitched more complex and challenging material. The chapter-long discussion helps explain why so many promising Midler vehicles, like her proposed Lotte Lenya biopic, were never made.

Allison J. Waldman's large-format picture book *The Bette Midler Scrapbook* (Secaucus, NJ: Citadel Press, 1997) is a breezy overview of Midler's career in movies, television, recordings, and the stage, mostly through credits, review quotes, and brief comments. There's a chronology of major events in her life, a listing of Midler movies that never got made, a selection of favorite Midler jokes, and even a trivia quiz. Midler has never been at a loss for words, and the book's most interesting feature is a compilation of extensive quotations (none sourced or dated, unfortunately) by Midler on everything from her family to her looks, from AIDS to psychotherapy (she's not down with it). More assembled than written, the book lives up to its name as a colorful scrapbook of the Midler life and career.

Like Collins and Mair, Mark Bego rolled *Bette Midler: Still Divine* (New York: Cooper Square Press, 2002) off his celebrity-bio assembly line. (It was sandwiched between his Cher and Bonnie Raitt books.) But like Baker and Spada, Bego is also a fan, and a general sense of excitement and discovery accompanies his telling of the Midler story. There's a good accounting of events surrounding her misbegotten sitcom. Bego's interviews with Buzzy Linhart and Moogy Klingman, coauthors of "Friends," give insight into her friendships with the two men. Klingman's fascinating reminiscences about the sessions he and Midler did at his studio for her third album, *Songs for the New Depression*, provide a first-person glimpse into Midler's creative process when she was recording for the first time without Barry Manilow's guidance. And it's the only Midler bio to include citations for its sources. Bego's fast-track publishing schedule apparently didn't leave time for editing, and *Bette Midler: Still Divine* is littered with all kinds of easily caught misspellings. It's Woody, not Wood, Allen. It's Loretta Devine, not Divine. The cinematographer on *Divine Madness* is William A. Fraker, not Franker. Midler's friend and *The View* co-anchor is Joy Behar, not Bahar, and on and on. Midler's New York Restoration Project is variously referred to as the Manhattan Restoration Project and the New York City Preservation Society. The worst blunder is spelling Haselberg two different ways—on the same page.

The longest-running, most extensive online source of information on Midler is **bootlegbetty.com**, operated by Mister D, Don Bradshaw. It's easy to go down a Midler rabbit hole, following links to articles, reviews, and photos from the far reaches of her career. (If you want to see images of the star in *The Who's Tommy* in 1971, this is the place.) It's not an elegantly constructed site; some of the links are dead, and the navigation is sometimes clunky. But there are links to Midler's social-media sites, to pages and pages of Soph jokes, to a list (long and extensive) of songs Midler had a hand in writing, and, best of all, to Bradshaw's video clips from throughout Midler's career available both on YouTube and on the Bootleg Betty Facebook page. Over fifty years of Midler performances, interviews, acceptance speeches, Q&As—if they're available, they're here.

A Bette Midler selected bibliography must also include her own writings. Her European tour following the filming of *The Rose* served as the basis for her 1980 memoir *A View from a Broad* (New York Fireside, 1980, reprinted by Simon & Schuster with a new introduction, 2014), a crazy quilt of photographs and mordant anecdotes written in the voice of the Divine Miss M, who emerges as a new-generation Auntie Mame. Midler's bawdy wit and genuine erudition, along with some winsome and touching stories, make the slim volume an unexpectedly delightful and moving read.

The Saga of Baby Divine (New York: Crown, 1983), an illustrated children's book for adults, reads like a creation myth for the Divine Miss M. The title character enters the world with a head of red curls, rouge and false eyelashes, high heels, and a jaunty flowered diaper, uttering just one word: "MORE!" Her staid parents are aghast at their new arrival (her mother even declares her "trashy"), but Baby Divine has three fairy godmothers who come to her rescue. Resembling a trio of retired Harlettes crossed with the Three Wise Men, these down-at-the-heel divas teach Baby Divine to shrug off anxiety and despair and realize her fabulosity through song and laughter. Their lesson plan culminates in a socko performance showcasing Baby Divine's life-affirming song-and-dance skills that convinces her parents how special their new baby really is. Baby Divine ends the story contentedly sleeping, swathed in a luxurious feather boa. Written in a series of rhyming four-line stanzas and accompanied by ravishing Technicolor illustrations by Todd Schorr that recall classic Disney cartoons, *The Saga of Baby Divine* is a small treasure. Its witty, literate wordplay and show-biz-savvy references (Darryl F. Zanuck, the Folies Bergère, Renata Tebaldi, Anna Pavlova) make it as much fun for adults as for children. Its story of empowerment for anyone who falls outside the mainstream continues to resonate, summed up by the Three Wise Women: "Make sure that your Life is a Rare Entertainment! / It doesn't take anything drastic. / You needn't be gorgeous or wealthy or smart / Just Very Enthusiastic!"

The Saga of Baby Divine is so delightful that it's regrettable Midler didn't follow it up for nearly thirty years. *The Tale of the Mandarin Duck* (New York: Random House, 2021), with photographs by Michiko Kakutani and quirky ink drawings by Joana Avillez, is another children's book but one with an adult perspective. When a rare, multicolored Mandarin duck appears in the Central Park lake, it stuns New Yorkers off their cell phones, and they begin to experience the beauty of the city and their fellow urbanites all over again. Midler's jabs at people glued to their cell phones is like shooting fish in a barrel, but in the end, this magical duck's tale is a fable worthy of New York City penned by one of its contemporary champions.

Index

For the benefit of digital users, indexed terms that span two pages (e.g., 52–53) may, on occasion, appear on only one of those pages.

Klein, Calvin, 86–87
Klimt, Gustav, 119–20
Klingman, Moogy, 21, 75–76,
    77, 101
Koch, Ed, 162–63
Kornbread, 160

Labelle (singing group), 40
Labelle, Patti, 40
Lady Gaga, 129, 173
"Lady Madonna," 15
La MaMa Experimental Theatre
    Club, 5, 25–26, 67
Lamour, Dorothy, 35
Lane, Nathan, 166
lang, k.d., 90–91
Lange, Jessica, 152
Lansbury, Angela, 91–92
Laub, Lindy, 153–54
"Laughing Matters," 54, 93
Lauper, Cyndi, 85
Laurents, Arthur, 121
Layton, Joe, 34–35
"Leader of the Pack," 15, 71, 81, 137
Lee, Michele, 165
Lee, Peggy, 13–14, 97–98, 100
Lennon, John, 69–70, 90
Lenya, Lotte, xix–xx, 4–5, 33, 73, 93,
    157, 164
Leonard, Elmore, 160–61
Leong, Terry, 17–18
"Let It Snow! Let It Snow! Let It
    Snow!," 98
"Let Me Drive," 84
"Let Me Just Follow Behind," 76
Lethal Weapon, 163–64
"Let's Shoot the Breeze," 41, 119–20
Letterman, David, 126
Levin, Ira, 169
Lewinsky, Monica, 54
Lewis, Jenifer, 109
Lewis, Jerry Lee, 118
Limbaugh, Rush, 54

Linhart, Buzzy, 21
Lion, The (nightclub), 16
Little Me, 130–31
Little Touch of Schmilsson in the
    Night, A, 32
Live at Last, 78–79
Logan, John, 61–62, 63
London Palladium, 42
Long, Shelley, 144–45, 163
"Long John Blues," 41
Lost Horizon, 130–31
Love Machine, The (Jacqueline
    Susann), 165
"Love Me with a Feeling," 135
"Love TKO" (Teddy
    Pendergrass), 94–95
Lovely Me: The Life of Jacqueline
    Susann (Barbara Seaman), 165
Lowe, Rob, 149–50
Luce, Clare Boothe, 171
Ludlam, Charles, 5–6, 23, 31–32, 50
"Lullaby in Blue," 93–94
"Lullaby of Broadway," xiii, 32,
    74, 106
LuPone, Patti, 91–92, 128
Lypsinka, 50

MacColl, Kirsty, 95
MacGraw, Ali, 63–64
Mack and Mabel, 25–26
Mackie, Bob, 42–43, 116
MacLaine, Shirley, 139
Madison Square Garden, xxiv
Madonna, 15, 86
Mahler, Gustav, 47
Majestic Theatre, The, 42
"Make Yourself Comfortable," 79–80
Mamas and the Papas, The, 69–70
"Mambo Italiano," 96–97
Mamma Mia!, 170
Manchester, Melissa, 80, 101
Manhattan, 153–54
Manhattan Transfer, 32